theatre@risk

Also by Michael Kustow

The Book of US
Tank, An Autobiographical Fiction
One in Four

theatre@risk

Michael Kustow

Methuen

Published by Methuen 2000

1 3 5 7 9 10 8 6 4 2

First published in Great Britain in 2000
by Methuen Publishing Limited,
215 Vauxhall Bridge Road, London SW1V 1EJ

Copyright © 2000 Michael Kustow

The author has asserted his rights under the Copyright, Designs
and Patents Act, 1988, to be identified as the author of this work

Methuen Publishing Limited Reg. No. 3543167

A CIP catalogue record for this book
is available from the British Library

ISBN 0 413 73820 5

Typeset in Goudy by MATS, Southend-on-Sea, Essex

Printed and bound in Great Britain by
Creative Print and Design (Wales)

For Shaike Weinberg

'I am Weimar, a little adulterated by the Middle East'

He felt something ultimate was missing,
some unutterable fulfilment
the very lack of which
gave his yearning the boundless radiance
that seemed to flood his whole being.

Robert Musil, *The Man Without Qualities*
Translated by Sophie Wilkins and Burton Pike

Contents

Acknowledgements

To all the theatre-makers, for fielding my questions: Peter Brook, Peter Hall, Tony Harrison, Ariane Mnouchkine, Alan Ayckbourn, Robert Lepage, Pieter-Dirk Uys, Rina Yerushalmi.

Fiona Shaw, Simon McBurney, Mark Ravenhill, Peter Sellars, Jean-Claude Carrière and Alan Sinfield spoke to me for a BBC Radio 3 series, *Dionysus and the Mighty Mouse*, which became the seed of this book. For letting me use parts of their interviews, and for commissioning the series, I am grateful to Richard Bannerman. To BBC Television and Harold Pinter, thanks for allowing me to quote from his *Open Door* programme about the NATO bombardment of Serbia.

Trevor Nunn, Adrian Noble and Mark Rylance spoke at the National Theatre Studio Forum on the speaking of Shakespeare, which Trevor called as he set about forming a classical ensemble at the National. I am grateful to him and to the other participants for letting me quote their words, to Lyn Haill for her editorial work on the tapes and transcripts, and to John Barton for inviting me, and for much else over five years of fruitful and entertaining work together.

Michael Earley, my publisher and editor, held up a sharp mirror reflecting the book that I was trying to write. David Buckland staged what I do as the jacket photograph. Dragan Klaic kept up a critical and heartening flow of e-mails from Amsterdam. Liz Hornby deftly copy-edited my manuscript, making me feel well cared for. Jane let the book and its author into her life.

The author and publishers gratefully acknowledge permission to print extracts from the following: Robert Musil, *The Man Without Qualities*, and Bruno Schulz, *Street of Crocodiles*, Picador; Tony Harrison, *The Kaisers of Carnuntum*, *The Labourers of Herakles* and *The Trackers of Oxyrhyncus*, and Ted Hughes, *Shakespeare and the Goddess of Complete Being* and *The Oresteia*, Faber & Faber; Jean-Pierre Vernant, *Myth and Tragedy in Ancient Greece*, Zone Books; Eugenio Barba, *Land of Ashes and Diamonds, My Apprenticeship in Poland*, Black Mountain Press; Heathcote Williams, AC/DC, Calder Publications; John Seabrook, *Deeper, My Adventures on the Net*, Simon & Schuster; John Naughton, *A Brief History of the Future*, Weidenfeld & Nicolson; C.P. Cavafy, 'Waiting for the Barbarians', from *Collected Poems*, Chatto & Windus; Bertolt Brecht, 'New Ages' and 'Everything Changes' from *Collected Poems*, Caryl Churchill, *Serious Money*, Mark Ravenhill, *Faust (Faust is Dead)*, and Simon McBurney and Theatre de Complicite, *Mnemonic*, Methuen.

Introduction

From new transmitters came the old stupidities.
Wisdom was passed on from mouth to mouth.

Bertolt Brecht, 'New Ages'

This is a book about theatre passion – my passion for the kind of theatre which excites me, both as an art and as a model of living together. It comes out of my own search to satisfy those passions in the theatre of my lifetime. For half a century I have tracked down performances and occasions of theatre, often in distant and offbeat places, with keen anticipation and in hope of shared pleasure. This prolonged hunt has also been driven by a desire to grasp theatre's essentials. Some of these quests and questions are inner ones. Where is theatre born in us? What does it light up? What is its voice and how does it speak? Others are social and public. How is theatre nourished, and how stunted? What would be lost if theatre was rolled back in the new Millennium by our society's dominant version of modernity – informational and global, managerial and market-led?

I write as an insider and an outsider, as a producer who writes and a writer who produces. At twenty, like the proverbial boy who runs away to join the circus, I talked my way into a French theatre troupe. Later, I joined the Royal Shakespeare Company and then the National Theatre at their beginnings, with an intervening foray as an impresario for the avant-garde. At forty, after a year as a director and literary manager in American theatre, I left theatre to become a television commissioning editor in the nascent Channel 4. There I tried to keep faith with the values of theatre and get it on the screen in a variety of ways. Today, as an independent producer, I am engaged in the Sisyphean task of getting on a fifteen-hour theatre epic about the Trojan War in America, England, Europe and as a television serial. On one level, this book questions: Why do I keep doing it? Theatre has always been my touchstone, and sometimes my work. It has never quite become my vocation. Maybe theatre for me has been a way of following Polonius' instructions to his son Laertes: 'By indirection, find directions out.' And perhaps that is not such a bad motto. A world which is becoming increasingly directional – though it hides behind a rhetoric of free choice and pluralism – needs the waywardness, the sense of special occasion and exception, which are at the heart of true theatre.

So in this book by a wayfarer, through and around theatre, don't expect to find a straight path. Prepare rather for a collage of accounts and critiques; profiles and testimony of some of the leading theatre-makers in the world; reportage cross-cut with analysis; memory of theatre occasions grafted onto interview and polemic. Certain theatre-makers – principally Peter Brook, Ariane Mnouchkine, Peter Hall, John Barton, Tony Harrison, Pieter-Dirk Uys and Simon McBurney – stand out. They do so because they have become exemplary, for me, of singular qualities of theatre in a century ending in homogenisation. Brook, the sensuous spiritual searcher. Mnouchkine, the mother of a troupe; what Joan Littlewood might have become in a better culture. Peter Hall, appetite linked to social passion and classical rigour. John Barton, sharing Shakespearean language with generations of actors. Tony Harrison, a poet in the theatre, rescuing the urgent example of classical Greek theatre from its class curators. Pieter-Dirk Uys, cross-dressing for democracy, in a satirical celebration of theatre's transformative powers. Simon McBurney, leading the most cosmopolitan theatre group in Britain, and anchoring their work in the play and disciplines of the body.

Despite such pioneers and re-inventors, things have got harder for theatre in my lifetime, and may get harder still. Though it charts setbacks and even some disillusionment, this is not an apocalyptic book. I can see theatre surviving around me despite the costs it exacts from the many artists who give themselves to it. But increasingly the real stuff happens in outposts and offshores, not in the cultural or commercial mainstreams. The concern behind this book is that vital theatre is being brushed aside by indifferent waves of modernisation, by the separateness created by screens big and small and by the sapping of public life and occasion as terminal connections take their place.

The central nervous system of individuals and society under global capitalism, underpinned by information technology, is changing. This is having its effect on all the arts. The status of theatre in our regimented cities, the dynamic connection between drama and democracy, which briefly and preciously existed in Athens over two millennia ago, are being eroded. Theatre, like democracy, is far from being killed off. But it may be undergoing life-threatening mutations. Of course, there are alternative, grass-root uses of the new media, and they are engendering challenges to the consensus. But for the rest of my lifetime, I can only see the landscape of the expanding 'wired world' looking uniform, corporate and mercantile. And even at its most fluid and anarchic, what the 'information society' creates is exchanges of information, not sharing of experience. To the extent that theatre is the most social performing art, I am therefore warning about endangered theatre, theatre subsumed by webs and networks, *theatre@risk*. But to the extent that theatre is planted in our nature, I am also celebrating the people who, in the teeth of the tide, and sometimes even surfing the tide, go on doing it because anyone's theatre passion, once ignited, will not be quenched.

I could have chosen to start this journey in many places, recounted countless examples of theatre in a mutating world. The example I have chosen, because it obsesses me so at the time of writing, is *Tantalus*, a theatre epic for the start of the new Millennium. In present theatre circumstances it is a completely unreasonable project, but as a cautionary tale it may reveal some

truths about where we are now. I start with a journal, a
surveillance camera report, on myself as a producer in action,
persisting well beyond what common sense would dictate, driven
by theatre passion to bring *Tantalus* into being.

Michael Kustow
December 1999

Part One:
Theatre of War

Pitching Troy

Easter 1999   Amsterdam
This week the Minister of Culture in Belgrade announced that
the city's theatres would stay open during the NATO bombardment, and that admission would be free. 'It is inspired,' she said,
'by British behaviour in the Blitz. The show must go on.'

To a British person of my generation, born three months after
the war began, this brings back iconic images. Not so much of free
theatre in the West End, perhaps, though that may well have
happened, as of the much more memorable newsreel of Dame
Myra Hess playing sonatas for free in the National Gallery;
Beethoven against the bombs.

On Easter Sunday, Maggie O'Kane writes in the *Guardian*
about an orchestra playing popular patriotic music in a square in
bombed Belgrade, under the headline *A City Battered But
Unbowed*:

> A poster taped to two brass drums reads: 'Happy Easter,
> European Union and the United States of America. We are
> singing under your bombs. What are you doing? Are you
> sleeping well?' In the middle of the square a mixed volleyball
> team plays in jerseys with a black and white target marked
> on the back and across the road at the National Theatre
> someone has put up a notice that reads: 'This is a shelter of
> the spirit'.

That trope again; it has a dying fall.

On the keyboard of tropes played by pop journalism and
theme-park history, how much more readily music comes to hand

than theatre to typify the resistance of spirit against violence.
Newsreels in spring 1945 lingered on the courage and dedication
of opera singers getting a Mozart performance together for
starving opera-lovers in the bomb-shattered skeleton of the
Berlin Opera House. Music is pure spirit, *geist*; music brings
sacredness in its wake. The spirit rises, cathedral-like, against the
downpour of destruction.

But the Belgrade Minister of Culture refers to theatre, not
music. And in so doing, she plucks a heartstring, pulls up an
image of theatre in the thick of things, theatre assembling citizens
at times of national crisis and testing, that I find irresistible. God
knows what those free Serbian theatres are performing. Probably
something kitsch and nationalistic, or some boulevard comedy to
wipe away people's cares. Maybe it's a smiling, dancing, singing
vaudeville, with lots of girls wearing next to nothing. Does the
Minister know that wartime London theatre's most defiant motto
– 'we never closed' – came from the Windmill, home of nude
revue? Probably not; it's too cheeky, too *louche* and double-
meaning to occur to Milosevic's Minister of Culture. Anyway,
most of the independent writers and directors in Belgrade theatre
have fled or been removed, so these wartime theatregoers are
hardly likely to be seeing a Serbian version of *Oh, What A Lovely
War!* And yet the invocation of theatre nourishing and rousing
the populace persists.

I have come to Amsterdam to stay with my friends Dragan and
Julie Klaic this Easter so I can recharge my batteries, depleted by
a plethora of producing, and recover this book about theatre,
which has been barged aside by my daily barrage of blurbs, calls,
pitches, e-mails, exhortations and manoeuvrings. I want to stand
aside for a while from the adrenalin, rage and calculation that go
with being a producer, the only way I know of being a producer,
in any event. I want to rescue my prose from the epidemic of
adjectives and the swish of superlatives that swamp it when I am
cajoling potential partners around the globe. I want to explore
why theatre has still got me by the throat.

I met Dragan at the start of the 'nineties, at a conference on
European culture in the Felix Meritis Centre in Amsterdam. This

short, bright, delicate, sardonic fortyish theatre professor from
Belgrade climbed onto the stage and, in the accents of an
American-educated central European Jewish intellectual, delivered an elegy for his country and a prediction of its devastation.
He was Cassandra, recast for a Woody Allen film. He gave a detailed, desperately calm account of the triggering of a murderous
process, already begun. It was to lead from intellectual and
cultural disputes to torching houses and extirpating people who
were different:

> Artists, writers and intellectuals were suddenly plunged into
> isolation in a disintegrating country. Airlines, trains, road
> transport and telephones one by one ceased to operate. A
> hysterical preoccupation and active involvement with the
> war and its politics, on which many held forth to receptive
> audiences, substituted for the development of new works
> and their public presentation. The purges in cultural
> institutions were ferocious: independent voices and
> 'ethnically unreliable' personnel were eliminated; others
> went into silent internal exile; many fled or were driven out
> of the country.

This became Dragan's own fate, as he must have realised that
spring in Amsterdam; Cassandra is never blind. As he wrote later,
in one of his many attempts to make sense of the war, 'One-time
guardians of the Communist ideology turned virulent nationalists
and, allied with anti-Communist traditionalists, attacked ideas,
then individuals, then turned to gutting libraries of unsuitable
books.'
His voice went on without respite, pitiless for himself,
displaying the teeth-clenching betrayals of his own caste,
pitiless for us, with our distance and detachment until a crisis
becomes a catastrophe. 'The younger intellectuals who fled
mobilisation,' he concluded, 'together with the children who
remained and were exposed to the war with all its hatred and
intolerance, and the distorted propaganda that made up their
education, are a lost generation. It will take a long time for the

theatre that can reshape the collective consciousness to appear.'

Dragan had come to Amsterdam that day from Belgrade, where he was professor of drama at the university. He was a Central European theatre intellectual, the conscience and Socratic questioner of the foremost Yugoslav directors and writers who were his contemporaries, and who respected him as a partner, almost a collaborator – a collaboration between doers and thinkers which would be unthinkable in Britain.

When I next met Dragan, the crisis had hit him. It was the end of 1991. He had arrived in London, and called me from where he was staying with relatives. He had been advised to leave Belgrade in a hurry, he said. If he stayed more than a few days, the military would have taken over the checkpoints at the airport, and he would not get out. He had to wind up as much as he could, make arrangements for his wife and daughter to follow on soon after, and choose what books and clothes he needed. I imagined the panic, and attempts at calm, of this articulate Cassandra, Cassandragan, going along his bookshelves, collecting framed photographs, pebbles from beaches; today in London, tomorrow on his way where?

Because he is good at what he does, because he's cosmopolitan, because Amsterdam and Dutch culture are relatively open, Dragan was appointed as Director of The Netherlands Theatre Institute. The Dutch imagined he would bring the place into the twenty-first century, which he is doing. With a dashingly displayed collection, a hands-on library and the calm spaces and tranquil garden of its merchant's mansion on the Keizersgracht, it's about the most seductive gateway into theatre studies I know.

Now that it is Kosovo's turn to go through the grinder, I come to Amsterdam to stay with Dragan, and his wife Julie, a psychoanalyst who has become a specialist in treating refugee trauma, and their daughter Nora, named after Ibsen's heroine.

When I arrive, their spare room is occupied by one of Dragan's students fleeing Belgrade to avoid conscription. So I stay in the Transit House, a rooming-house out of Isherwood's Berlin stories. The walls of my room are plastered with posters for the Sarajevo Film Festival. On the computer in the room is a letter to the Soros

Foundation, seeking funds for a theatre piece about Sarajevo. I spend two days there, having long talks in the kitchen with appalled young men who couldn't or wouldn't get back home. One day the frantic mother of one of these taut young men telephones from Australia, trying to track down her son. I move into Dragan's appartment, try to be inconspicuous in the anxious flurry of phone calls and e-mails, and start to write this section of this book.

Even in this city of still water, curved brick and placid, studied façades, the link between theatre and war chafes. As the radio tells me how Kosovar Albanians are being pushed into railway trucks like the Jews in the Second World War, I read about an Amsterdam theatre, the Hollandse Schouwburg, founded in 1893, and decide I must see it. After a shaky start doing operettas, it became the centre of theatrical life in The Netherlands until the First World War, featuring leading actors in such plays as *The Merchant of Venice*, *Tartuffe* and *Uncle Vanya*.

Among the greatest hits of the Schouwburg were a premonitory play called *Ghetto* (1899); *The Wandering Jew* by Jaap Van Dam (1922); and what sounds like a stirring melodrama for an audience with a seafaring history, *Op Hoop van Zegen – By The Grace of God, A Sea Play* (1900), 'the story of a fishing boat whose owner knows it is no longer seaworthy and which indeed goes down with all hands.' The Act Two curtain-line is 'We pay dearly for fish.'

Set on the edge of the Jewish district, between diamond-traders' houses, the Portuguese Jewish Synagogue and the zoo, the Schouwburg attracted many Jews to its performances. When the Germans occupied the city, they did not create a ghetto. They relied on a meticulous system of registration and control, identity cards and, finally, the yellow star. In 1941 the Hollandse Schouwburg was renamed the 'Joodsche Schouwburg'. Only Jewish performers could play there, and only Jews came to see them. The Great Jewish Entertainment Orchestra under Bernard Drukker, made up of musicians who couldn't play anywhere else, played desperate light music that autumn.

In 1942 it was requisitioned as an assembly-station for the city's

Jews before they were deported, under the pretext of their going to work in Germany, to Westerbork transit camp and then to Auschwitz and Sobibor.

Penned away from their fellow citizens for days behind the neo-classical columns and caryatids of the Schouwburg's façade, stuffed into its plush boxes and orchestra stalls in the dark, obliged to defecate among gilt *putti* and velvet drapes – was it even worse for Amsterdam's Jews, many of them the theatre's former patrons, to remember the tunes and plots and performers of harmless, heartfelt evenings spent in this place? If they had been herded into the iron and concrete stadiums – the Vel' d'Hiver in Paris or the football fields in Chile, the places where persecutors customarily choose to collect their victims – would they have been spared that last sarcastic twist of the knife, that reminder of the good old days, when 'We pay dearly for fish' was as serious a curtain-line as theatre could deliver?

Theatre and war is also what has driven me here to take a deep breath. Theatre and the Trojan War, to be precise. For the past two years, I have been producing – which at this stage means trying to raise nearly two million pounds for – *Tantalus*, a cycle of ten plays about the Trojan War by John Barton, lasting nearly fifteen hours in all, to be performed, if I succeed in getting it together, in the year 2000. It has taken over more and more of my working life, taken more out of me than I anticipated. In the last weeks I have reached the stage where my normally boundless appetite for explaining and enthusing others about this outsize theatre project has begun to curdle. My zest is beginning to turn into a reluctance to pick up the phone or hit the keyboard with yet another digital declaration for co-producers and foundations, ministers and millennial maestros.

I'm burning out, I tell myself, as I wake up, my head instantly filled with lists of the next ten steps to push the Sisyphean boulder up the hill, who to wheedle, who to prompt, to conceal from, to connect, to inform (I start drafting appeals and descriptions while I do my lengths in the pool) and switchback calculations about which of these things to do first. It's a frenzy that can only be stilled by more activity, which builds up its own momentum that produces more frenzy overnight.

Theatre and war, theatre about war, a passion for theatre born after the war; I glimpse myself fighting to bring this theatre juggernaut into being like a demented general leading a campaign, but with no power except persuasion, and no weapons except fax, e-mail and an answering machine in a house at the foot of Highgate Hill. But you can make yourself a labyrinth anywhere; this is the one whose source and exit I am trying to find.

This Easter will be a watershed; if I can't get the funding together, *Tantalus* will fall apart. It's been a tough journey so far.

Autumn 1997

I go to see John Barton two or three times a week, now that we are working together again. He lives and works in a mansion block in New Cavendish Street, with stained-glass windows on the landings, tucked between Broadcasting House and the Chinese Embassy. The lift is the kind of gated polished mahogany cage an art director might choose for a Hercule Poirot period thriller, the plumbing is vintage Agatha Christie.

John has a head which would look good above a ruff in an Elizabethan miniature. Bearded, blue-eyed and crowned with a vigorous rug of hair which belies his near-seventy years. A contender at Queen Elizabeth's court, or a very polite earl or duke, who plays a Machiavellian game with finesse. 'Political' is one of his favourite words, but in the sense of a game played subtly and with a kind of Zen calmness. Perhaps he assimilates it to cricket, which he watches avidly on television, second only to *Newsnight*, whose nightly grilling of politicians enables him to relish rhetoric and tactics under pressure.

John does not, however, have the dress sense of an Elizabethan earl. His wardrobe seems to consist of three grey or grey-green cardigans, which he rotates, an all-purpose pair of trousers and a set of shoes with their backs trodden down. He shuffles down the corridor to greet me, a beaming, intelligent man coming out of his lair. I follow him into this study, Prospero's cell lined with learning, and with the texts of all the theatre he has made.

Black box-files clad the walls, containing nearly forty years'
work as director, adaptor, teacher, writer. The scripts, in various
drafts and stages, go back to *The Wars of the Roses*, his adaptation
and tailoring of all Shakespeare's English history plays, with
which he and Peter Hall forged the ensemble and style of the
Royal Shakespeare Company in the early 1960s. They include
what I think of as his explorations of English nobility – *The
Hollow Crown*, an ironic but not unsympathetic portrait of
royalty, and the *Morte d'Arthur*, Thomas Malory's encrusted
account of King Arthur and his chivalric knights, which John
still loves to perform. By heart, relishing the chewy language as if
he were dipping into a fountainhead of English from a time when
it drew deep from both French and Anglo-Saxon sources. John is
a language junkie. His conversation drips with jokey Tudor *anons*
and *goodlys*, and reminders of Indo-European derivations.
'There's a linguistic link between Fate and fact,' he tells me as a
throwaway. He's mentioned 'a great language epic' which he
intends to get back to when we've completed the job in hand.

Casting my eyes along the shelves as I settle into his heaped
and overheated workspace (some conjunction of complaints in
the legs, back and neck, requiring the continual attention of
osteopaths and masseuses, makes him keep the place at tropical
temperatures), I am reminded that he's directed his own
translations or versions of Ibsen, Calderón, Byron, and hearing
him speak about them I know that what he tracks down are the
contradictions and ironies, above all the 'argument' of each play.
At first I don't get what he means by 'argument', and try to
assimilate it to Aristotle's 'action' or Stanislavski's 'through-line'.
But argument is the plain word for the plain thing he means – the
wrestling of a play, within a speech or a sequence of actions,
which drives it forward. Its grappling, always adversarial, always
engaged, either with other protagonists or directly with the
audience. John is a theatre man, nurtured on Shakespeare; before
he will even consider 'sub-text', he wants to plumb everything
that can be found in the text itself. The words are the character,
he tells actors who ask him about their character's motivation.

I met John when I joined the Royal Shakespeare Company in

1963. Peter Hall had invited him to join the company from King's College, Cambridge, where he had been a don with huge aspirations to become a director. The actors were sceptical at first, and occasionally brutal, but John grew from being seen as a tolerated academic visitor to a respected and much loved theatre person. One of the reasons why he was loved was his cultivated eccentricity, a kind of permanent parody of common-room quiddity. Another was his genuine absent-mindedness and physical unawareness. For a man who was good at arranging stage fights, this was often astonishing. Actors still relate the legend of John giving them notes after a run, tipping back on his chair at the very edge of the stage, talking and smoking non-stop, and then going over the edge into the dark front stalls with a crash, but with the stream of words unabated. This was irrefutable evidence of the life of the mind in that hot-house of appetite, fear and ambition which goes into the making of a play. Bringing John on was one of Peter Hall's most generous and constructive acts at the outset of the Royal Shakespeare Company.

I had taken to John, loved the sensuousness and mock-scholas-ticism and passion of his *Love's Labour's Lost*, and got really excited about a Sunday night he put on at Stratford-upon-Avon in 1964. It was a long double bill of the US Senate Foreign Affairs Committee hearings into the conduct of the Vietnam War – General Westmoreland's cross-examination was its highlight – paired with John's adaptation of *The History of the Peloponnesian War* by Thucydides. The Greek historian's anatomy of the moral morass of the war between Athens and Sparta 2,500 years ago threw a quizzical and ironic light on the pre-processed and tech-nocratic speeches of Westmoreland and Pentagon 'experts'. At a time of feverish denunciations and justifications, John's double bill, performed by the same actors who were playing the kings and king-makers, the rebels and rhetoricians of *The Wars of the Roses*, was a classical and historical gaze at a current convulsion, and one that could only have been done by a publicly funded repertory company. It was citizens' theatre; it gave citizens the means to judge and argue for themselves.

Thucydides became the means by which John Barton and I

made contact again. When the Gulf War loomed at the end of
1990, I called him up and said, 'John, it's time to dust down your
Thucydides for a new war.' We had met in the interim, when I
was in charge of arts programmes at Channel 4 television, first
during the shooting of his Shakespeare workshop series *Playing
Shakespeare*, then when he came with an American director to
discuss a television version of *The Greeks*, his marathon
adaptation of Euripides, Homer and Aeschylus into a saga of the
Trojan War.

In 1990, I told John I thought we should do his Thucydides
adaptation for television, and get it on air before the war started.
With relatively little persuading, and the directorial skill of Jack
Gold as a guarantee, Alan Yentob at BBC2 took a quick decision,
and *The War That Never Ends*, as we retitled it, went out the
weekend before the war began. Preceded by a documentary overture of Bush, Saddam and the gathering of allied armies, it made
a powerful impression, troubling people with its timeless account
of the ambiguity of principles and pronouncements in the run-
up to a war and the inevitable degradation of idealism in its
pursuance.

After doing *The War That Never Ends* on television, we took
it back into the theatre again, staging it on Sunday nights at the
Young Vic, where the Royal Shakespeare Company was playing,
and following each performance with an often fierce debate.
Among the politicians, historians and peace activists who took
part were Tony Benn, Enoch Powell and Rana Kabbani. John
would join in the open discussion from a vantage-point in the
horseshoe-shaped auditorium, untangling his legs to saunter on
stage and ask pointed questions about how human beings
actually behave rather than how ideologues and activists would
like them to behave, and gently insisting on the difficulty of
knowing the truth about anything, and yet having to act. In this
he was like Socrates, and he played Socrates in each performance at the Young Vic, having spliced in that bit of a Plato
dialogue in which Socrates makes the fiery young commander
Alcibiades, Athens' main hope against Sparta, question all his
certainties. I shall always think of Socrates in the John Barton

mould: very good-humoured, extremely polite and ruthlessly consequent.

After Thucydides, we sustained our friendship. I felt that John appreciated my restlessness about getting things done, my frequently quixotic choice of projects which went against the current, and my resilience to his Socratic questioning. I also felt he found me amusing. He gently mocked me when I went into overdrive, and I enjoyed amplifying my indignation when I had been dealt some especially outrageous blow. If one mark of good friends or collaborators is to supply a mirror for each other, John and I are good partners. Which is one of my main reasons for slogging on with *Tantalus*, ten years after John started writing it.

But before *Tantalus*, indeed as the genesis of the production of *Tantalus*, we worked together on *Playing Shakespeare USA*, a new version of John's Shakespeare workshop television series, but with American actors and intended in the first instance for American television. John had for some years been giving Shakespeare workshops in America, at New York's Public Theater, at the Shakespeare Festival Theatre in Stratford, Connecticut, at the Guthrie Theater, Minneapolis. He had helped Mel Gibson play Hamlet in Franco Zeffirelli's film. The book and video of his Channel 4 series had become essential material for American teachers. He had been cast as the Shakespeare guru, the man from Stratford-upon-Avon, the guy who knew the secrets about Shakespeare you couldn't learn from the Method. So when Kevin Kline, who had played Henry V and Hamlet at the New York Shakespeare Festival in Central Park and was John's biggest fan in the American theatre, suggested that John did an American TV version of *Playing Shakespeare*, John asked me to produce it for him. It is out of that collaboration that I find myself trying to set up *Tantalus*.

October 1997

John is still struggling with the last three plays. Or maybe four, because he is continually conflating and folding them together. 'Once I get the argument right, I can write,' he says. I tell him about the remark made by the fourth-century BC Greek comic playwright Menander. 'I have the play,' he said, 'now all I have to do is put the words to it.' Tony Harrison, another shaper of words, plots and arguments prompted by the ancient Greeks, told me that. John nods sagely.

I've now read the first five of his projected twelve ninety-minute plays – until recently there were twenty – and I'm hooked. There's a grim yet humorous inexorability about the story, as he binds together divine interventions and human attempts to escape or defer what is destined. Great figures of the myths and extant tragedies, of Homer and Hesiod, bump into characters who have been little more than marginal walk-ons in the previous literature of the Trojan War, and their presence makes accepted interpretations pivot into something new.

John's modesty makes him say that these characters have been prompted by clues and glimpses in what he refers to as 'the sources', which he says he will one day spell out. But I think he's a playwright for the first time in his life, embarked on a dramatic vessel nearly a decade in the making and so demented in its ambition and dimensions that he takes cover behind the more familiar disguises of adaptor and scholar. Of course there are things I don't like or follow or understand. Before we get to the war itself, there's what feels like a two-hour exposition, in which couplings and antagonisms of gods and humans, matters of miracle and wonderment and grudge, spiral down relentlessly, but leisurely, to the house of Atreus and its war. John stubbornly and cunningly defends it, saying he knows it's long, but everything depends on his getting the final play right.

Tantalus is a puzzling piece. Although its matter, the matter of Troy, prompted some of the greatest plays of fifth-century BC Athens, from Aristophanes' *Peace* to Euripides' *The Trojan Women*, its story and its ethos have nothing of the classical in them. *Tantalus* is, if anything, pre-classical, its story dating from hundreds of years before fifth-century BC Athens created democracy and gave its signature to what we have called classical Greece. They read as utterly modern plays, written in spare verse, in simple language, alert to the savagery of our times. And, in their inversion, their turning-inside-out of the characters and actions we have inherited from legendary Troy, they seem decidedly postmodern. Truths about the war and its meaning become relative, moral conclusions are unravelled.

None of these labels really matters or fits. What comes through is a wry comprehension of human manoeuvres, allied to the pathos and passion of creatures caught in the web of war, its elusive causes and unforeseeable, unending consequences. The women especially, whose roles are majestic, seem to embody John's fierce stoicism, a tenderness tormented into rage or tears. And in the character of a grizzled Poet, more evidently John's *alter ego*, he finds a voice for his rueful awareness of the relentless but infinitely slow whirligigs of time. Now I can see why his shelves are full of books of about how carbon dating proves that our familiar historical landmarks are wrongly situated in the great flow of time. But John is no armchair philosopher or Spenglerian fatalist, seeing the world with pity bordering on resignation. He's a dramatist, with the theatre's multiple focus, portraying life's events and choices as blips in the continuum and yet utterly, compellingly important to mortal beings.

Tantalus is also a play about theatre itself. Going against naturalism, its dozen leading roles will be doubled by eight actors. It could be a reassertion of the strength of the company, the ensemble, and an example of the creative power of actors in a culture of screen behaviourism and personality. And finally, even though he hasn't finished all the plays, there's one massive fact about the whole undertaking. It's already clear, and John's obsessive line-counting as he shifts scenes and passages from one play to another bears this out, that *Tantalus* is going to be about fifteen hours long.

Isn't the whole thing a gigantic folly? What am I doing getting drawn into this behemoth? How could actors ever be persuaded to give two years of their lives to it? Or audiences to go the full distance with it? Could one, in an age of soundbites and three-minute attention-spans, count on people's unmet need for a big, enveloping, extended experience? Something that has the immersive quality of opera, but speaks to the mind as well as the senses, and is more in the world we inhabit? Could I use the advent of the Millennium to urge other theatres (for it's certainly going to need partners) to join us in going beyond the norms?

I've crossed the threshold, from *one* to *I*, I've started to think about *how*, not *whether*; yes, I'm hooked. The Royal Shakespeare Company, of which John remains Advisory Director, has financed his writing of the plays over the past nine years. They will be able to put further money or services into the production, but by no means the whole funding. Now they agree to pay me a small fee to find co-producers and partners for *Tantalus*. I start by writing the Basic Blurb. John raises an eyebrow when he reads it, but only queries one or two of my more heated claims. His mild comments about my salesman epithets recall other critics over the years: John Goodwin, the Royal Shakespeare Company's head of press and publicity, putting his pencil through my 'lapel-grabbing prose', and Andrew Motion doing the same as my editor on a previous book, murmuring, 'I can see you've written too many blurbs.' I must have in mind some notional customer, impassive, easily distracted and not very impressed. It makes me reiterate and underline, fall into ardour. I ask Peter Hall to write a foreword. He writes:

> The power and potency of Greek myths do not need me to define them. They remain at the centre of world culture, and particularly European and North American culture. To re-unite with John Barton to make a huge piece of epic theatre is therefore the most modern gesture I can think of, although the myths John has revived date back to our origins as a species. When we survey the Greek myths, their irony, debate, contradiction and willing embrace of ambiguity all help us to understand our puzzling present in terms of the past. They are rattling good stories; they are also absolutely at the centre of our political and psychological thinking, our ideas of family and power, male and female, war and peace, today. Theatre remains the most immediate form of communication because it is alive. The actor telling the story or singing a song or drawing a picture is the oldest means of knowing. It is what children do naturally. It is primal.

I write my own sales patter, and once again become the Willie Loman of a perversely unfashionable project. I can hear an imaginary off-screen narrator sonorously rolling out my prose, but I don't know any other idiom with which to address culture ministers, sponsors, funders, presenters, co-producers and foundations across the world:

> *Tantalus* is a ten-play saga about the Trojan war [I write] which has captivated human imagination since Homer and Shakespeare. The war continues to mirror political, moral and personal behaviour today, at the end of the Millennium. As well as the war itself, *Tantalus* is about family revenge and the intervention of the gods in our lives. And finally, it is about hope and fear, the feelings with which we approach the millennial turning point. Over the past decade, *Tantalus*, which lasts some fifteen hours in all, has been written by John Barton. It will be directed by Sir Peter Hall and designed by Dionysis Fotopoulos. The full cycle will receive its world premiere in 2000.
>
> The duration of *Tantalus*, the size of its characters, their actions and passions, are on an epic scale. *Tantalus* works as a powerful plot, a family saga with constantly surprising reversals and perspectives, and a war drama with all the pain, pity and blame of war. With this saga, John Barton has gone beyond his admired work as an adaptor of Shakespeare and other classics, and come into his own as a playwright. His re-creation of the whole mythical sweep of the story is provocative, immediate and gripping. *Tantalus* will show that, even in this age of screens and keyboards and digital communication, the hunger for a great story, full of human hope and contradiction, enacted by characters who take us further than our everyday lives, remains unquenched.

November 1997

I have lunch with Peter Hall, in the bistro at the back of the Old Vic. He eases himself into the chair, bigger and rounder than when he first hired me at Stratford-upon-Avon over thirty years

ago; I've also come to look weightier, though less like the sad-
faced spaniel I resembled then. There's still something feline
about him, in the soft voice, something almost feminine in the
curving gestures – immediately belied by the belligerence with
which he attacks opponents, and his pleasure in attacking.

Today he is beaming. The Peter Hall Company, an ensemble
dedicated to the classics which he is running at the Old Vic, has
given him further delight. Not only does it provide him with the
chance of rehearsing all the time, which he says he lives for,
opening plays back to back, running his actors from one role into
another; not only has he jettisoned for the sake of the actors'
salaries most of the stage design that used to cost thousands of
pounds to construct and change over; not only does he keep the
place open seven days a week, with new plays watched by young
audiences on Sundays and Mondays at a £10 top price, thus
proving his contention that the theatre audience could be
transformed if a ticket cost no more than a paperback; he has also
managed to solve the problem of King Lear's followers.

With a small company, and unable to afford extras, he couldn't
see how he could give Lear the unruly retinue of hunters with
which he bursts into Goneril's house and demands hospitality, for
himself and all his people. You can't skimp on theatre extras in
this scene; Goneril beats Lear down, arguing that he doesn't need
so many servants, that her own servants will look after him, until
he explodes, seizing on her reiteration of the word 'need'. 'O
reason not the need,' he cries, comparing her flimsy gorgeousness
with the rags of beggars, and opening up one of the play's fault-
lines, as Lear going down nags away at need's multiple meanings
until he confronts his own bedrock needs in the devastation of
the storm.

'I got the bodies I needed on stage by asking the Old Vic stagehands if they would consider coming on as Lear's servants, for a
bit more money,' he tells me. 'We had a full company meeting,
with the actors' and stagehands' union representatives, and
everyone agreed. I'd never have been able to do that at the Royal
Shakespeare Company or the National. There's a real company
spirit now.'

This makes me think it's less likely that he'll consider directing John's *Tantalus*. Why should he give up for a year or more the only classic repertory company in a historic London theatre, now more than breaking even and affording him great satisfaction? But I think he's the only one to do it, I tell him, not just because he knows John inside out, has already created a Shakespearean theatre epic with him, can stand his ground when John digs in his heels and support him when he has doubts, but also because his own path in theatre, ever since he staged Tony Harrison's *The Oresteia* in masks at the National, and even more since he left the Royal Shakespeare Company and the National to run his own company, seems to point unerringly towards this classic and contemporary, timeless and political saga that John Barton has engendered. 'It's your idea of classic style,' I say. 'The masks of your *Lysistrata* and the Oedipus plays you did, the Greek and Shakespeare productions you've taken to the amphitheatre at Epidaurus, your collaboration with your Greek designer Dionysis Fotopoulos, your fundamental belief that extremes of grief and madness can only be contained and communicated within classic form.'

He starts to calculate how long his contract at the Old Vic has to run, gets out a diary to see how many weeks of rehearsal he would need for *Tantalus*, asks me whether I think John will ever finish it and whether it could really sustain for fifteen hours. He says he's worried that there could be conflicts between him and John such as they never had for *The Wars of the Roses*, because then he was in charge of the theatre. The last thing he would want is to do the piece and hurt his old and dear friend John. There's a mixture of care, generosity, realism and anxiety in what he says. Realism dictates that these questions and concerns will only become more than talking points if I can raise the necessary funds. I give him the nine plays that are now completed in first draft, urge him to read them and call John. He scuttles back to rehearsals.

The Royal Shakespeare Company has now put a value on *Tantalus*. On top of the money it has invested in John while he's been writing, it will contribute free rehearsal space, and 'the equivalent of the production budget for one-and-half plays at the

Swan Theatre', as Lynda Farran, the RSC's executive producer
and right-hand person to its artistic director Adrian Noble, tells
me. If I raise the extra two-thirds of the money, the production
would begin to open (it is too long to open all at once) at the
Swan at the end of 1999, and would be shown in its totality as an
RSC special venture in London later in 2000.

I start by thinking how I can find the extra funds in England. I
write to Peter Mandelson, the minister overseeing the
Millennium Dome project. The Dome and other millennial
projects are benefiting from millions of Lottery money. Surely
they can afford, surely they would like something from the art
form Britain arguably does best (I am tap-dancing on the rim of
chauvinism), and moreover, a theatre piece that challenges and
questions our millennial celebration, our industrialised euphoria?
Mandelson replies promptly, expressing generalised interest and
forwarding the correspondence to Jennie Page, chief executive of
the New Millennium Experience Company, responsible for the
contents and events of the Greenwich Dome.

I call her, and she tells me that it's frightfully interesting, and
that if it were only up to her, she personally would *love* to see it
and so would most of her friends, but the smallest performance
space they are planning is for 6,000 people, and *really* it's not
exactly, I don't know how to put this, not exactly the kind of
thing the masses – well, she doesn't actually talk about the
masses, but I get the gist. Live theatre, unless it's in the Lloyd-
Webber mould, isn't going to find a home in the Dome. I console
myself by saying that it will probably be impossible to create a
soundproof space there for John's words. And I shudder at the
prospect we might have had of doing a fifteen-hour play there,
even split over three evenings, and relying on the Jubilee Line,
still under construction, to get the audience there and back.

This brief brush with the Millennium celebrations is a
reminder that theatre thrives in city centres, in the press and
conviviality of work, residence and pleasure, not in a reclaimed
industrial site far from the centre, devoted to a millennial fair and
powered by technology that displays the wonders of the future
and ignores the weight of the past.

Too true, but I'm going to have to try harder for *Tantalus*.

January 1998
I turn to television. In 1982, when I joined Channel 4, I
persuaded Jeremy Isaacs, its chief executive, to invest £50,000 in
Peter Brook's *The Mahabharata*, then in its early stages of
development. Jeremy agreed, because he wanted Brook's
stripped-down version of *Carmen*, which both the BBC and ITV
were also after. He didn't know what this Indian epic Brook was
cooking up would be – none of us did – but he knew that
investing in it was a way of securing *Carmen* for Channel 4. Brook
filmed *Carmen* – in fact, he filmed it three times, each with a
different Carmen, since because of its vocal demands he needed
three casts to play it in the theatre every night. Channel 4 had a
good response to the three films, and eventually appeared as co-
producer of *The Mahabharata* when it opened at the Avignon
Festival in 1986.

This was an act of strategic investment, supporting a long-term
project to get a short-term property, and the Hindu epic came
into being as theatre in no small part because of an act of
corporate sponsorship of theatre by television. But it does raise
the question why there is so little stomach in the broadcasting
institutions, or in their regulators, to put what for them would be
modest funds into exceptional works of live theatre. It is, after all,
from the theatre that television drama draws so much of its talent.

Here was a British television station acting as partner in an
international theatre production which ran for six hours in
French. Each year when my cost controller examined my budget
and saw this £50,000 for the development of a project which
hadn't yet been realised, she said, 'Shall we write this off now?'
Each year, I said no. Eventually, after *The Mahabharata* had
become an English-language production and had been round the
world, we shot it in Paris in 1989.

The *Mahabharata* precedent is what makes me still seek
meetings with BBC2 and with Channel 4. But we are nearly a
decade on, there are five terrestrial channels and Rupert
Murdoch's tentacles. Competition, narrowcasting and channel

proliferation have become the watchwords of the day. Sport and movies are doing well in the new dispensation, but arts and cultural programmes are shrinking and mutating, more and more devoted to the celebrities of other people's agendas, or to landmark classics of ballet, opera or the nineteenth-century English novel.

Still, I think it is worth a try with *Tantalus*, and write to Mark Thompson, Controller of BBC2, and to Alan Yentob, the BBC's Director of Television. Peter Hall adds a letter to Sir Christopher Bland, the BBC Chairman. We make the same points: not only is *Tantalus* likely to be exceptional and extraordinary as a millennial enterprise, it is of such a scope and ambition that from the outset it needs sympathetic partners in the public sector of culture. We say we believe that the BBC, by virtue of its goals and ideals, even in a changing broadcast environment, should seriously consider becoming a co-producer of *Tantalus* by putting up some money now, and joining the venture with the Royal Shakespeare Company and others. It would then have a creative involvement, with a director and screenwriter in rehearsals, so that the eventual screen version could be developed organically, and not simply be the interpretation of a completed theatre piece.

Mark Thompson reads the scripts, and gives them to Simon Curtis, formerly of the Royal Court Theatre, who has been doing imaginative things with theatre scripts in a BBC2 slot called *Performance*, including Marlowe's *Edward the Second* directed by Derek Jarman, and with theatre directors like Deborah Warner directing her *Hedda Gabler* for the camera for the first time. Peter and I meet Mark and Simon in a rooftop bar at the St George's Hotel, looking down on Broadcasting House. It turns out not only that Mark Thompson has been taught at Cambridge by Anne, John Barton's wife, but that he knows Homer and *The Iliad* well, and appreciates what John has done in his reworking of the sources into original plays. This is a good start.

But it's also clear that BBC2 will find it very difficult to envisage even a relatively small development investment, when it cannot see clearly enough ahead. Although it has a planning cycle like every channel, it is, as a result of John Birt's rationalisations, entering a new process which will be 'schedule-led'. This means that the output to the viewer, in the form of a schedule, will determine what is commissioned. And that schedule is shaped by assumptions about what people want, never about what might astonish them. It gives more power to the executives and planners, and less to the creators and originators. Something as unprecedented and boundary-breaking as *Tantalus* is unlikely to endear itself to the planners and ideologues of the Corporation, even though BBC2 is meant to be its path-breaking, innovative and, yes, upmarket channel.

We leave the meeting with a well-let's-see in our ears. Peter seems a bit deflated as we go down in the lift. Perhaps he's right to be. When I ring Simon Curtis, who hadn't finished reading the scripts at the time of our meeting, he splutters admiration for Peter and respect for the scripts, but then he says, 'Look, it would consume my entire budget for a year.' I say, 'I know it would, but it won't happen that way, we're looking for support not from your budget but from the BBC as a public-funded, broadly cultural body. It's a political and strategic decision we're looking for. Your opinion about the value of the piece could help that.'

I get the name of someone in Microsoft who is interested in developing new educational material. I am convinced there could be a rich multi-media *Tantalus* for sixth-formers and university students. I write a letter to my Microsoft UK contact saying that *Tantalus* is going to happen, brandishing as many knee-jerk names of partners as I can and covering myself with the weasel phrase 'discussions are under way with'. Everyone in this business knows how much puffery is used to get big projects off the ground. It may be bad for my prose, but if I don't communicate as if it's about to happen, *Tantalus* never will.

The meeting with Channel 4 is more perfunctory than the BBC one. We meet Michael Jackson, who has just arrived from the BBC as chief executive. Bushy-haired, thin, unnervingly still, he listens to us expound our project. He seems so contained, so plugged into the Norman Foster high-tension steel container of Channel 4's new headquarters, such a media monk. *Tantalus* seems too unbuttoned in this context, too excessive and sprawling for a medium in which drama customarily means naturalistic surfaces, raw *verismo* or behaviourist intimacy. He smiles, a rather shy touching smile, and tells us that it sounds interesting, he's sorry he hasn't had a chance to read the scripts, and even sorrier that his new head of drama won't be joining the channel for a couple of months, and he'll have a lot to learn before he could take a major decision like this. So it's another wait-and-see. On the way out, John, who gave a five-minute account of how he came to write *Tantalus*, is mystified. 'Was he really interested? Or just politely putting us off?'

May 1998

John and I are in New York, to do his *Playing Shakespeare USA* workshops at Brooklyn Academy of Music. It doesn't look as if we're going to get them onto American television, despite the presence of Kevin Kline and Helen Hunt, who has just won an Oscar for playing opposite Jack Nicholson in *As Good As It Gets*, and is about to play Viola at Lincoln Center.

I've introduced John to Jac Venza, who runs the main arts and drama strand of American Public Television, which is so poor that it regularly suspends normal programmes to solicit money from the public, and spends almost as much time hunting and pleasing sponsors as making programmes. John tries to tell Jac, a theatre buff, about *Tantalus* when he discovers Jac has seen *The Greeks*, which was its matrix. His exposition is hindered by the appalling decibel level in the restaurant, which is crowded with voluble customers, histrionic waiters and shiny designer surfaces that amplify every hearty honk of laughter. Sipping his margarita faster, John's right eye gets more basilisk, which I have come to recognise as a sign either of mild anger or bewilderment or both.

The situation is not improved by the late-night arrival of Jon Cutler and his buddy Bill Shea. Jon I have met through John's theatre connections over here: he is the Barnum-like real-estate developer of the hitherto defunct Shakespeare Festival Theatre in Stratford, Connecticut, which is, he tells us, going to arise phoenix-like and renewed as the centrepiece of an entertainment/commercial/residential complex, prettily illustrated, as always, in his promotional brochure. Jon is also a producer, with two Broadway revivals to his credit: 'Lilian Hellman's *Little Foxes*,' he says, 'and the geriatric revival of *My Fair Lady* with Rex Harrison.'

Jon is ever-hopeful, soft-spoken, shy and immediately loveable, with something approaching reverence for John Barton and Shakespeare and the classics. He would be good casting as Sancho Panza to John's Don Quixote. He explains that he'd be honoured to work with us guys, and that his value in raising money for *Tantalus* lies in his extensive contacts. One of these, he whispers in my ear, is his companion Bill Shea, who is the son of the founder of the famous Shea Stadium, a hallowed baseball venue, and the place where the Beatles played their most famous US gig. Shea, who would not be out of place as a slightly threatening David Mamet character, has brought his bosomy girlfriend with him. She orders a plate of shrimps. It's getting pretty late. Jac Venza is not best pleased.

Next day he tells me he had been expecting an artistic discussion with John Barton, not a talk about deals and funding with two operators. But he agrees to write a letter to the headquarters of Public Television in Washington, stating his interest in WNET's becoming 'the presenting station' for *Playing Shakespeare USA*. This does not commit WNET, the New York public television station, to provide or raise funds, but makes the project more credible when we are fundraising and may give us access to a small amount of funding from Washington. I try explaining the tortuous American public television system to John, sitting in the gothic interior of his room at the Chelsea Hotel, where Thomas Wolfe and Arthur Miller lived and Dylan Thomas died. He wants to know why it's called public television when we still have to go out and find sponsors.

Meanwhile Jon Cutler, who has raised $50,000 from his investment associates to pay for John's workshops in Brooklyn, telling them it will raise the profile of their Stratford, Connecticut, project, holds out hope of raising serious money for *Tantalus* through his connections. He reels off a litany of corporate names – in telephony, insurance, electricity and banking – whose chairmen, or the sons of whose chairmen, or the number twos to whose chairmen he knows. He'll make a brochure – another promotional brochure – with the blurbs and letters I've given him. Well, he has raised dollars for *Playing Shakespeare*.

But there's nowhere near enough to make the workshops as television, even on the lean budget that our director, Oren Jacoby, has made. I spend the last few days before John is due to begin in a round of talks with cable channels, distributors and potential underwriters. There is some interest from a video distributor which, with the money we will get from Washington (whose Head of Cultural Programming turns out to be a John Barton *afficionado*), could just about cover the budget. But I can't tie it down before I have to leave for the Cannes film festival.

For while with my right hand I have been trying to propel *Tantalus*, with my left I have been trying to get *Pandaemonium* off the ground. *Pandaemonium* is a feature film about Coleridge, Wordsworth, friendship, betrayal, revolution, poetry and drug addiction. I combine these ingredients in different ways depending on who I'm pitching to. The consensus of this year's Cannes festival is that the pendulum is swinging against costume dramas, and however much we insist that it's not a classic heritage adaptation like the Jane Austen movies which have sprouted in the past year, I can see the downturned lip and filmed-over eye of the American sales agent or European distributor we are courting. Assimilation is the name of the game – if you can assimilate your project to a successful film crowned by the market and *Variety* magazine, you're in luck. If it assimilates to some turkey, forget it. I find myself saying, in the fabled thirty-second pitch you're supposed to make to grab interest, that *Pandaemonium* will be more like *Trainspotting* than Jane Austen. Well, our story does also pivot on drugs, even if Coleridge was hooked on opium and on poetry rather than cocaine.

With our director Julien Temple, who has been thinking about this film for years and lives in the West Country Quantocks, where Coleridge and Wordsworth spent their *annus mirabilis* and wrote *The Lyrical Ballads* and *The Ancient Mariner* and *Kubla Khan*, and with Nick O'Hagan my co-producer, who is young enough to plunge into this maelstrom of deal-making with zest, I put myself about the bars and parties along the Croisette, giving the pitch, switching from English to French, watching an aspirant French film-maker defer to a loud-mouthed, opinionated American huckster proclaiming how he loves the youth of Cannes and eyeing up a comely female *cinéaste*, while at the back of my brain a taxi-meter is ticking up how much this possibly fruitless trip is costing me. We do have one meeting which on paper looks promising, with Andrea Calderwood, head of production at Pathé, who we have already met in London, who has read and enjoyed the script and is a good friend of Robert Carlyle, the star of *Trainspotting*, who Julien has interested in playing Coleridge.

Carlyle, 'Bobby' to those in his circle, got mellow with Julien one evening in London, talked about the time he spent driving small theatre round the wilds of Scotland, and said he was at heart a serious actor and not just a star. He seems genuinely to want to play the part – as long as we get the money together in time, and his agent doesn't let one of the fully-funded American films get him first. Everyone here in the sunshine, beneath the lurid banners and billboards for Hollywood's socko boffo best, is juggling such provisional semi-commitments with money, time and weather – for if a film doesn't start shooting on a given date, it can wait a year for the right weather. When a film gets the go-ahead, it is, in industry parlance, 'green-lighted'. But the red light can keep you standing still for a very long time.

We meet Andrea and her Pathé colleagues on the front lawn of one of the big hotels. After some small talk and movie-huddle, she and her script reader give us a detailed, measured but positive response to the screenplay, ask some hard questions about the input of the BBC, which commissioned it, and about our advance against distribution. I'm listening, not saying much, for I'm aware here at Cannes that I might appear like some dinosaur from the public-funded world of art and culture, in blissful denial of market laws. After half-stifled guffaws at ineffable bullshit from some earlier potential partners, my colleagues begged me to stifle the irony until we had the money in the can, so I've learned to bite my tongue, though there's no need with these Pathé people. But when Andrea Calderwood says that Pathé likes the movie and will do it with us, I can't suppress a whoop, which turns the heads of various languid deal-makers across the lawn, as I rush indoors to collar a waiter to bring champagne.

Before I leave Cannes, I go to the office of Fox-Lorber, the video distributors who showed interest in New York in putting up an advance for *Playing Shakespeare USA*, and who are down here pitching their substantial catalogue of documentaries, educational series and art-house features. Kathy, a friendly, fast-talking woman, has been encouraging over the past few days. But now she tells me she's spoken to the owner of the company, who says he loves the project but can't possibly take a decision about it in the tight deadline we require. 'But it's only tight because John has to start on Monday,' I say. 'And he only has to start on Monday because of the availability of the actors. Do you know what it took to find a clear day for Kevin Kline and Helen Hunt?' Much head-shaking, but our last chance of putting John's Shakespeare workshops on television has gone, for now at least. I call John in New York, and Oren Jacoby, who has been making frenzied last-minute efforts, and tell them the television's off. This time John doesn't even want an explanation. He's too busy girding his loins for the three weeks of workshop sessions, which will now be for a devoted but tiny audience. Kevin Kline and Helen Hunt turn up anyway, television or no television. They spend a day working on the scenes of Orsino and Viola with John, who gets them to dig into the ironies beneath the courtesy and formality of the language.

June 1998
What is variously referred to as 'the front money' or 'seed money' for *Tantalus*, which has been provided by the Royal Shakespeare Company, is running out, and I am now beginning to subsidise the telephone, e-mails and fax, not to mention the time I am stealing from other pursuits. But I cannot let go, not until all alleys have become blind ones, and the thing has no future.

Paul Collard calls, saying he's heard about *Tantalus* from his mother. He's the son of Eleni Cubitt, a feisty Greek woman from Thessaloniki, widow of an English architect. In the eighties Eleni and I ran a production company called The Greek Collection, dedicated to bringing the classical Greek legacy into the modern world through all media. Eleni cajoled friends in power in Athens and members of the Greek community in London, and raised enough money for us to produce four films for Channel 4 for the 2,500th anniversary of democracy and for John Barton's Thucydides adaptation that BBC2 screened on the eve of the Gulf War. She was then unjustly victimised by vindictive and chauvinist journalists in the Athens press, who said the money should have gone to Greek artists and producers. Some even went as far as to accuse her of lining her own pocket. Her excitement in our work was equalled by her pain at being scapegoated by her probably jealous compatriots.

Her son Paul is as voluble and zesty as she is. After managing the Institute of Contemporary Arts in London, and running the North of England's year-long visual arts festival, he has now decamped to New Haven, where he's directing the city's annual festival of Arts and Ideas. A gifted cultural entrepreneur, he sees a possibility of getting Yale University to make a co-production investment in *Tantalus*. 'Yale will be celebrating its 300th anniversary in 2001,' he says. 'They will have extra funds for the occasion and are looking for a major event. I'd like to have a go at selling them *Tantalus* as a symbol of the culture the university stands for, and as something all the key departments – the School of Drama, of Classics, of History, of Philosophy – can get involved in. Seminars, lectures, workshops around your performances.' I send him the Basic Blurb, and new information to help his pitch.

Peter Hall calls, in some excitement. He's been talking to his friend Nikos Kourkoulos, director of the Greek National Theatre in Athens. Nikos has hosted the visit of Peter's *Oresteia*, *Cymbeline* and the *Oedipus* plays to the open-air theatre at Epidaurus, through which they have become good friends. Nikos is one of Greece's leading actors, married to the daughter of one of the great ship-owning dynasties of Greece, which means he's rich enough to have a boat with a twelve-man crew, and a private

helicopter and jet. In spite of all these privileges, Nikos has taken
on the often thankless task of running the National Theatre,
which means dealing with fickle politicians and bureaucratic
inertia. But it also means he has direct access to the Minister of
Culture.

'Nikos has arranged for me to meet the Minister to talk about
Tantalus,' says Peter. 'The only way I can fit it in with rehearsals
is to leave this Saturday afternoon and come back Monday. Can
you pay for the ticket?' I say yes, and then wonder how I'm going
to do it. Peter says he's too old and too large to travel economy,
and his charming assistant Corinne tells me that 'his hotel in
Athens' is the Grande Bretagne, which is Athens' answer to the
Ritz. I take a deep breath, remind myself to remind Peter of the
conditions in which we're working and of my own hidden
subsidy, and talk it over with John. John murmurs and shifts and
says, 'This is an emergency, a real chance for us. I'll talk it over
with my sister, and see if she can't help out with a loan.' He does;
she can, and thus becomes an angel of the production; Peter goes.

I meet him on his return, Monday lunchtime in a tiny Japanese
sushi-house in Brewer Street, behind the Piccadilly Theatre,
where the Peter Hall Company is now installed. The owners of
the Old Vic, the generous Canadian food and entertainment
businessmen Ed and David Mirvish, had decided that they
needed to rationalise their empire and had to sell it. Peter had
spent weeks trying to assemble a rescue package, getting words of
support but no promises from Chris Smith, our Secretary of State
for Culture, but had failed. The farewell performance had been
fiery, the goodbye speeches heartfelt and, in Peter's case, tearful.
Now, with the help of Bill Kenwright, the producer who has
worked with him before, he's picked himself up again and is
starting to do well at the Piccadilly. All this, and *Tantalus* too.

'The Greek Minister of Culture – his name is Venizelos – is
very bright and capable. Nikos took me to his office and we met
last night, Sunday night, and talked for an hour. It was a good
talk. He's an intellectual, professor of law at Athens University.
He understands *Tantalus,* sees that it's not a modern revival, but
a contemporary reworking of the myths. He wants to see the

budget, and might be prepared to match the RSC contribution. It's important for him that it tours in Greece to other ancient sites, including Thessaloniki, which is his constituency. He wants it to go to the Olympics arts festival in Sydney in 2000. It's clear he sees it as a feather in his cap, both domestically and internationally. Nikos tells me he's tipped as a future Prime Minister. I told him you and John would come out to meet him.'

There's some jubilation at the Royal Shakespeare Company, and a well-done note from Adrian Noble. Lynda Farran and her dedicated staff, starting a new Stratford-upon-Avon season and facing yet another financial crisis, buckle down and provide John and me with budgets and production and performance schedules. We have now reached schedule 27. John loves getting schedules done, making charts, doing line-counts. He needs to do them. It must be his way of dealing with writing blocks, with the immensity of guiding his great dramatic vessel into harbour. Schedules provide a mindless mathematical occupation that stills his anxiety.

Armed with our data, John and I set out for Athens. The Royal Shakespeare Company, encouraged by this first sign of progress, has put up a little more money, with a warning that it will be the last, and I have paid for our flights from it. John gets an aisle seat so that he can stretch out his leg. He's alarmed by flying; on the way back from New York, something happened to his chest – 'it blew up' is the phrase he always uses – and he was on antibiotics for weeks. At Athens airport, the light and the space and the surrounding hills are as welcome as ever, and Nikos' chauffeur takes us to the hotel. John holes up in his room, I go for a walk in the Pláka, failing to find the little shop of the antique dealer who sells Nazi memorabilia near the Agora. I swear I once saw the signed document of surrender of Crete in his window, flanked by SS dolls and vicious hunting knives.

At dusk the chauffeur returns to take us out to Nikos' club, an hour-long drive through the habitual clog of traffic. Nikos greets us, in white denim trousers and rolled-up shirtsleeves, the picture of a fifty-ish one-time matinee idol. He has that combination of strength and delicacy that reminds me of Albert

Finney. Like many actors, his bravura hides an inner insecurity. This may explain why he smokes like a chimney, is tense as a harp-string, and shows pleasure by explosions of laughter. Or maybe it's because of the cares of running the Greek National Theatre.

Over dinner by the side of the club's pool, he seems to take great pleasure not just in John's exposition, but in John's character. Sometimes John, with his hermit humour and old-fashioned charm, has the effect of a secret, because totally unexpected, weapon. Later, Nikos tells me emphatically, 'I *adore* John.'

We meet next morning at the offices of the Ministry of Culture. Nikos is now wearing a suit, and with him is Dionysis Fotopoulos, who Peter has asked to design *Tantalus*. Dionysis has worked with every Greek director who matters, and with many leading directors abroad. He has probably done every play in the canon of Greek tragedy two or three times. He has the face of a wicked cherub, grey-blue eyes and silver locks, and a quality at once cuddly and impassive which is said to have a serious effect on young women. He commands great respect in government circles, as an artist, an international success and an oracular authority.

The Ministry is a 1960s building, but redolent of a much older Central European bureaucracy. Byzantine, perhaps. In the lobby and corridors there are groups of men in check shirts with five o'clock shadows, muttering and smoking heavily. Security guys? Porters? Casually dressed drivers? As lift doors close, a boy carrying a hanging tray with four tiny cups of thick Greek coffee shoehorns his way in. For sure, we are in what nineteenth-century Western Europe called 'the Levant'.

Evangelos Venizelos, the Minister, is heavy-set – well, actually fat – and young, I'd put it at early forties. His features, set in a well-fleshed, compacted face, are intent, and it's soon clear that he has a rapid, impatient intelligence. He quizzes us on the nature of John's text, he wants to be assured that these are new plays, not adaptations of the classics. John gives a lucid reply. Venizelos wants to know where the rest of the money is coming from. I say that if Greece agrees to match the Royal Shakespeare Company's promised contribution, we should have two-thirds of the budget. With the Greek National Theatre and the RSC involved, I say, it should be easier for me to get the rest from other co-producers, from the European Union – 'I know Mr Pappas, the head of the culture section of the Commisssion,' he says – or from America, where Yale is examining it as a cornerstone of their tercentenary.

'What about Australia?' he says. 'There are 800,000 Greeks in Australia, the biggest community outside Greece. I'd like it to go to the Sydney Olympics Arts Festival in 2000.' Fine, I say, even better if they can put up some money as co-producers, not just pay the costs of presenting it. 'And I would like you, Mr Barton, to come back and meet some of my professor colleagues from the classics department of Athens university. You must explain to them that you have not just done another modernising of our classic drama, we are wary of that, but a *new imagining* of the myths, Mr Barton.' I know why he is insisting on this point, and say so; 'If you help us, Mr Venizelos, we have to avoid the Greek newspapers saying that you are giving a lot of good money away to foreigners to misinterpret your ancient plays.' He nods rapidly, already catching another train of thought: 'We should organise a colloquium, yes, maybe first in Athens and then in Yale, called The Survival of the Myths in the Information Age.' Nikos looks pleased at the performance of his English duo.

Venizelos is an enthusiast, I think, shrewd and sophisticated and doubtless ambitious for sure, but certainly giving every sign of a willingness to support *Tantalus*. Dionysis mutters what must be a laconic recommendation, and the Minister then asks Nikos to give him a report on the budget, after which he will make his decision. I say we really need a response in eight weeks if we are to secure the remainder of the funds, secure the talent and start rehearsing as planned in June 2000. I have a feeling this will be the first of many receding deadlines.

It's nearly noon. John is desperate for a drink. Dionysis, who has flown in from Munich where he's preparing a production with Peter Stein, has invited us for lunch at his house across the bay, near the classical amphitheatre of Epidaurus, which could be a venue for *Tantalus*. Nikos has offered the family helicopter, and drives us to the airport. On the airstrip, surrounded by a fleet of people's private planes, the pilot and co-pilot introduce themselves. One is called Geoff, the other Brian. They look like RAF airmen in 1950s British films – decent, good-humoured, stiff upper lip. They fly us over a turquoise sea. John has opened his briefcase in the cabin and is struggling to mix mineral water with a miniature bottle of *ouzo* he has bought at the airport. Dionysis looks on, more impassive than ever. I look down at boats scudding through the shining sea, and wish I was on one.

The landing in Dionysis' village is dramatic. Geoff and Brian bring us down on the village football pitch, raising a deafening clatter and a major dust-storm from the pitch. Angry neighbours on its perimeter try to pull their windows shut against the dust, coughing and shouting and shaking their fists. We jump out and walk on, Dionysis, more deadpan than ever, in the lead with his baggage over his shoulder, John loping in the rear with his briefcase probably stocked with more *ouzo* miniatures and me feeling foolish and wondering when we get lynched.

We get lunched instead, by Dionysis in his local taverna. Burly local men come over, shake him by the hand, slap his back, he offers drinks, there seem to be no hard feelings, perhaps the place is proud of their incorrigible local hero. He makes an assignation with a young actress to meet after tonight's dress rehearsal at Epidaurus, and thereafter seems more relaxed. John tries to have a serious talk with him about stage design, but as Dionysis is either monosyllabic or skittish, John soon looks bemused.

'Too hot to go now to Epidaurus,' Dionysis announces. 'You come to my house, we sleep, maybe swim.' Dionysis' house, further round the bay, is hung with masks, maquettes and sketches. The sketches have a sure rapidity, the masks are serene or paroxysmic. On the couch lies a bikini, on the wall an erotic surrealist nude. John elects to sit on the terrace and snooze. Dionysis gives him a couple of monographs of his prolific designs to read, and he dutifully turns the multi-coloured pages of Dionysis' imaginary worlds realised on the stages of the world. From the sea, I look up and watch John, scrutinising the books and then raising his eyes to squint at the bright afternoon sky. He must be going through the pain of separation as his long-gestated baby is about to be seized by other, possibly rougher, hands.

Towards sunset, we go to Epidaurus, a spatial miracle. Twelve thousand spectators can sit in a half-spherical bowl, and everyone feels close. I climb up the uneven stone steps, sit near the back row of stone benches, look down into the playing space, and it seems to come at me. How to have both epic size and intimacy with such numbers is still mysterious, how to create an acoustic of such fullness and closeness a puzzle, though I remember Denys Lasdun, who based his National Theatre Olivier auditorium on this space, saying that one of its secrets was the number of asymmetries and irregularities in the making of the space. No doubt its location, high above a long valley curtained with cypress trees, also has something to do with it. Epidaurus is a theatre with authority.

And that may be why it's not right for *Tantalus*. Maybe it's too classical, too consecrated by generations of reinterpreted ancient tragedies. Standing on the spacious circular *orchestra* where the chorus once stomped and swayed and sang, I know for sure that what John has nearly finished is a modern piece, in which the gods are as unreliable as the humans, in which the lyric and the choric support but are finally eclipsed by the ironic and the argumentative. That may be why this chastening theatre, especially haunting as light fades and birds sing in the darkening trees, may be unsuitable for *Tantalus*. I have an image of it being done instead in a building site in central Athens, or even an archaeological site, though we'd never get permission. An unfinished place, rather than the classical closure of Epidaurus. A place surrounded by the clutter and tackle of uncovering, investigation, reconstructing.

Late summer 1998
The pace slows a little, I have time to turn to my other projects. For *Pandaemonium*, I start to write more advocacy prose for the application we are making to the Arts Council Lottery Film Fund. It's time also to start launching Tony Harrison's *Prometheus*

film into the world. I go with my fellow producer Andrew Holmes to a meeting at Film Four Distributors, who will handle our film, which defies most of the norms in today's film business, having no stars, no love interest, no cute plot, no feelgood factor and being 95 per cent written in rhyming couplets, an awful lot of them. The Film Four people are eager to make it work, but wary; they must apply most of their resources to plugging the more mainstream films whose punchy posters deck their walls. We decide to start by trying to get the film to a British and – with a French subtitled version – an international film festival. If successful there, the film will collect reviews and the beginning of a reputation that will encourage foreign distributors to take it on for their own territories.

Over the next few weeks we get a negative response from the Edinburgh Film Festival, whose director wishes Tony's visual poetry matched his verbal brilliance, and grudging admiration from Derek Malcolm, the *Guardian*'s former film critic, now advising the Venice festival, who finds it visually brilliant but too long. They may be right – though they can't both be right– but I can't help thinking of the number of occasions over the years where a work was so radically new and different that its first viewers literally couldn't see what was there. Beckett's *Waiting for Godot*, Pinter's *The Homecoming* were both derided and dismissed by all but a few when they appeared. Now they are part of the landscape.

Eventually *Prometheus* is accepted by the Locarno film festival in Switzerland. Tony has been fine-tuning the film up the last minute, putting in a provisional ending because, despite promises and pressure, we have not been able to get a firm date for the demolition of some Yorkshire cooling-towers Tony needs to round off his film. So as a result of wheelings and dealings in Doncaster, Andrew is unable to get a print finished and despatched to Locarno in time, and we are relegated to a slot in the festival's final week.

The bleary-eyed film-gobblers who do turn up to our two screenings are moved to tears and heated debate. Marco Muller, director of the festival, gives us a celebratory lunch, goes down on one knee in homage to Walter Sparrow, the septuagenarian actor who incarnates the Promethean spirit of defiance, and tells me how much he loves the film and how we could have got a better slot and much more coverage if it had arrived sooner.

At breakfast in Ascona, where as a producer I am billeted with most of the distributors, I make the rounds of the terrace, handing out promotional postcards and peddling *Prometheus*. People listen politely, consult their screening schedules, but most of the key independent distributors have left. I console myself and switch out of street-trader mode by going for a walk through the woods around the hillside conference centre where we are staying. Peering through the windows of wooden huts under the pine trees, I see strange costumes, rough Tolstoyan shirts and flowing Isadora Duncan gowns. I see photographs of long-haired women dancing eurhythmically in unison, muscled youths baring their bodies to the dawn. I see theosophical diagrams on the walls, a print of a sturdy oak, the Tree of Liberty, its roots in Plato, its branches in the nineteenth-century labour movements, its twigs in anarcho-syndicalism.

It clicks: I am staying on what was at the turn of the nineteenth century Monte Veritá, the most famous and determined Utopian community in modern Europe. These huts have clearly been turned into an on-site museum, and I resolve to find my way in before I leave. Peddling my wares in the marketplace of industrialised stories and pictures, I feel so far away from the passionate simplicities of these bearded vegetarians and nudist earth-diggers of a century ago, these pioneer abstract artists and fresh air worshippers, beetle-browed therapists and affirming homosexuals, building a kibbutz of experiment, a sanatorium for a continent's perturbed spirit, on the southern slopes of north Europe before World War One slithered it into the mud.

Autumn 1998

The Greeks come to London to talk about the *Tantalus* budget. We have an all-day meeting in Adrian Noble's office at the Barbican, accountants speaking to cost controllers, managers to managers. Next day, Saturday, we meet at Nikos' London flat, a

Mayfair penthouse. Nikos is angry. He believes the Royal Shakespeare Company is loading some of its routine costs onto the budget. The figure they have put in for the costs of keeping John writing for nine years astounds him. 'And there's also an item for author's royalties!' he booms. Under his assault, Lynda Farran wilts a little, admits that the royalties shouldn't be there because John has waived them, but defends her corner. She's ready to reduce the development costs charged to the production, but that, she warns, will reduce the RSC's total input, and therefore also the Greeks' matching contribution. 'So be it,' Nikos indicates, clearly still feeling that his theatre is being rooked.

The real sticking point, however, is the cost of touring the production. We have worked on the normal assumption that the hosts for each of our appearances once the whole work has been premiered will bear the costs of bringing and presenting the production, and will keep the box-office take. This is routine practice when theatre productions go on tour, or indeed play a long run. For reasons we cannot understand, Nikos and his team insist on putting the full costs of presenting the show around the world into the budget and not counting any ticket revenue. This, as I point out, will push the budget close to an impossible £5 million, an impossible target for most theatre productions except for a long-running musical, which unlike *Tantalus* is not fifteen hours long and does have the possibility of going into profit. As this circular argument proceeds, with the Greeks remaining obdurate, Peter musters all his persuasive power and John looks as if he's wishing he were somewhere else. We agree to disagree. It doesn't bode well for Nikos' report to his Minister.

A *deus ex machina* arrives, like Apollo descending from the heights to ease and arbitrate human woe. His name is Donald Seawell, he is an 85-year-old American, a governor of the Royal Shakespeare Company and a fan of John's. John has just had a letter from him, offering to finance the television series of *Playing Shakespeare USA* we failed to get off the ground this spring. He will shortly be in London and wants to meet. 'Let's tell Don about *Tantalus*,' says John, and writes back saying we also have a new project to discuss and he will bring me to the meeting.

Donald Seawell is cat-like and silver-haired, with a papery voice, a lawyer's precision and a Turnbull & Asser tie. We meet him in his suite in his London lair, the hushed and distinguished Connaught Hotel. I tell him the last time I came here was over twenty years ago, to have lunch with Barbara Schall, Brecht's daughter, who shared her father's epicurean tastes.

Don got to know John when as a young producer he had brought over two Royal Shakespeare productions to America – Clifford Williams' *Comedy of Errors* and John's parade of English kings and queens, *The Hollow Crown*. He and John reminisce about the high and low points of that tour a quarter of a century ago, and Don tells how he managed to get *The Hollow Crown* performed in the White House auditorium for President Kennedy and his guests. 'The President, who was always being compared with King Arthur and his court, loved the show,' says Don. 'But Adlai Stevenson was absolutely besotted with Dorothy Tutin, who seemed to enjoy him. He had to fly off next day to Moscow. A few days later, the phone rings. It's Adlai: could I arrange for him to take Dottie out for dinner when he comes to London? I was pleased to.' Don stops, and lets the climax of the story tell itself in silence, like a curl of cigar-smoke.

By allusions and references, Don fills out his life, to make us realise who we're dealing with. A young lawyer, who became attorney to the Securities and Exchange Commission, who interrogated witnesses at Nuremberg and wrote speeches for Roosevelt. A passionate theatre fan, who began to represent the stars of his time – Noël Coward, Gertrude Lawrence, Alfred Lunt and Lynn Fontanne – in his legal practice, and soon became more manager than lawyer. One of the pioneers of the movement for an American National Theatre. Proprietor and publisher of the *Denver Post*, which he sold profitably, investing the money in building a five-stage theatre complex, the Denver Center for the Performing Arts. You wouldn't want to be cross-examined by this soft-spoken steely man. But he's a card.

He is ready, he says, to wholly finance the making of John's Shakespeare workshop series, providing it is shot at his Denver centre, and carries Denver's name as the promoter of the Shakespeare tradition into schools and colleges, onto television and CD-Roms. John and I give Don profuse thanks. Then he asks us to tell him about *Tantalus*, and we do our by now well-rehearsed act. He listens motionless for five minutes, then asks if he can read the scripts.

I invite him to come to the *Tantalus* workshop, which is starting at the National Theatre Studio next Monday. 'We've got together a group of actors,' I explain, 'and for two weeks, with Peter Hall leading it, we're going to work through John's text, reading a play a day, discussing it, turning it this way and that, re-reading it, to give a taste of this material which is so extensive it's hard to handle on the page.' Don says he'll come on the afternoon of day one, before he flies back home.

Monday morning at the National Theatre Studio in the Old Vic Annexe: the usual effusive, boisterous greetings of actors starting a new piece of work. Many of these actors – Norman Rodway, Jane Lapotaire, Harriet Walter, Penelope Downie, Lisa Harrow, John Carlisle, Oliver Ford-Davies – are Royal Shakespeare Company alumni, and have been through seasons at Stratford-upon-Avon and London together, playing kings and courtiers, penetrating Shakespearean heroes and dazzlingly articulate Shakespearean heroines. They are classically-based actors, holding the craft they learned from John Barton and Peter Hall as a sheet-anchor against the wild winds and follies that can rock an actor's life.

Peter arrives in a broad-brimmed black hat, and is soon hunched into a corner with his mobile. He has told me he's in dispute with his producer Bill Kenwright, the guarantor and backstop of the Peter Hall Company, in which Kenwright seems as determined to exercise his authority over Peter, by all means possible, as Peter is to resist his bullying. It's only his allegiance to the actors, to his lifeblood of rehearsal, I think, that enables him to put up with the daily sniping and obstruction. If the falling-out is as final as it looks to be, Peter is going to need *Tantalus* even more.

The days roll by in the long, low-ceilinged rehearsal room, with everyone sitting in a circle, script and pencil in hand, digging their way into John's stuff, finding its voice, its form and, yes, its argument. Impassioned questions and objections are made, terrier-like worrying at the levels of reality and representation of the gods is aired, all characteristically met by John with a courtly politeness and a rooted insistence that there's nothing they're raising that he hasn't raised for himself, even more toughly. 'When John digs his heels in, he can be immovable,' Peter mutters to me.

Ethnically cleansed Kosovars are pouring across the Balkan borders. I go to the Old Vic on a Sunday night for a benefit in aid of the Red Cross Kosovo Appeal. Theatre de Complicite – Simon McBurney, Marcello Magni and Jozef Houben; an Englishman, an Italian and a Belgian – are reviving A *Minute Too Late*, their clown show about death. Simon is the man out of step, our representative in the ever-unfamiliar rituals of death and remembrance. Not knowing what to do, always getting it wrong, singing too late or too loud, too soft or too soon, he becomes a compendium of our clumsiness in the face of mortality. He meets Jozef and asks him what he does in life. 'I'm an undertaker,' is the reply, which sends Simon into contortions of inarticulacy. The undertaker insists on giving him a lift, thrusts him into the hearse – four chairs in the light – and off they set, with a recumbent corpse on the back seat, and a drum and bass beat on the hearse radio. Everything goes double speed, and their synchronised bodies are thrown about by corners taken at speed. The corpse slumps over their shoulders, is unceremoniously shoved back. It's the oldest comedy of all, out of Chaucer and Rabelais, dancing on the threshold of death.

Simon returns to his solitary bedsit, carved out of air – coat-rack, gas hob, chest of drawers – by the two other actors. Then it's hysteria again, as Simon visits the hospital for news of his sick wife. A white-coated medic with a clipboard reels out clichés of reassurance, but Simon demolishes them with a flailing eruption of pure panic, tongue uprooted with terror so he can only flap like a mad doll, baying and moaning, rooted in real terror, these seismic explosions triggering a horrified laughter.

If that were the sum of A *Minute Too Late*, it would be a

remarkable enough series of turns on death's tightrope. But there
has been something more. Early on, at a wake, when nobody
knows what to say or how to stand, suddenly a 1940s swing band
strikes up in the parlour of the deceased, and the three actors
glide into a perfectly executed, exhilarating dance routine. This
exuberant chorus line has nothing logically to do with death, but
everything to do with the pleasure of defying it and dancing in its
face. And that awareness of joy and extinction, that urge to
outface reality, is what makes this piece theatre.

The performance over, Simon holds up his hands for silence.
He tells how the company had been in Macedonia performing
The Three Lives of Lucie Cabrol, a play in which there was a gypsy
song. A woman came up and said she had written the song. 'The
woman sang to us, and we sang for them,' says Simon. 'That was
how we began to get involved with the Balkans.' He winds up his
introduction to the young Red Cross worker who is making the
appeal with the words, 'There is an interconnection between us
all, we are umbilically linked to our brothers and sisters.' That too
is the voice of theatre.

At the National Theatre Studio, I come in and out of the workshop, for I am trying to keep up with the other aspects of my life as
a producer, notably *Pandaemonium*. We have now received the written report of the Arts Council Lottery Film Fund assessor, another
independent producer. It's pretty favourable, raising an eyebrow at
the tightness of the shooting schedule, but liking the screenplay and
giving us good marks for production planning (thanks to my fellow
producer Nick O'Hagan). In the evaluation of our production team,
the assessor writes a sentence about me which I've been chewing
over: 'He has an enviable record of quality production in theatre
and television, but, forced to choose an adjective to describe him,
not even his best friends would come up with "populist".' Should I
consider having this carved on my gravestone?

Early in the final week of the workshop, there's a breakthrough.
Peter, who has been duetting and debating, often heatedly, with
John after each read-through, has been hammering away at what
John's chorus of young women is, where they come from. John,
who has previously written stage directions suggesting they are

refugees after some natural or man-made catastrophe but has now deleted the suggestion, rebuts any attempt at seeking character or motivation. The breakthrough comes when Peter has a visual image of modern young women on a Greek island beach who have come on an archaeological field trip, and are drawn into the story, become its characters, under the influence of a drunken, randy old poet who emerges from a cave which has 'numinous' (one of John's favourite words) powers.

It's as simple, as disbelief-defying as that. Maybe drama flourishes on such insubstantial, fairy-tale, once-upon-a-time pretexts – the magic wood in which whoever enters has a midsummer night's dream, or Prospero's enchanted island.

Encouraged by this, the group, which is now swinging like a Basie band, pushes on to its next discovery: how much irony there is in John's text. Peter gets actors to replay speeches with new attention to the levels of language, the gear-changes, the antitheses and oppositions – all the battery of Shakespearean devices which he and John have brought to the surface and embodied in these actors over the years. The transformation is immediate. Irony doesn't make these exchanges cooler or more detached, but richer and more emotional, as if the knots and nets of language revealed by contrast the unspeakable extremes straining beneath. It's this tension, this counterpoint, which make *Tantalus* a classical as well as a modern piece.

On the last day of the workshop, we invite guests – Adrian Noble, Lynda Farran and all the RSC people who have helped us; European festival directors who I've asked, in the hope that they will present or even co-produce *Tantalus*; young directors, other actors. Don Seawell, who read all the scripts in two days in the Connaught, came, watched steadily, looked pleased; the general secretary of Yale University stayed for a while with a potential donor, and smiled a lot. When you're money-hunting, you hang on people's facial expressions. The notable absentees are Nikos Kourkoulos and any potential Greek patrons. Until he has resolved his budgetary differences with the RSC, Nikos is politely but firmly boycotting the workshop.

We've chosen two plays to present as rehearsed readings in the

round: *Priam* and *Helen*. They work wonderfully. Priam's twisting
and turning about whether or not to invite in the Trojan Horse
becomes an emblem of any leader skewered on incompatible
choices, and overtaken by events that lead to disaster. The trial
of Helen of Troy as a war criminal subverts her Homeric and
Shakespearean stereotype, and has a lot of wry laughs.

I ask for people's responses immediately after the performance,
and turn to Adrian Noble. Off the cuff, though he has known and
supported John's work for years, he reels off a list of things he
appreciated; 'but the main thing, even in this impromptu setting,
is that the text stood up with dramatic life, the script became a
living play for these circumstances.' Bob Palmer, running the
'Brussels 2000' millennial festival, is enthusiastic; I will go over
and see him in Brussels. Jon Cutler has brought over and
introduces me to Tim and Tom, one from the New York Council
for the Arts, the other a California-based playwright who, Jon
tells me, 'made a packet on Wall Street, and can get us to Gordon
Getty, who's loaded.' I go home elated, but wrecked, and worried:
I'm talking up *Tantalus* to all these money prospects, like a real
estate salesman in David Mamet's *Glengarry Glen Ross*. But the
money has long ago run out, and I'm worried about the phone
bills.

The week after the workshop, I circulate a rallying memo to all
our visitors, and those who couldn't or wouldn't come:

> The atmosphere at the Old Vic annexe during these days
> was that of a laboratory, an impassioned, sometimes
> anguished symposium or a bear pit, with actors plunging in
> with arguments and questions as well as performance. The
> workshop gave us a real sense of the extraordinary theatrical
> creature John has produced, and galvanised us all.

As Adrian Noble wrote to Greek Minister of Culture
Evangelos Venizelos following the workshop: '*Tantalus* is a
project I've been involved in for nearly 18 years, but this was
the first occasion when actors stood up and read the plays
aloud. It was a thrilling experience, because quite
miraculously literature became drama before our eyes. We

discovered, not only that the stories remain some of the greatest known to humankind, but that John's plays are witty, politically relevant, profoundly moving, and quite clearly inspire tremendous performances from our very best actors.'

The creature called *Tantalus* not only has legs, it has a head and heart too. As producer, I now have some serious deadlines ahead. If we are to get Peter and the actors to commit eighteen months of their lives to *Tantalus*, starting rehearsals in June 1999, I need as things stand to have the majority of the funding in place or strongly pledged by the end of January 1999.

By return, I get a reply from Don Seawell: 'Denver Center for the Performing Arts will invest $1 million in *Tantalus*. I am ready to put £350,000 in your account immediately to cover development costs.'

I send back a prompt thank-you to our saviour from Colorado. By the skin of our teeth, we continue.

January 1999

On the road again, this time to America, with Peter and John. Our itinerary takes us to New York, New Haven and Denver. John will peel off to Minneapolis, where he's giving Shakespeare classes to a company about to start *Julius Caesar*; Peter has a date in Los Angeles, where he is casting two Shakespeare productions he will do back to back. I'm staying in the turn-of-the-century splendour of the Harvard Club, replete with tusked and antlered big-game trophies, but otherwise a dead ringer for the Athenaeum. Off the plane, I do a dinner meeting which Tim has arranged with the director of Lincoln Center Festival, who can't promise much at this stage. Peter arrives late and fuming off a delayed flight.

Next day I'm up early, step out into West 44th Street to get the city's throb. Waves of young men and women flood out of Grand Central Station, dressed for the office in designer or cloned-designer garb, carrying customised coffee and a sandwich made

with one of twenty ethnically distinctive breads. If postmodern is
the culture of surfaces, more and more of New York has gone post
modern. I gravitate towards an older, shabbier coffee shop, where
the waitresses still have Central European accents and don't greet
you with a bright beam.

Peter comes in from the next-door Algonquin, whistling to
himself, which is usually a sign he's preoccupied or worried. The
feud with Bill Kenwright is still dragging on, and he won't be
continuing the Peter Hall Company after his final production in
April. If *Tantalus* doesn't happen, he'll have to scurry around for
well-paid work to meet his commitments. John is worried that
Peter's getting into the habit of working too fast, and he believes
his anxieties about money are partly of his own invention. John,
who is staying at the Chelsea as usual, arrives in a taxi, and we
get to Grand Central, with John not walking too well, to go
to Yale.

I plant them in a nouveau coffee shop, and go off to get
beverages. When I return, I'm struck by the contrast between
them. Peter, *bien en chair*, is wedged up to the table; John, gangly
and contorted, perches perilously on the edge of the seat. They
are arguing. John has woken up thinking that the credits of the
play are not honest: 'It shouldn't read, "Written by John Barton",
but "Devised from the sources by John Barton".'

Peter pours cold water on his friend: 'John, you're being
absurdly modest. Of course, you wrote them.'

'But you don't know how much I've taken from the sources,'
John murmurs, writhing but firm.

'Every playwright draws on sources, John,' I say, thinking that
the closer his play gets to being done, the more scary it must be
for him, labouring so long to make his own plots and words after
years adapting and directing other people's.

As we get up to go to the train, I suddenly see them as the two
main characters in Pinter's *No Man's Land*. Peter is Hirst,
originally played by Ralph Richardson as a fluent, masterful top
dog, the executive in a perfectly cut suit. What's Hirst-like about
Peter is his social combativity, the feline ease with which he
seems able to direct and dominate situations – and the fact that

he directed *No Man's Land*. He seems unquestionably capable. John is Spooner, the frail, gentlemanly poet of little magazines, originally played by John Gielgud in old socks inside open-toed sandals, a misshapen tweed jacket and a raffish cravat. Spoonerishly, John is tougher than his surface would imply; he maintains modesty and manners in a brutal world, but his gentleness doesn't hinder him from fighting his own corner, with a strategy as wily and polite as the Socrates he admires. If I were looking at myself from outside, I'd find something of each in me. Hirspoonster, perhaps. With a sense of disaster at the door underlying all I do.

On the Amtrak train, which trudges through unlovely Connecticut commuterland, we read the latest Monica Lewinsky headlines and Peter talks about his forthcoming Los Angeles *Measure for Measure*. 'I'm going to set it in the eighteenth-century White House Oval Office,' he says gleefully. 'Think of Angelo abusing his powers in that setting. And the Duke, that manipulative mystery-man nobody knows how to interpret – I cracked it the other night. Woke up and realised he's the Marquis de Sade, an experimenter in human nature. Makes perfect sense in the eighteenth century.'

John nods, and looking at these two men who have reshaped Shakespeare production for our age, I know they know that such a concept is only the first step. It has to be tested against the text, the fibre and stitching of Shakespeare's language, taken into the body and the breath and the mind. That's the difference between them and the more recent generation of conceptual directors, subsuming everything to some overriding concept which is embodied in scenic design, but under-explored in words. The method works well in opera, where the music articulates what meanings music can, and it makes great photographs in glossy theatre magazines like the large-format German monthly *Theater Heute*, in which every production looks like a masterpiece. But unless the spoken text is mimed, it's pictorial drama for a predominantly non- or anti-verbal age.

It's been snowing in New Haven. John's canvas beach shoes, which he swears are the only thing his feet feel comfortable in, dampen in the drifts. Hearty greeters from the Yale Drama School and Long Wharf Theatre pile us into a van for a tour of possible playing spaces. We see the Shubert, a Broadway try-out or tour venue. It's a smaller version of the Palladium, a gold and ginger-bread jewel-box, which has too many showbiz associations for the primal piece of theatre we are dreaming. Then there's Long Wharf, a thrust stage which would be perfect but is 250 seats too intimate; a tennis centre which would be good for a Chinese mass demonstration spelling out the face of Chairman Mao in coloured flags; and the University Theater, which feels as if it might have been a chapel in a previous life, but has the requisite size, depth and contact with the auditorium.

We are transported to the office of the president of Yale. The only oval thing about it is a huge table, which would have served well in Peter and John's *Wars of the Roses*, whose central stage furniture was a gigantic steel-mesh-clad council table, at which England's warring factions slashed their way to ascendancy, their sharp words clearing the way for their sharper swords. On the walls are oil portraits of Yale's founding fathers, the Donald Seawells of the age, wearing benign or shrewd expressions.

Richard Levin, Yale's president, arrives, a trim, suited man with the brisk smiling attentiveness of a successful surgeon. He turns out to be a Shakespeare enthusiast. 'When my wife and I spent a year at Oxford,' he tells Peter, 'we saw every single Royal Shakespeare production.' I know that President Levin's wife teaches Homer's *Iliad* on the Yale undergraduate foundation course. With the Homer and the Shakespeare connections, we could be in with a chance.

Paul Collard, who is seated across the oval table, has already cleverly caught Yale's interest by suggesting that their year of tercentenary celebrations be planned in three 'chapters': Where We Come From, Where We Are, Where We Are Going. *Tantalus* would be the cornerstone of chapter one, in autumn 2000. I launch into my Platonic picture of how it would be if we brought *Tantalus* to Yale: not just the performances, but around them workshops with the students of the Drama School, lectures, debates and symposia with members of the departments of

History, Philosophy, Literature, Architecture, a new production of John's *Peloponnesian War* script with the Yale Repertory Theatre company. It could be a feather in Yale's cap, I say, not merely to present this marathon drama in the USA and have Yale's name shipped around the world, but to tie a theatre production into the interconnections of classical Greece, which have shaped it as a university. I sound like a glossy brochure, but I do in more than part believe this. And part of me yearns to bring our nomadic vessel into the brief harbour of a university. Through the window the Gothic bulk of Yale's halls, cathedrals of learning modelled on nineteenth-century Oxford, look reassuringly monumental under snow.

Peter adds his considerable persuasiveness. Listeners round the table lean forward to follow this soft-spoken but fervent Englishman with a 'Sir' before his name – 'Sir Hall' this morning's taxi driver had called him, lining him up perhaps with America's jazz aristocracy, King Oliver, Duke Ellington, Count Basie. And Sir Hall, on tenor and alto. Just before I left to teach theatre at Harvard nearly twenty years ago, an English friend who had taught at Columbia warned me, 'Remember, when they love you in America, when they say they love your voice and your manners, they're loving you for your species, the species Englishman, not for yourself.' Let's hope that old-country charm works for us.

President Levin, clearly pleased to have one of his heroes in his office, replies that the deadline is very tight, but that he will energetically pursue Yale alumni who have done well, are interested in drama and would like to help their alma mater's tercentenary in this way. Potential patrons are discussed, and two seem hopeful. One has made a lot of money setting up Dream Works, Steven Spielberg's new production company; the other a steel millionaire who financed the building of the Royal Shakespeare Company's Swan Theatre, and who sounds even more likely.

John has already slipped out to go to Minneapolis. Peter goes back to New York, to audition more American actors for his Shakespeare plays. I decide to stay overnight, to see people and sound out the New Haven scene. I go to Long Wharf Theatre to see the premiere of a new American play by an Asian-American author. It's about the fate of a Chinese actor, one of the greatest players of women's roles, during the Cultural Revolution. His daughter, a young actress in the now agit-prop Peking Opera, is a Red Guard, and has been ordered to chastise and re-educate her own father. It could have been a resonant play about the urge to repress theatre. But the young playwright settles for a personal melodrama: violence wreaked on family bonds by pitiless politics.

The audience, largely middle-aged, white and professional, takes it aimiably enough. There is the tidiness of response that I got to know when I worked in American theatre, and which comes from a ticket subscription system. Without getting its core audience to subscribe at the start of the season to a multi-play subscription, theatres like Long Wharf couldn't make ends meet. But the penalty is that audiences turn up because they have contracted to do so, rather than because they have heard about the play through the press or word of mouth and are really passionate to see it.

In New York, I have a meeting with the man who works for Gordon Getty, whose oil fortune could easily solve our shortfall. The prospects, he says, are encouraging. There will be a meeting with Gordon about *Tantalus* in San Francisco. I head out for Denver with Peter in a stretch limo with smoked-glass windows, driven by a muscled, hip black chauffeur out of a James Bond film. 'This is what the casting people provided me with,' says Peter, a little uneasily; but not unduly.

There's a minor crisis at Denver airport when he discovers he's left his DVD camera, with all the material he shot of the auditions, in the plane. But it's restored, and we drive into Denver, through big empty plains rimmed by the Rockies. The Denver Center for the Performing Arts is an imposing cluster of interlocking theatres around a busy central piazza. It's much better than a shopping mall, but its architecture is selling theatre to a society that understands shopping malls and their principle of concentration. Donald Seawell and his artistic director Donovan Marley proudly take us through the foyers and

auditoriums, with the touring version of *Rent* in one and a Derek
Walcott play in another. It feels gutsier than the Long Wharf.

The next two days melt into a succession of meetings and
plannings with Don and his colleagues. We choose a theatre, a
750-seater, draft a schedule, talk about building a duplicate set in
their workshops to save the cost of transporting ours. Don is not
only a courtly patrician, with a scathing dismissal of the
mediocrities of both Democrats and Republicans who are
scrambling to give their two dimes' worth of opinion on the
nightly television news about Clinton's crimes and mis-
demeanours; he's also a *bon viveur*, and keeps us nourished with
champagne and crudités as we sit in his huge office with its
memorabilia of Noël and Gertie and a bygone age of the elegant
impresario. John looks positively cosseted. Peter becomes more
expansive. Don reconfirms his commitment to putting in a
million dollars to *Tantalus* and to financing the television
Shakespeare workshops. Toasts are made to our future millennial
collaboration. The Denver Broncos win the US Superbowl, and
Don's office, indeed all his theatres, go berserk. Real broncos are
bucking on the other side of town, where the annual rodeo is in
full swing. The space that stretches to the far Rockies makes me
walk taller; a cliché, but true. If there's an upside to this odyssey
of getting *Tantalus* to happen, this must be it.

Spring 1999
It begins to splinter. On several fronts.

The Lottery Film Fund turns down *Pandaemonium*. For
business, rather than aesthetic reasons: they don't find the
undertakings we have obtained from distributors sufficient. The
Film Fund may not be able to recoup its investment. It's chicken
and egg, of course; the film is unusual enough to make distributors
want to wait and see before guaranteeing any more than a
cautious advance. But they like it enough to encourage us to
reapply. Back to the persuasion game.

The regional theatres of the British Film Institute, which were
set up to provide alternative outlets for non-commercial,
distinctive, creative, authored, independent, innovative film – all

the adjectives we have used to mark ourselves out from the market for the past twenty years or more – have seen Tony Harrison's *Prometheus* and, for the most part, give it a wide berth. One is them is even reported as saying they can't see why anyone should want to see it. Since underfunding has caused most them to become distinguishable from their local multiplexes only because they show many of the same films but a week later, it's not surprising. Back to the persuasion game again.

Am I doing something wrong? Hopelessly out of step? Blindly kicking against the pricks? Flogging a dying horse called theatre?

Gordon Getty turns down *Tantalus*. I don't even get a reply from him, but from an assistant. 'Mr Getty has asked me to say . . .' A week later, the same assistant sends me the annual report of the Getty Foundation, showing the many-faceted work it is doing with fine art museums and multicultural art history and art appreciation for ethnically diverse kids. Clearly, despite all the encouragement from his henchpeople, I've been barking up the wrong tree.

The Royal Shakespeare Company is worried about its deficit, its future. There are rumours of surgical cutbacks, even whispers of closure. A series of Arts Council meetings will tell how bad things are. I ask Lynda to tell me if *Tantalus* is going to fall victim to the crisis, the moment she knows anything. Peter talks about the RSC needing *Tantalus* to restore its image for courage and daring. 'If I were still running the RSC, I'd scrap some of the repertory and do *Tantalus*.'

I go to Brussels for a talk-shop about artists and society, funded by the European Commission for Culture. I take the opportunity to pitch *Tantalus* to one of the seasoned European culture-crats. She tells me there could be some money for *Tantalus*, under the aegis of the Kaleidoscope programme, but I will need four member states to be involved, performances must begin in 1999 and I must get our application in by the beginning of March.

The RSC has reduced its budget (and its input). Nikos Kourkoulos seems happier now. Peter and I join him in Athens, for another meeting with Minister Venizelos, to whom Nikos has explained the new and improved situation. Waiters in the restaurant in Kolonaki shimmy and defer to Nikos and his wife, who are clearly superstars. Nikos, smoking his twenty-fifth cigarette of the evening, gives us a relaxed rendezvous for next morning. 'No need to rush; the Minister is always later.'

Next morning turns out to be the one morning the Minister is not late. Peter and I arrive, and find Nikos already in the Minister's office, looking pale. There's an atmosphere of rush and urgency. It turns out that Venizelos has been summoned to the Prime Minister and has only fifteen minutes for us. I begin to outline the new situation and its deadlines, when the door opens behind me and a bushy-haired man dressed in an old cardigan comes in, followed by a young woman in a white coat carrying a leather box. They rush past us, open the box, Nikos gets up, takes off his jacket and rolls up his shirtsleeve. He's having his blood pressure tested.

'When he came in, he fainted,' says the Minister, speaking fast, intently, under pressure. 'I called my doctor from his home. Nikos will be in good hands.' Nikos goes out of the room, I guess to have a cardiogram in the corridor. 'I want to help *Tantalus*,' says the Minister. 'I am ready to match the Royal Shakespeare Company contribution. Forgive me, I must go. There will be time to talk without pressure.' He starts to get up. It's true that moments of high drama or decision affect time, either speeding it up or slowing it down. This time it's *molto allegro*, no question. 'Let's shake hands on that,' says Peter, clutching at something to mark the pledge. We all stand and shake hands, including Nikos, who still looks mask-like. Why does a rich man and a successful actor like him need the aggravation of running his National Theatre?

Back in London, we do our sums again. Now that Getty has turned us down, we will be short of money even with the Greek contribution. Peter suddenly calls up and reveals a plan which will save us money – and probably cost him some artistic satisfaction. 'If I direct it all myself, the rehearsal period will be much longer than if I "chair" a group of three directors and we do it collaboratively. Less time, smaller fees and salaries. Each director will take one-third of the piece, or one aspect. I've already spoken to Mick Gordon, who runs the Gate, and was at our workshop. Comes from Belfast, sharp as a pin, has worked with Brook, is up for anything. He says, "Peter, count me in. We have a lot to learn from you, and we'll bring you the hottest talents of our generation." ' Mingled with his regret at not being able to put his signature directly on the whole cycle is excitement at this dynamic, combustible group, working across two theatre generations.

John is immediately worried about the implications of Peter's bold plan – with each actor playing several parts, will there be enough of them free at any one time to make triple rehearsals work? His admiration of Peter's impetuousness and his mistrust of it tug at each other. I say to him that we've reached the point where we just have to make it work, that it's becoming a choice of doing it for the money we're likely to raise, or not doing it at all. He nods, reiterates his worries, says he's already worked it out with parallel rehearsals involving two directors and will now draw up some more charts of actor availability for three.

Ten days later, all our plans are once more torn up by the roots. The word *catastrophe* is commonly used as a synonym for disaster, usually in reference to war, flood or earthquake. In its original use in Greek drama, however, it had a more precise meaning, and described an action or process. 'The change or revolution which produces the conclusion or final event of a dramatic piece; the dénouement', says the OED, tracing the etymology to the Greek word for 'overturning'. Well, we are now reeling from a sudden overturning; and since it is a modern convulsion, born of a thoroughly contemporary conflict, it has hit us from a completely unexpected quarter.

A man called Ocalan, leader of the Kurdish armed struggle against Turkish repression, has been kidnapped from Greek protection in Kenya by a Turkish snatch squad. I'll say that again, as simply as I can, to help it settle into my own mind: some Greeks, antagonists of the Turks, gave sanctuary to the most hunted Kurd in Turkey in Athens for a few days, unofficially, not even with the knowledge of the Prime Minister, apparently. When he found out, he insisted that Ocalan be moved out of Greece but kept under Greek protection while asylum was negotiated with another country. Ocalan was on his way to Nairobi airport in the Greek ambassador's car when they were ambushed.

The agreement we had with Minister Venizelos for *Tantalus* is now in peril. Venizelos is no longer Minister of Culture. Three ministers were fired in the wake of the debacle in Nairobi, and Venizelos has been promoted to Economic Affairs and Tourism as a result. The legitimate demands of a national minority, which I support, and the request for asylum, which is the starting point of Aeschylus' *The Suppliants*, one of the earliest and most telling Greek tragedies, have dealt what may be a catastrophic blow to our modern saga of the war between Athens and Troy.

I spend the next month chasing Venizelos in his new ministry, faxing him about honouring his deal or getting his successor at the Ministry of Culture, Elizabeth Papazoi, to do a 'co-production' with their two ministries jointly funding *Tantalus*, which will cost her less and which he can justify as part of his 'Athens 2000' millennial celebrations, the cornerstone of his tourism campaign. No fax is answered, no call returned, Nikos is puffing with frustration, Dionysis tells me his old friends on high aren't answering his calls.

Adrian Noble calls to tell me that the end of March really is the RSC's final and definitive deadline, because they have to go to press with their winter 1999/2000 season. 'How are you feeling?' he asks. 'Guarded,' I say, and I tell him of my persistent but so far unavailing approaches. 'We're trying the Whitehall route,' he says. For a moment, I don't understand what he's talking about. He explains that he's writing to Chris Smith to approach his opposite number, the new Greek culture minister, to speed a decision.

I put the phone down and call Eleni, who is now secretary of the British committee to return the Parthenon Marbles. When she hears that the RSC is asking Chris Smith to mediate, she goes into hoots of laughter. 'Chris Smith is public enemy number one in cultural circles in Athens,' she says. 'Asking him to intervene on your behalf could kill *Tantalus*.' I call Stratford-upon-Avon, and manage to get Adrian to pull the letter to Chris Smith out of the fax machine, and revise it. Eventually, the approach is made by our ambassador in Athens. Nikos says Elizabeth Papazoi seems to be taking it more seriously. But she says she won't know whether she has enough money to consider *Tantalus* until the end of March, which would neatly coincide with the RSC deadline. But I know it won't. Nothing in this enterprise does. Tantalus was imprisoned by the gods in a pool of stagnant water, with a tree of delicious fruit nearby. Whenever he stretched out to pick some fruit, the wind rose and blew the branch just out of reach. I know how he feels.

Peter comes back from Los Angeles, where he's been going round schools, looking for teenagers to play the fairies in his *Midsummer Night's Dream*. He would like a Latino Peaseblossom, a Chicano Mustardseed, a Chinese Cobweb. 'This maths teacher who has a passion for Shakespeare took me into his classroom and showed me his kids in the *Dream*. Some of them were really wonderful. And he says that after working on Shakespeare, they get better at mathematics.'

I have heard nothing from Yale, so I start nudging. If they are talking to their rich alumni who might be sympathetic, wouldn't they like Peter to come over and give them the pitch? They wouldn't; they are very confident. One day, they are less confident: the theatre-mad steel millionaire who single-handedly paid for the RSC's Swan Theatre apparently won't fund *Tantalus*. He seemed such a good prospect, I say, couldn't we help them with a follow-up approach from the RSC itself? No, says the Secretary of Yale; he was adamant. She sounds dashed. Another week later, their last prospect has melted into air saying he'd rather fund a new roof to Yale's library than back a play. There's the rub: people want their names on something lasting, not transient theatre; and people in the entertainment business especially want solid neoclassical pillars housing priceless books and manuscripts. Drama they know about already; they make drama every day.

Because of the uncertainty about the Greeks, whose participation we need along with two other European Union countries, I haven't got down to doing the application for

Brussels, and have let their deadline go by. I'm surprised and pleased to get a letter from the culture-crat I pitched to, saying she's sorry I haven't applied by the due date, but in view of the interest of the project, they can grant us exceptionally an extra month to apply. I buckle down to fill out the application forms for the Kaleidoscope fund. There are reams of them, drafted in a floating all-purpose lingo that can encompass everything from theatre productions like ours to the formation of networks to assess opportunities for minority identities in 'the European cultural landscape'. So it's more pitch and persuasion, and I try to make it fresh one more time, like a *madame* parading her girls for clients.

But catastrophe hasn't finished with us yet, it comes knocking at the door again. I'm halfway through the form-filling, with Bill Wilkinson, the wily and forthright former RSC finance director (who has such a passion for theatre he has directed forty productions for his amateur drama society in Warwickshire), when the mother and father of corruption and nepotism scandals blows up in Brussels. Forced by the European parliament, the EU Secretary General and the entire body of Commissioners resign.

This happens while I'm trying to persuade the Dublin Theatre Festival to become our fourth partner. Is somebody up there trying to wrongfoot me? Zeus? Jehovah? Is *Tantalus* becoming as jinxed a play as Shakespeare's *Macbeth*, which is such a source of real-life accidents and catastrophes that actors, trying to fend off the evil eye, refer to it only as 'the Scottish play'?

I'm feeling completely wiped out, but it just won't let hold of me. I go to the press conference of the 'Shadow Arts Council', a pressure group and watchdog for the interests of artists which, at the instigation of publisher John Calder, we have been trying to set up. Peter has become its chairman, and in the front bar of the Old Vic, his former theatre, he makes a disarming and passionate speech to the arts journalists, which shows no sign of how worried he is about the future of *Tantalus* and his own future.

Afterwards, John Tusa, the managing director of the Barbican Centre, to whom I have proposed *Tantalus* for autumn 2000, comes up and says how sorry he is that *Tantalus* won't be happening. I realise that the RSC's letter saying they can't do it now, but give it every support and are ready to do it in autumn 2000, is being interpreted as a close-down message. I assure him that's far from true, and he tells me that in that case, I ought to hurry to get in an application for some of the nine million pounds the Arts Council is holding for special projects or strategic developments or something not yet fully defined; it sounds as if it could be for *Tantalus.*

So I take another deep breath, feeling like an ageing nag whose flanks need goading, and I call the Drama Director of the Arts Council, get some more information, though still scant, and pump out another rationale, another prospectus, another irresistible justification. Neither this nor the Brussels application will bear fruit before June. We may well get the deal together, but just too late to hold the people together.

I come to Amsterdam for Easter and respite – though that's hardly the word, since I'm staying with Dragan and Julie, whose flat is now the target and focus of thirty e-mails a day, anxious calls to his mother in blitzed Belgrade when he can get through, and a procession of émigrés and expatriates calling to each other from the four corners of the world through the webs and networks of the digital domain. Their talk, their panic, their rage, their impotence, their attempts to master their fear, their consumption of the daily blanket-bombing of information all firmly put into perspective the setbacks in my one-man campaign to get John's plays on.

We watch nightly television of the Kosovar Albanian refugees, pictures which stun words. Later, I think these women and children are descendants of the fifty Egyptian women who populate Aeschylus' *The Suppliants,* beseeching the Greeks to give them asylum from their crazed husbands, stranded in some holding centre while the city decides whether to take them in. I wonder whether there will be any Aeschylus of our times who will be able to express so pitifully the agony of the defenceless and anatomise so pitilessly the reasoning of the powerful and ask hard questions of the gods.

I come back to London, I plug on as the bombs pound away and the suppliant refugees are chased every which way. I write a letter to the two Greek Ministers, urging them to see me before the deadline goes and *Tantalus* collapses. Even if you can't afford the whole amount because you have a war on your doorstep, I say. Even if meeting the 'convergence criteria' for joining the European Union is squeezing you tight, I think. I round off the letter with an appeal which is Churchillian in spirit, but also a memory of what was happening as I grew up in the war:

> During World War Two, when I was a child and London was being bombed, one of the things that kept the spirit of British people alive was the performances of classical music and drama in theatres, galleries, concert halls all round our country at a time of crisis. Joining us to produce *Tantalus*, which itself speaks of the moral dilemmas of war and politics, would be a similar affirmative gesture in our world of violence and fury.
>
> Greece has always understood, and undergone, these afflictions, and sought to make sense of them through its theatre. I ask you to join together to deliver the crucial funding to *Tantalus* this month because of culture, because of tourism, because of keeping the Greek name in view in the world. But above all, because an international venture such as *Tantalus* with Greek participation would affirm that humanity needs drama and poetry, and not just violence and politics, to survive.

I copy the letter to Sir Michael Llewelyn-Smith, our ambassador in Athens, who, at Adrian Noble's request, has already nudged the Greek culture minister. Could he help again, help me to get a meeting with Ministers Papazoi and Venizelos by the end of this month? Maybe I've been alluding to Myra Hess performing Bach and Sybil Thorndike's wartime Medea in an unconscious playing to the gallery where Sir Michael Llewelyn-Smith sits.

Jon Cutler has been trying to call me from America while I've been away. He has a new scheme, new target via his network of contacts. 'There's this guy called Kurt, who can get me to Nathan. Well, actually to Nathan's uncle, and then to Nathan. Nathan is number two to Bill Gates. Microsoft Bill Gates. I want to go for the whole thing: *Tantalus*, *Playing Shakespeare*, an ongoing relationship between Microsoft and the Royal Shakespeare Company. Let me hook you up with Kurt.' Which he does next morning, with a conference call at breakfast time (for Jon, 4am, he's a time-shift sleeper). Kurt – deep-voiced, stentorian, with a hell of a racket in the background – intones that he's in a nightclub in Los Angeles and that's Pink Floyd playing in back. He machine-guns out some advice – go and see this one, call up that one, tell them I said so, who are you dealing with in Greece. When I say the Ministry of Culture, he goes quiet, but only for a second. I say that Peter Hall is in Los Angeles doing two Shakespeare plays, and if the scheme is really a possibility, I would come to LA with Jon and meet Kurt and the Microsoft people. At which point, he pulls an old Hollywood stunt on me, by saying he doesn't know when he can fit in a meeting, he's very busy. I say that if he can't find an hour in the next two months for Sir Peter and me, it's not worth talking. 'What's the name of the plays?' he says. *Midsummer Night's Dream* he knows, but I have to say *Measure for Measure* once or twice, the line's bad. Once again, I find myself inside a David Mamet play, talking to operators with hooded eyes.

But I'm also talking to Her Britannic Majesty's representative in Greece, who you don't find in many Mamet plays. I call the British Embassy in Athens, and get hold of Sir Michael's assistant. My heart drops when she tells me it's his last week in the job. Yet another Tantalistic twist of the knife. But he has a farewell party tonight, she says, and both Greek Ministers will be there. He'll do what he can, as will the head of the British Council.

Jon Cutler calls again. From the sound of his voice, I know he's got other people hooked up on a conference call, and sure enough, he tells me he has Kurt and someone called Jeff on the line. 'Where are you now?' I ask, looking out my window at the bunched clouds and slate tiles. 'We're in Las Vegas, it's 5.45 in the morning, and that's Stevie Wonder in the background,' says Kurt, the man who's going to lead us to Microsoft-man's uncle.

There's a silence, the kind of silence that means who's-calling-who-and-what-is-there-to-say. I decide to start, and say I've spoken to Peter, who would be ready to do a properly prepared meeting with Microsoft in Seattle or LA, to discuss *Tantalus*, *Playing Shakespeare* and a possible relationship with the Royal Shakespeare Company, which still has to be discussed with them.

This doesn't seem quite to chime with what Kurt thought we'd been hooked up to talk about. He starts telling me about the new generation of high-definition recording trucks which he's just seen at this Las Vegas convention, and how more and more stations and networks are converting to 'hi-def', and how he likes our stuff but he'd like to 'retune our package', and that Microsoft isn't the only game in town, and we could be talking to PBS and to the Arts and Entertainment channel.

At which point I raise my voice and say, 'Look, I don't need you to tell me about American public television and cable channels. I spent nearly ten years at Channel 4 trying to squeeze out of your public television a fraction of what the BBC spends in a year, it was blood out of a stone. And I don't need to be told about hi-def; we have trucks in Europe, the Japanese system, I taped an opera on it. What I thought we had, Jon, what you led me to believe Kurt could lead us to, was a top executive in Microsoft, because Microsoft have already shown their interest in quality things – encyclopaedias and museums mostly, but who knows? That's what I thought I was getting.'

There are whoops and yells of approval. This Englishman is some goddam hard case, they must be thinking, he keeps raising his voice, doncha love it. I just can't lose. Except my energy. All this deal-making, this skirmishing and manoeuvring, which takes up so many hours and days and months in America, can leech your energy down to zero, and still buoy you up with the adrenalin of anger.

My friend Peter Gowan, a professor of political history, has been writing against the clock about the genesis of the war, and now e-mails his text, *The Western Powers and The Balkan Tragedy*. It's an intricate and impassioned sleuthing-out of the motives of states, especially the USA, since the break-up of Yugoslavia, following through their interests to a conclusion of bombs in Belgrade and pogroms in Kosovo. Peter's text keeps referring to 'the Yugoslav theatre', meaning 'theatre of war operations', but I keep hearing actors and plays.

Dragan's e-mails keep coming. I can chart his anxieties, his pain as he learns of the loss of landmark after landmark to the smart bombs. Maybe the ghost of Samuel Beckett should come back and write a sequel for Dragan: Krapp's Last E-Mails. I get two, three a day:

> When I heard the other day that the official Television, locally known as TV Bastille, was hit in Belgrade I was not surprised and my capacity for empathy was in the first instance somehow tamed by all the unpleasant memories of this place of power, staunch regime control, paranoia. Belgradians underwent a change of heart, it seems: several times in the last years they demonstrated against the government-controlled television and threw eggs at the office wing that remained undamaged; yet after the NATO attack they marched in protest and laid flowers at the ruins. TV Bastille, once seen as a house of lies, is becoming a monument of patriotic defiance.

> Ugly as it was, this bridge they have just bombed was part of my childhood and adolescence. The consequence of the bombing was that windows were broken in that part of town and there was no running water around, even the large hospital on the nearby hills of Fruska Gora, some 900 beds, was without running water for a while. This did not make the awful lot of Kosovo Albanians easier and – surprise, surprise! – did not prompt the brave Novi Sad citizens to start an uprising against Milosevic.

> What's next, I wonder, the Serb National Theatre, the Modern Gallery of Pavle Beljanski, the old former

Synagogue or the Petrovaradin fortress itself, a 17th-century, Austrian-built complex of former military installations converted to restaurants, museums and artists' studios?

In the evenings, when I succeed to reach my childhood and adolescence friends who still live in Novi Sad to share their anxiety and mumble in the phone some unpersuasive words of consolation, I realise their children might end up writing and reading another sort of literature, permeated with a sense of abandonment, anger and hatred. The emotional maps of Novi Sad, Belgrade and other cities – and not just their physical panorama – have been altered.

The combined effect on me of Peter Gowan's meticulous unmasking, of Dragan's tormented sadness, his wife's weary treatment of refugee traumas at an asylum-seekers' centre and the bewilderment and anxiety of the 'post-Yugoslavs' I met in Amsterdam make me want to do something, something in my own field of activity, which is art, which is currently mostly theatre.

Sitting in this sunny attic from where it all emanates and circulates, I write a proposal for a theatre piece about us and Kosovo. Another would-be rallying text:

I am writing to a group of theatre-makers and friends to propose that we find a way to make a theatre piece over the next few months about 'Kosovo And Us'. A timely but more than topical piece which could be playing on Thursday, September 9, 1999, sixty years after World War Two started. This is a call from a producer and writer to find out whether there is sufficient interest from colleagues to justify raising the means of production for such a show.

My personal experience of theatre in a war comes from being a participant in the show called US, which at the height of the Vietnam War was created for the Royal Shakespeare Company by a group of theatre people led by

Peter Brook. *US* was made in great heat, but it had the rhythm of theatre, not of the journalism that engulfed us, then as now.

Everyone who receives this will probably have some parallel experience or impulse to make theatre in a time of war. Theatre can give a voice to the voiceless, a platform to dissident opinions; it can dramatise contradictions, link the personal and the global, collage together aspects separated in the media of news and fact; it can find metaphors in the harshest facts, reach beyond reportage, make fact into song. It can face the worst things, the things that stun speech, and still go on speaking.

It might turn out to be a show which may not play in a theatre at all, because, while it is not 'commercial', public-funded theatres might be scared of harming their subsidy because of its politics. It might happen in London on the forecourt of the Imperial War Museum. It might perhaps be financed and presented by a network of European war museums. What are such museums going to display when they mark the fiftieth anniversary of NATO?

I know this could be acting-out rather than action. I know I'm inviting overload by doing this, on top of *Tantalus* and all my other tentacular projects, the full tray of goodies every independent producer must have, for most of the projects will go down. Neither this new idea nor *Tantalus* is a bread-and-butter idea, aimed at a market with a reasonable chance of finding buyers. Both of them are about theatre, about finding an urgency for theatre. Why am I still pushing at this possibility? The world's against it, for sure. Since I started work, culture has become more homogenised, 'product' more standardised, audiences more stratified and targeted, the industry of 'leisure' more organised. Who needs theatre events that cross categories, deny definitions, trespass across boundaries?

In Denver, where Donald Seawell has put his life into building a theatre centre, a couple of teenagers stirred by Internet bomb recipes and white supremacist conspiracies, screen killings and inadequate human contact, gun down their schoolmates. I'm not a superstitious person, but it's beginning to seem as if the gods have got it in for *Tantalus*. Wherever it sets foot, something goes wrong. In Athens, ministers are fired, in Brussels all the civil servants resign, in Denver there's a bloodbath.

I call Nikos, to see if he can push for our meeting with the Minister in Athens before the deadline. He says he's thinking of resigning from the Greek National Theatre. 'I can't even get an answer from the new Minister of Culture to my requests for our own theatre. She doesn't return calls. People are saying the Ministry of Culture's bankrupt. I don't need this. I'm thinking of going home, spending more time in the pool with my kids.' I joke that we'll do *Tantalus* together with him as an independent producer. But it's worrying. I keep pushing away, book my air tickets, and then de-book them when the former Culture Minister says he doesn't think he should meet me until he's consulted with the new Culture Minister, the one who doesn't answer calls, though presumably she'll have to answer him. Another week's delay. By then, there may be NATO ground troops shipping into Salonika. Will Greece be able even to contemplate taking part in *Tantalus*? And yet the Trojan War – the war in the 'Trojan theatre' – must be told and retold. Continued retelling in theatre brings people together and can make them see the difference between what changes and what is essential.

Donald Seawell has made a huge offer. Since the hoped-for funding from the RSC, the Greek government and Yale university has bit by bit failed to materialise, he announces that Denver Center for the Performing Arts will fund *Tantalus* one hundred per cent. There are two conditions: that the six months' rehearsals and the world premiere take place in Denver; and that Peter Hall make up his mind very fast.

I keep pushing Athens for an answer. Meanwhile, I go to the Old Vic, Peter's old playground, and see its bright young general manager, Michael Morris, about *Tantalus* playing a three-month season there in autumn 2000. 'It will be after Greece,' I say, ' after Denver, before Brussels and Dublin,' I say, and my sober double mutters inside my head, *None of which may ever happen.* But Michael, who has read half the scripts, is very keen and positive. He tells me Stephen Daldry, artistic director of the Old Vic, is even more so, and is talking about ripping out the stalls and filling the Vic with sand to make the beach and seashore where *Tantalus* happens.

But Athens is not looking so hot. Peter Chenery, the head of the British Council in Athens, keeps up the request for the two Ministers to meet me, but is clearly troubled by the Balkan situation, with Greeks siding with their fellow-Orthodox Serbs and protesting on the streets against the NATO bombing. He doesn't think the Ministers will make *Tantalus* much of a priority, and adds that security has been increased at the British Council offices after bombs against British premises in Athens and Thessaloniki.

The Arts Council of England meets to pick its criteria for the strategic fund. I have been hoping that they would take a deep breath and invite us to apply. Instead, we will have to wait another month while further work is done polishing the criteria. I write to Anna Stapleton, Head of Drama, who has been sympathetic:

> Good to know that the Council meeting went well, and I look forward to the refreshed criteria. I fear, however, that *Tantalus* may have fallen apart by the time Council gets its framework right. The word 'strategic' worries me, perhaps unnecessarily. Tantalus isn't strategic, structural or criteria-based: it's the perhaps final flowering of two men who have reshaped British theatre.
>
> Why do we British think it fair to support institutions, and so hard to back individuals? Peter, who has created the major public theatres in our country, surely deserves more at this stage of the game than to have to slope off to pick up the offers he has turned down to keep time free for *Tantalus*. And so does John. There isn't a major British actor who hasn't learned Shakespeare at, so to speak, his knee.

Not exactly laid back, I know, but I'm beginning to feel there's nothing to lose.

Protests against NATO, and Britain's leading role in it, mount in Greece. At Thessaloniki, protesters turn NATO road-signs back to front, and British troops, aiming to reach the airport, end up in a fruit market, where they are pelted with figs. Distinctly not a welcoming climate for an Anglo-Greek collaboration on a theatre production.

On BBC2, Harold Pinter is given half an hour by the Community Programmes Unit to make a 'counterblast statement' against the NATO war. Wearing one of his charcoal suits and a black shirt, and standing in a studio with NATO and target insignia, he gives it all he's got, using his deep actor's voice and generating great heat and many irrefutable arguments. Seeing him in full flood reminds me of the evenings we spent round a big table when we were all associate directors of the National Theatre under Peter Hall. I was struck, then as now, by Harold's rapid gear-changes to indignation, his sudden adrenalin glee when denouncing error or folly. At one meeting, Jonathan Miller announced he intended to stage *The Importance of Being Earnest* with Lady Bracknell played by a man. 'If Wilde had wanted it like that, Jonathan, he would have said so,' growled Harold.

On television now, he hits the same note of sarcastic criticism. Addressing people who will say that something needed to be done about the Kosovar Albanians, he says, yes, but to do it, and to justify this bombing, you need moral authority. Then he launches into a litany of questions, at machine-gun speed:

What is moral authority?
Where does it come from?
How do you achieve it?
Who bestows it upon you?
How do you persuade others that you possess it?
You don't have to bother. What you have is power. Bombs and power.
And that's your moral authority.

In Harold's fury, I hear not only the voice of an artist, but of one of theatre's wiliest critics of war: Falstaff, critically catechising military honour in *Henry IV Part One*, on a battlefield strewn with corpses:

> What is honour? A word.
> What is that word 'honour'? Air.
> Who hath it? He that died o' Wednesday.
> Doth he feel it? No.
> Doth he hear it? No.
> 'Tis insensible then? Yea, to the dead.
> But will it not live with the living? No.
> Why? Detraction will not suffer it. Therefore I'll none of it.

The same sceptical, Socratic dialectic and ironic dismissal from black-clad Pinter now as from Shakespeare's rotund Falstaff then. Theatre rhetoric, arguing with the more dishonest linguistic masquerades of politics and war.

Quite a few answers to my proposal to make a theatre piece about the war. Mostly positive, but there's no equivalent of Peter Hall's RSC deciding to make a piece about Vietnam, though I ask Nick Kent at the Tricycle, after his supremely civic stagings of the trials of Nuremberg, Srebrenica and the Stephen Lawrence inquiry. Without a host theatre, it will not be taken seriously. Dragan, who in 1993 produced an immediate piece of émigré theatre about the siege of Sarajevo, grapples with the challenge.

I do despite everything keep thinking about your theatre appeal. Theatre can't handle war too well, I mean the horror of military interventions and their consequences. What theatre can do well in a documentary format is to expose the media lies and machinations, to theatricalise the rhetoric of propaganda (BBC TV being gung ho, CNN working as a global rumour mill, Yu media translating everything into antifascist rhetoric of WW2, Russian media sliding into conspiratorial paranoia . . .). A production with 50 screens with TV news and projections of front pages of papers from all around the world.

On making theatre out of this war: I have a lot of ifs and buts, like where do you get the concentration, the peace of mind, the uplifting energy to reach the metaphorical level? Yet I'll remain involved. To start with: Sloba and Mrs as Macbeth and Lady M, Père et Mère Ubu. Then guilt and anger. All this anger for being bombed, for being treated as perpetrator even though a victim. But guilt; for what was done, for what was not done (everyone could have done more), for the indifference to the misfortune of others manifested in the past.

I talk to Peter in California. Don Seawell is pushing him to respond to his offer. If American Actors' Equity agrees, Peter would be able to have some leading English classical actors in the predominantly American cast. Peter wonders what level of American actor would turn down TV and film offers to spend six months in Denver working on a fifteen-hour theatre piece, but, since Don has been such a steadfast supporter, he knows we must explore it. He is halfway through writing his article about John that he has proposed to the *Guardian*, using the anniversary of John's forty years with the Royal Shakespeare Company to bring to the attention of the public – and, we hope, of benefactors – the plight of *Tantalus*. He will send me a draft so that together we can sharpen its advocacy.

Peter's piece arrives. It's written with the warmth not only of a long-lasting creative collaboration, but a lifetime friendship that began when they were both students at Cambridge making theatre:

John directed with precision (amateurs need often to be told what to do, rather than inspired into doing it for them-selves); arranged awesome fight sequences (I regret to say I sent him to hospital when my Tybalt fought his Mercutio); and acted with a strange combination of glamour and fubsiness which was irresistible. His old men were all

Shallow, his young men strangely vulnerable and dear. He was brilliant and eccentric and utterly obsessed by the theatre. He chewed razor blades at rehearsal while his actors watched, mesmerised, as he slowly turned the blade over and over on his tongue. Often, there would be a tell-tale trickle of blood at the corner of the mouth.

He fell over chairs, fell off stages, broke cups and glasses and chewed cigarettes. But there was nothing shambolic about his work or the clarity of his perceptions. It was crystal-clear. He was from Eton, but you'd never have known it. He was the best advert for individuality a school could ever have. He hated conformity, class or dogma. He was sceptical, yet moral; unpolitical, yet committed. I acted with him, directed with him and argued with him. He was responsible for giving me my first solo production as a student. After half a dozen more, I graduated and started directing professionally. From the start, he gave me something to measure up to.

Five years later, I was about to run Stratford and create the RSC. It seemed natural to ask John to join me. In the next few years, much was written about the RSC's aesthetic – about its post-Brechtian sense of realism, its cool and witty style, its post-imperial, not to say left-wing philosophy. In truth, our clarity and our lack of romantic sentiment, even our ability to get audiences to understand Shakespeare's dialectic, was born entirely out of the precision of our text work, with John Barton doing training, training and yet more training. In those years, if John was not quite my artistic conscience, he certainly tried to make me live up to my standards.

Maybe for Peter as well as for me, this *Tantalus* odyssey is turning not just into a sea of troubles, but into a mirror; of friendships, principles, commitments, passions. Then Peter turns to the current state of play:

So why isn't it being done? Well, it will be, finally. It has been nearly financed several times over the last two years. But, ironically, it has always failed at the last fence. It is a vast undertaking, not in the cast or the physical production, but in time. It will take six months to rehearse and a year to play round the world. It is essentially an international subject and it needs international collaboration. The RSC have contributed a great deal over the years, but they cannot do all of it now without curtailing their normal programme.

So for two years, Michael Kustow, John and I have been running round the world seeking co-producers. I have sometimes felt that not since Wagner built a theatre at Bayreuth in order to give the first performance of *The Ring* has anything so daft been attempted. He found King Ludwig; we haven't, not quite.

The producer in search of a patron as crazy as mad King Ludwig of Bavaria gets a call from Alex Bernstein, the chair of the Old Vic Trust. The producer of a Trojan War extravaganza in a time of war has been faxing Mr Bernstein for help from private foundation. The sums are too great, says Mr Bernstein, and we are anyway fully committed well into next year.

The producer of one of the dafter theatrical enterprises since *The Ring* gets a late-night call from Peter in Los Angeles. He is sitting with Donald Seawell and his colleague Donovan; they have been going through the plan for rehearsing and mounting *Tantalus* in Denver with a mixed cast of American actors and expatriate British ones who have a 'green card' allowing them to work in the USA. Peter, who had previously told the producer that spending six months rehearsing and performing in Denver would be 'a deal-breaker', now says that it looks as if it could be made to work within the budget, that rehearsing in New York would be too costly (we need three rehearsal spaces concurrently, for a start), and that he is still worried that senior actors of the calibre the leading parts require would not come for such a long time to Denver and then London and elsewhere. 'But it turns out that my casting director for Los Angeles is the same as the one Denver uses. So we're going to explore how likely such a commitment might be from the right level of actor. The trouble is, by the time we find out, it will be too late; I will have to have made a decision.'

'So it's a leap of faith?'

'It is,' replies Peter, ruefully.

When the producer gives John Barton an account of the developments, John's reaction is that the schedule is too short for such a mammoth piece of work, and that there's a danger of wishful thinking by Peter about what can be achieved, because of all the financial pressures on him. 'I'll be able to demonstrate this in a few weeks, when I've finished my charts of cross-casting and actor availability,' he says.

The producer says that there's not enough time, that there's pressure for a decision from everyone, and that the situation is beginning to resemble John's play five, in which King Priam worries about how to test whether the Trojan Horse can be trusted, and while he's working it out, the Horse is dragged into the city.

'And the result wasn't exactly a stunning success,' murmurs John.

The millstones of anxiety grind through the weekend. Peter in Los Angeles doesn't return my calls. When I get through to his assistant, I find out his 'voicemail' automatically picks up calls while he's speaking, but doesn't let him know he has calls unless he checks it. Another digital coercion, another wait. John is in Cambridge, more and more convinced that it would be fatal for Peter to accept Denver's offer, as generous as it is. As the prospects seem to shrink, John's voice acquires a strength and sureness, like Richard II accepting the inevitable. Facing defeat, he becomes truly heroic. Peter calls back at my daybreak, his 11pm. I have to ask him to speak up; his voice keeps dipping into his boots. Don is insisting on an answer in twenty-four hours. He tells Peter that he cannot hold back the future programming of his theatres any longer. He reminds him that he is putting nearly $5 million into *Tantalus*, in cash and indirect subsidy. He has also firmly rejected the idea of rehearsing in New York, which might attract more actors. He has the facilities in Denver to house and rehearse the whole company, he's said, and he doesn't see why they should stand idle.

Peter has canvassed the actors with whom he is working at the Mark Taper Forum in Los Angeles, and its director. They all tell him what a risk he's taking. He has spoken to Rosemairie Tichler at the New York Shakespeare Festival, who knows more than anyone about American actors and the classics. She warns him that he'll be lucky to get really good actors for such a long engagement, and in Denver too. He is also worried that American Equity allows any actor to walk out of a theatre production at six weeks' notice. 'Imagine trying to replace a senior actor who is playing four massive leads,' he says.

I tell him that John will support whatever he decides, and is already resigned to its not happening in England at least, during the year 2000. 'He'll put in a speech about the arbitrary dating of the Millennium,' I tell Peter. But he sounds too burdened to take the joke. I tell Peter that I am going to try to reach Adrian Noble at home, just see whether there might be some formula whereby the RSC takes the project in, for 2001. He doesn't sound too hopeful about that, either.

That evening, I get hold of Adrian, who is happy, he says, rehearsing *The Family Reunion*. 'Very simple verse – three stresses and a caesura to each line – but it gets hold of you.' I explain the crunch point we have reached, and gently ask whether there's any alternative the RSC could offer Peter at this moment of choice. 'Of course, we want to present it, and of course we'll bring a "dowry" to the table. But the problem has always been finding the rest of the money. And surely it would be so again. I think Don's offer is the best chance John is likely to get, and he should seize it.' I tell this to John in Cambridge, where he has spent the day making progress, he says, on the final play. He wants to be called, but I tell him time is running out before tomorrow's deadline, give him Peter's number, and he says he'll call him. I imagine him making a last plea to Peter not to accept if he's not happy, and throwing his work at Peter's feet, to pick up when Peter, who has already booked himself up with plays and operas for much of 2001, will be free to do it. I also imagine Peter deciding to go ahead, in some degree because John has urged him not to.

My hunch turns out to be correct. At teatime next day, Peter calls.

'I've decided,' he says. 'I'm going to do it.' His voice is resonant, his rhythm up-beat.

'Mazeltov,' I say, 'What about the American actors?'

'One thing I know: they won't crumple under the pressure. My only problem with my actors here is that they do everything I tell them to.'

'Are they too reverential?' I ask. 'Maybe you must do something disreputable. Like getting into a car on Hollywood Boulevard with a hooker. Then they'll think you're just another piece of jumped-up British trash.'

He chortles, a good sign.

We talk about things that now have to be done, and I ring John. Initially, he doesn't leap for joy. It's as if he's been attuned to it not happening, and still pinning hopes on some future production, when Peter is free, and the RSC able to take his work into its bosom, for which it was conceived. He brings out his not-unjustified list of concerns, above all the shortness and intensity of the rehearsal period, with its danger of traffic-jams and overwork. I say that he's going to have to balance his misgivings with his wish to give Peter every support. I think, but do not say, that Don's offer is probably the only chance he will have of seeing *Tantalus* staged in his lifetime.

A gleeful e-mail from Dragan arrives.

Did you know that in the Moscow Theatre *Satyricon* there was an old actor called Nikolai Kustov who used to work with Meyerhold? In the late sixties he gave unofficial workshops on bio-mechanics as he remembered it (how much could he really demonstrate, he was old). All the workshop marketeers of bio-mechanics picked up the stuff from this guy Kustov. So you have a (slightly tangential) link to the maestro. Ha!

The producer takes a breath, and constructs his own catechism:

Why do I spend such time and emotion on such Utopian projects?

Why do I hold to such faith in theatre, when the planet is ruled by screens big and small?

Why do I go on seeking for some truth in theatre, where I feel more a fellow traveller than a family member?

Why do I try to import what I see as the truths of theatre into any work I do?

What is this theatre-essence that I keep hunting? And how was it implanted in me? In anyone?

Part Two:
Essentials of Theatre

In Our Nature?

My nature is subdued
To what it works in, like the dyer's hand.

Shakespeare, Sonnet 111

The hand stained by the dyes it uses to transform skins and fabrics is Shakespeare's image of himself as a theatre-creature. It seems to come out of a low moment of unworthiness, when the traffic of emotion and transformations, make-believe and manoeuvring which was his life as an actor-writer-manager felt like a betrayal of his self. But it's an arresting image, because it's irreversible. The dyer cannot get the stains out of his skin. His nature is submerged in the theatre, has taken on the colour of theatre, is branded by theatre.

When I look at the faces of actors, worked by the lifelong passage of emotions and actions, or the longevity of energy and shared excitement in theatre directors, when I see playwrights riding on the here-and-now reception of their play before a live audience, I see one way in which theatre is central to human nature.

And when I sense the anticipation of an audience, the speed with which they seize on an allusion, an echo, a plot twist, a charged syllable, a simply achieved transformation before their very eyes, I see evidence that theatre is inscribed in our nature, a latent faculty which in the right conditions may flower in anyone. You don't have to become an actor, a playwright or a director to find the theatre in yourself.

But what is my own proof of this belief, in my own experience? It begins in memories of my father's shop.

Seeing Theatre de Complicite's staging of Bruno Schulz's *Street of Crocodiles*, set in a miraculous shop, all its ingredients felt very familiar. The *pas-de-deux* between picky customer and affable but inwardly contemptuous salesperson, the *corps de ballet* of shopworkers, suppliers and customers, bales of cloth choreographed into continents and cosmologies – Complicite's dynamic and vertiginous staging bespoke tides of imagination too big to be contained in a clothes shop. I knew what they were like because I knew my father in his shop.

My father's shop was also his theatre, where he transformed his work into a kind of play. Once a week, he stayed late at the shop, window-dressing. Sometimes, in school holidays, I stayed with him. He had a pincushion on a strap round his wrist, he had a reel of fine twine to raise sleeves and make jackets fly, to spread skirts, suspend shirts at angles to each other, build up a frozen ballet of garments in the lit proscenium of his shop window.

On the glass-topped counter, through which you could see drawers of vests, socks, gloves laid out in neat ranks, he had set little pots of poster paint in the anarchist colours of red and black, with flat-nosed brushes, thick and thin. I watched him swiftly and confidently paint prices and slogans on cardboard. The slogans brimmed with superlatives and exclamation marks, they were the script and the finishing touch to his weekly retail repertory theatre, of which he was the producer, designer, and playwright.

My father poured his gifts – for window-design and scene-painting, and for music-hall patter with the customers – into that shop in south London. He ran his shop with the manic zeal of a true impresario, shouting at his long-suffering brother, fussing the local shop-girls, strutting out front between walls of hanging clothes to gee-up the punters, as I learned to do. When I discovered Bruno Schulz's father, another hyperactive fantasist of the shop floor, I recognised the same engorged imagination at work in Drohobycz and Bermondsey:

Grown tall with fury, his head swollen into a purple fist, my father rushed like a fighting prophet on the ramparts of cloth and began to storm against them. He leaned with his whole strength against the enormous bales, heaving them from their places. He put his shoulders under the great lengths of cloth and made them fall on the counters with a dull thud. The bales overturned, unfolding in the air like enormous flags, the shelves exploded with bursts of draperies, waterfalls of fabrics as if touched by the wand of Moses.

The customers of my father in Bermondsey and of Bruno Schulz's in provincial Poland may have seen them as middle-aged men selling clothes. But they saw themselves as protagonists in a titanic drama of the circulation of goods, money and emotions, despite the shortcomings of suppliers, the unreliability of helpers, the knavery of rivals and the fickleness of customers. Is this so different from the over-abundance of energy I pour into my work as a producer?

My father made me see the bridge between theatre and his shop, theatre and his street, which became his thrust stage. Standing out front, shouting 'Come on in, darling', his showman voice joined the chorus of cries in Tower Bridge Road, vying with the shouts of the stall-holders – the fresh egg stall, the fruit and veg, the fish and poultry. The whole street felt like a theatre, with the passing trade our audience. There was comedy, backchat, flirtation. Its pub's regulars still included dockers from the Pool of London; its missionary outpost, the South London Salvation Army, was like something out of *Guys and Dolls*, to help the poor and combat the evil drink; its cinema, the Trocadero, was an Italianate extravaganza.

Later, when I went to Italy and saw the piazza in action, I recognised the conviviality I had known as a child. When I came to Roger Planchon's theatre in a district of Lyon, in a 1930s Front Populaire building, sandwiched between the municipal swimming pool and library, flanked by a bustling street-market and little bistros, I had the same feeling of a place for people. I never had that feeling of intersecting life, work and art when I worked at the National Theatre, though Tom Phillips' poster announced in ringing tones (and lettering more studied than my father's) 'The National Theatre is Yours.' It might have helped had there been low-cost housing right next to the National on the South Bank, with shops, school and playground helping to make the place less of a 'dedicated' culture zone. Proximity might have got our neighbours through our intimidating doors. Instead, we got skateboarders from the estates across Stamford Street, the IBM headquarters was built where there might have been housing, and the homeless set up their cardboard cities, until a monumental IMAX cinema pushed them out. I am glad to have had that taste of the theatre of the street. And my father's frenzy reminds me of the madness and obsession of getting the show on. He taught me that play is fight as well as fantasy, that you need to be a bit crazy to transform your world.

Is theatre grounded in our nature? What are the essentials of theatre? Does its mixture of truth and artifice, physical presence and transformation into metaphor, seriousness and frivolity, reflect some mixed human essence? In a time of genetic modification and brain-altering chemicals, of multiple channels and information overload, can the instinct that makes us play and play along with theatre remain untouched? I asked a group of leading theatre-makers how theatre began for each of them.

Tony Harrison, poet, playwright and director, who yokes the intensity of classical Greek theatre with the common touch of music hall, found his essence of theatre in pantomime:

My very earliest experience was of the last days of variety, pantomime and music hall in Leeds, at the Leeds Empire, the Variety and the Theatre Royal. When I was doing my play *Square Rounds*, which involved magic, I went to a magic consultant, and I talked to him about one of the most theatrical things I remember. I was very, very young, and it was in a show that was called *Pete Collins' Would You Believe It?* It included Belgian giants who put babies in their shoes and people who wrestled with crocodiles. And there was this act, this great *coup de théâtre*, which probably turned me on to theatre. It was in the days before our computers and there was this great bank of lights and buttons, like they imagined a computer station in the fifties, and a professor with wild red hair, wearing a white coat, was pressing buttons. As he pressed the buttons, a very slim robot in a suit walked on. There were steps in front of the stage like a mounting block. So they pressed and pressed, he lifted his foot and went up a step, and it all seemed so elaborate and so difficult that the whole audience applauded when he got to the top. The professor came from the back of the electrical gear to take a bow and the dummy turned round and pulled off the head of the professor.

I thought uuh . . . And I have never forgotten it. The only time that reminded me of it was in the Moscow State Circus. There was a clown in a big coat and he had monkeys and one of them ran into the audience and jumped onto this woman's lap. Through dumb show, the clown said come up and I'll recompense you for your shock. And he brought her down into the ring and put her behind a screen. She came out with this glorious mink coat and she swaggered round the ring and suddenly this man blew a whistle and the whole coat disintegrated into about forty live minks. And I just went 'Whoooa!!!'

I love those kinds of transformations and the metamorphoses of pantomime. In pantomime you had the tradition of the Dame, a man playing the woman, the Principal Boy, a woman playing the man, there was all that kind of theatricality.

Those experiences in childhood came simultaneously with my beginning to learn ancient Greek at the age of eleven or twelve. So I was seeing Laurel and Hardy live at the Empire or these *Would You Believe It?* shows. And at the same time I was struggling with the beginnings of learning ancient Greek. Almost all the serious theatre that I have done has been mediated through the popular theatre I was excited by and thrilled by and gob-smacked by when I was a child.

What was it like when he saw 'a proper play', I asked Tony:

> I couldn't quite believe it when I first went to a proscenium
> play. In the pantomime people talked to you, they said
> 'Hello' and they pointed and picked people out of the
> audience. When I went to my first proscenium play when
> everybody talked to each other and smoked cigarettes and
> took drinks from the cabinet, I thought Hey, I'm here, I'm
> sitting out here. Even now I can't bear seeing proscenium
> theatre, however good it may be. I can't bear the idea that
> the audience is there on sufferance and is witnessing
> something that the actors are unaware of.

Simon McBurney, actor and director, leads Theatre de
Complicite, a very un-English theatre group. Their productions
have included work by the Polish prose-poet Bruno Schulz, the
Russian absurdist comic Daniel Kharms, John Berger's *The Three
Lives of Lucie Cabrol*, about the life of a tough little French
peasant woman, and Durrenmatt's *The Visit*. Like many of
Complicite's performers, Simon was formed by the French master
mime Jacques Lecoq. He not only has a mime's plasticity, but a
sharp awareness of the life of the present moment and actors'
ability to transform the space around them. In the Olivier
Theatre, where he staged *The Caucasian Chalk Circle* in the
round, his eel-like twining round a chair as he dished out
sentences as Brecht's anarchist judge Azdak conveyed both the
pleasure of a life-long underdog enjoying power at last, and his
anxiety that his luck couldn't last.

For Simon, theatre also started with the pantomime.

> I loved it, I really loved it. I grew up without television so my
> mother used to write little plays and we put them on. Next
> door lived a woman, a professor, who wrote a study of *The
> Fool*, which may have had something to do with it. Going to
> the theatre was a very big deal, if you didn't have television
> and rarely went to the cinema. When we went it made a
> profound impression on me. I don't ever remember taking a

decision that I was going into the theatre. I just suddenly found myself doing it. I was invited to do the opening night at the Comedy Store in 1979. I came from that generation of rock concerts where live performance was mixing into music: the rock world stole the language of theatre and used it very cleverly. From the 'sixties onward, rock concerts became not only about the music, but about an event. That helped me become a performer.

Mark Ravenhill is author of *Shopping and Fucking*, a devastating play which tapped into the desolation of the Thatcher generation growing up in a world of sex, drugs and transactions. Seeing it transferred from the Royal Court Theatre to the West End, it felt to me, one of the older members of the audience, as if it were touching a similar nerve of pain and bruised hope as John Osborne's *Look Back In Anger* had done for my generation.

For Mark, theatre began in his own sitting room.

The family that I was brought up in was not very wealthy. We didn't have any money to go to the theatre, so my brother and I started making theatre before we knew what it was. My dad was working in a factory and would bring home large cardboard boxes, which we used to cut out into shapes, trees and mountains, pretend to be characters and invite people to come and watch. From when we were about four to eight we put on plays in a theatre, although we didn't really know what we were doing. We just put the chairs at one end of the room because that seemed the place to be and stood in front of the cardboard mountains wearing special clothes, and made up stories. For us it just came out of childhood play and games. It was only later that we found that you could pay to see people do this or that you could do this as a job. We felt incredibly liberated. It was hard work, but rewarding when an audience came to see it at five o'clock on a Friday.

In Montreal, actor and director Robert Lepage is one of the

most original *auteurs* in today's theatre. Coming from Canada, a country patchworked into different linguistic identities and ethnic communities, Lepage is acutely aware of marginality. He makes theatre that dances on frontiers. Stories seem to have been collected at random, joined and cross-cut with the haphazardness of life. The work is composed, rather than written and then performed. It looks highly technological, but the technology turns out to be very simple, a network of hand-held tools supporting a live, often solo, performance.

Lepage believes theatre speaks to us because we all play, we are all players. But this sense of play is being trimmed and tamed in a morally troubled and technologised society.

In French we use the word *ludique* to describe playfulness, the way a child plays. That playfulness was extremely present and fundamental to theatre for centuries and centuries. Suddenly the twentieth century comes around and this guilt-ridden society, the western world, is ashamed of something, post-war guilt or whatever, so suddenly the theatre belongs to the psychologists and the psychoanalysts. Suddenly there is only one kind of reading of theatre, which is the reading that actors do, not players. I admire and appreciate actors, I love seeing good acting, but there is way too much of it going on. In most of our theatre, players are less welcome than actors and there are very few of them left.

Lepage sees theatre as a continual see-saw between the soliloquy of aloneness and the collective encounter:

A man alone on stage, whatever he talks about, he talks about loneliness. Theatre is also about meeting, about not being alone. When Berlin was reconstructed after the war, one of the first things they did was to reconstruct the theatres, because people wanted to gather together. Theatre is a meeting point. Cinema is much more about one character intimately linked to another person in the room but theatre is the meeting of an architect and actors and

writer and designer. So there is this community thing and
inside it there is this soliloquy relationship with the
audience. That's why the theatre is this fantastic three-
dimensional form of communication.

In a strong theatre experience, the never-fixed border between
subjective and collective can blur, pointing to another way in
which theatre-making and theatregoing mirror our nature. They
give us a rehearsal of what being a realised individual in a rich
society might be. For Peter Hall, who has spent his life making
mini-societies called theatre companies, making a play is an act
at once personal and social:

> I think the act of making a play has for so many years been
> central to my life that I can't imagine living without doing
> it. There are a whole variety of reasons for this. Firstly you
> get paid quite good money to live in the head of a great
> genius, if you are doing Chekhov or Shakespeare or
> Aeschylus. You get to know an artist and his genius by
> articulating him in a way which no study would ever give
> anybody. You can't do a play without making a healthy
> social group and in a sense the act of play-making is a
> metaphor of a decent society, both in terms of the way that
> you support each other, and the way that you respect each
> others' creativity. The sentimentality about companies of
> actors is that they all love each other, which is of course
> rubbish. The strength of company work is partly the
> definition of how you dislike each other, because of your
> reservations about somebody's talent and way of working. So
> it's about community knowledge both good and bad; I think
> it's quite a good metaphor of living.

In Tel Aviv, Israeli director Rina Yerushalmi has restored
theatre to her country's native language. In a two-evening staging
of the Old Testament, four years in the making, she has made a
Hebrew and universal theatre by planting it in the violent
contradictions of emotion and thought that can be found in the

Hebrew Bible, once it is removed from the grip of religious regulators and simplifiers. Her young company is the outcome of all the ethnic mixtures and encounters of her country. She wants to test the necessity of theatre in our nature and society.

I still don't know whether theatre has anything to offer in the present century. But I want to examine it, to understand in which sphere of human existence theatre is simply imperative, because otherwise the human being loses something of itself. Not a social activity in the sense of having to preserve culture, but rather a matter of humanity's well-being. In some way theatre still activates creativity in us. The actor must perform in a way that activates the audience's inner world, not present it with a ready-made experience. We can create a 'virtual reality' on a computer. But are we not moving away from creating it as a group experience? Society needs to 'exercise imagination', and it appears it also needs to do so together, not just individually.

The theme of theatre threatened and of the need for something more than routine entertainment finds a ferociously funny form in Comic Potential, Alan Ayckbourn's fifty-first play, opening in London in the last months of the twentieth century. It's set in a television studio in the near future. A daily soap opera is being performed, not by actors but by 'actoids', robots programmed with a narrow repertoire of speech and gesture in which endless episodes can be clothed. You wonder how much difference there is between this dystopian soap, ground out by mechanised mannequins, and the actual afternoon soaps that already fill out the schedules around the world, placebos against depression.

Ayckbourn's ferocity begins when Jacie ('JC' for Juvenile Character), an actoid playing a nurse, begins to push at her limits. Her artificially intelligent break-out from her fellow actoids begins with manic laughter at seeing the funny side of things. Then the soap's director, a superannuated movie-maker, teaches her the art of the double-take, as perfected by Jack Benny and

Zero Mostel. Since JC is a quick learner, she disrupts that day's maudlin episode by inserting massively inappropriate double-takes. The vampirish TV executive, dedicated to profitable predictability and the exclusion of originality, hits the roof.

But JC is also going beyond her limits because she has 'fallen in love', whatever that is for 'her', with a young scriptwriter, who spirits her out of the studio and into the city. On the run, holed up in a knocking-shop hotel room, she reaches into her memory bank for words to match her unfamiliar feelings of being in love for the first time. Terrified, all she can dredge up is a patchwork of soap-opera fragments and scraps of old songs, but nothing personal, nothing from inside, for there isn't any inside to an entertainment robot. And how much will be left in us, Ayckbourn seems to ask, if what most people get as drama is as automated as much of it is already?

When the erstwhile movie director teaches JC the art of comedy, he concludes, 'Two things make comedy. Surprise. And anger.' *Comic Potential* runs on surprise, the disturbing surprise of seeing human behaviour aped by automata, and – in the wide-eyed radiance of Janie Dee's performance – the enchanting, playful and moving surprise of watching JC's innocence, eager to experience much more than she knows. But equally, Ayckbourn's comedy is fuelled by anger, anger at the reductive machinery that keeps this launched spirit – or any awakened aspiration – on a leash of conformism and uniformity.

Ayckbourn writes and stages his funny, serious plays in a theatre-in-the-round, a converted cinema in Scarborough of which he is Artistic Director. I went up there to see one of his annual plays, and found that when he stops long enough to think what needs theatre meets, it's both community and a non-literal way of seeing. Theatre-in-the-round is the ideal medium for this:

> It's exactly the sort of theatre that's important these days. Not only are you on top of the actor and therefore very much part of what happens, but you're also sharing that experience with other members of an audience. It's also that sophisticated thing that theatre is: not only perceiving the

action but also perceiving other people perceiving it, and enjoying that shared perception of it. And when a show really works, whether it's laughter you're sharing with someone or horror or alarm, the fact that you know that you're sharing that experience is a very exciting and, I think, life-enhancing thing to do. When you come out you feel . . . well, right back to the Greeks, you feel that your emotions have been stretched and purged. That's why I think that theatre is about humanity. It's not about car-chases, it never can be. It's about the people in the cars, never about the vehicles.

Ayckbourn speaks of a communal happiness, within the theatre company, and between the stage and the house:

There is the odd masochistic actor that likes to be flayed, but most actors work far better when they're happy. Sometimes you have to give that corny old note to actors and say, 'Well guys, you've got it all together now, but the one thing that you haven't got is any joy in what you're doing. You're just so worried. And stop frowning, because an audience is coming in and they'll just smell that fear and that uneasiness and they'll get shifty!'

Fiona Shaw, an actress of tragic depth and intelligence, speaks with similar intuition of the way basic elements of our nature – time and silence and expectancy – can become charged up in theatre:

Fundamentally we have a terror of silence, and yet the theatre is built on silence. Peter Brook is very interesting about this; he said recently to me that all great religions in the world have one thing in common: they are the pursuit of silence. But, he said, it is not the silence of the leaden coffin, it is the silence of anticipation. That moment before. And of course music is full of that pause before the beat, before the pianist plays; that moment when you know that you're alive because the universe is crackling with anticipation of itself.

It was time to talk to Peter Brook in Paris.

I sat with him, in the tiny cabin of his office in his Bouffes du Nord theatre in Paris. Wearing a blue denim shirt which intensifies the light blue of his eyes, he was sitting very still, hands clasped, a containing position, like the mid-sentence suspended pauses while his mind searches for the exact word, riffling through the differences between French and English, the two languages into which he, like Beckett, digs.

I had worked with him, had my horizons opened and my sense of what matters altered by him, over three decades, from his 'Theatre of Cruelty' workshop season to his recent neurological chamber pieces about the mind's afflictions and persistence. All the diverse, sharp edges of his work point to one centre: theatre as a means of probing our nature, and its origins in human stuff.

I could imagine him a monk in saffron robes, though there's nothing chaste in his eyes and mouth; or a psychoanalyst like his brother, listening to confessions and professions; or a Socrates, gleefully picking up a thread from an argument and drawing it deep into re-examination. His paradoxes have deepened but not changed since I first met him thirty years ago, and in a typically paradoxical gesture he gave me a copy of *In Search of the Miraculous*, Gurdjieff's mystical manual, on the first night of our fiercely political *US*. *US* managed to upset just about everyone, including the US ambassador of the time. 'Will the Ambassador walk out if he comes to the first night?' the Lord Chamberlain, then nearing the end of his rule as theatre censor, asked Brook. 'Not if he stays to the end,' Brook blithely replied. He meant that the complexity of part two might mollify his outrage at the anti-Americanism of much of part one. That is Brook's version of the story, anyway: it has the tinge of a well-turned Zen anecdote.

In his recent work, *The Man Who* and *I Am a Phenomenon*, Peter has gone to the works of two great neurologists, Oliver Sacks and Alexander Luria, to explore the landscapes of the human mind, in its disability and its over-abundance. In these chamber works, poised at the very edge of theatre, he let the experimental reticence of these scientists of the mind colour his own craft. The sparse means of these pieces – three or four actors playing patients and doctors in turn, a few chairs and tables, a couple of video screens – focus into the interior of the mind, the characters' and our own. That, Brook is saying, is where theatre, play, pattern, recognition, thought and emotion themselves, begin. It is as if, after a cavalcade of productions across the main stages and opera-houses of the world, he were paring down his implements to make what Christopher Marlowe called 'a great reckoning in a little room'. Only, dialectician that he is, in his greatest theatrical profusion he has always placed the counterpoint of rigour, quietness, stillness, simplicity. You cannot think of any polarity about Peter which he has not thought of, turned over, played with, already. In his memoir *Threads of Time*, a particularly passionate sentence gives a glimpse of the forces struggling inside his fierce equanimity:

> The meaning of chaos, the need for order; the wish for action, the power of inaction; the silence that alone gives sense to sound; the necessity to intervene and the virtue of letting go; the balance between inner and outer life; the dilemma of what to give and what to withhold, of what to take and what to decline – then, as now, I was driven by these shifting themes.

As I got to know him in the 'sixties, I began to see Brook the director mirrored in key characters of the plays he did, especially the ones he staged several times. The two mirror-figures that kept coming up, of course, were Prospero in *The Tempest* and the Duke in *Measure for Measure*. Both are directors, stage-managing an action that, after some hair-raising twists and turns, leads to a revelation and to justice. Both show a director's excitement – indeed, I remember a moment in Brook's French *Mesure Pour Mesure* where the Duke had to rein in his own manic enjoyment in his inventiveness, in danger of stifling itself in its own ingenuity. Both set up an experimental process to test human conduct. It is hard to imagine either without a group of people to

lead, mould, bring into shape, for both the magus and the theatre
director live best when they are acting with, acting upon, others.

But since Brook has begun to rein in his overt theatricality in
order to bring consciousness itself more directly into a theatre, he
seems less the conjurer of images, more like a Sacks or a Luria, a
doctor working on behalf of the patients, and from their view-
point; a doctor who is also a patient, a master who is also a pupil.
This is a movement which began in 1970 with the turning point
of his life and work, the move from London to Paris, from the
triumph of A *Midsummer Night's Dream* at the Royal Shakespeare
Company to Les Gobelins, a disused tapestry workshop in Paris.
He was determined to make a radical new departure, to start out
again with nothing taken for granted. It was as if a prodigal child,
blessed or even imprisoned with a profusion of gifts, reached
maturity, and decided to put himself out in the wind, the way
Lear thrusts himself onto the wild heath. Like Lear, he divested
himself of authority, and joined the multiracial group of actors on
the floor, trying to do exercises with a bamboo pole as well as
them.

He moved to France, because he was able to find funds there
which were not available in Britain. Britain subsidises institutions, not individuals. There's a 'fair play' factor which prevents
the British backing people, even people as proven and talented as
Brook. It calls itself democratic, but it's parsimony by another
name. The French, by contrast, with a tradition of state
patronage stretching back to Louis XIV's authoritarian court,
have the habit of godfathering outstanding individuals, even if
their system runs the risk of vain partiality and court intrigue.

Brook set up the International Centre of Theatrical Research
in Paris as a multinational laboratory. His interest in what
humans have in common across their cultures has expanded into
a grappling with the evolution of the human creature itself. I ask
him if he thinks we have theatre in our nature, and if he, as a
particularly searching director, has it in his nature. He begins
another of his long, looping answers:

Yesterday I was looking at an eight-day-old baby and

watching her moving her head and arms, groping, looking round. It's very clear that the human organism functions by trying to understand and interpret, second by second and even millisecond by millisecond, all the vast amount of stimuli coming from outside and inside. Genetically one sees that no baby, no human being, is equally endowed with the entire spectrum of human possibilities. That's why at the beginning of the work of our International Centre, it seemed so important to bring people of different races and cultures to work together. Each one of them has his own series of qualities to bring to a human potential which nobody possesses as a whole. But one begins to possess more when people from different backgrounds work together: the fan opens and the range is wider.

He turns from the child and the theatre-group to the play-goers, and sees a dialectic deeper than binary oppositions at work.

Sometimes the audience says, we are like children, we love the theatre because we go into a dream, we are taken out of ourselves. What does that mean? Is every human being so dissatisfied with themselves and their lives? They go to the theatre and the theatre becomes the opium of the people, the consolation, one's taken and taken out of oneself. Or there is the painful, very moving confrontation, almost like on a psychiatrist's couch, where one is shaken by being brought right into oneself. The true experience is when the two contradictory experiences happen at one and the same time.

He thinks 'distilling' is the best way to describe what a director does. The most telling memory I have of this side of him is an improvisation he gave the actors in US, the collectively created show we made about the Vietnam War, America and our British selves. The story that gradually came to the surface, out of a collage of scenes, tableaux, songs and dramatised research, relied on a thread of suicides by fire that linked the defiant Buddhist monks of Vietnam with Quaker pacifists in America and a young Englishman ready to immolate himself out of a confusion of protest and despair.

The acting problem was, how on earth to represent committing suicide by fire? The actor's stock phrase 'getting into the skin of my character' felt like an obscenity. Brook asked six actors to line up against one wall of our rehearsal room. 'I want you to try to walk to the other side of the room,' he said. 'But with each step you take, you must imagine you are sacrificing one of your senses. So you will have to decide whether to give up sight before touch, hearing after taste.'

The actors stood up – and remained standing for minutes on end. You could see the inside struggle in the tension on their faces. After fifteen minutes, one of them managed to take one step, in a silence that had become suffocating. After half an hour, perhaps three steps had been taken. Nobody was able to take the steps needed to reach the other wall. But the friction, the inner grinding, that came from asking yourself, like Artaud's performer tied to the stake, what was the essence of your nature, what would be the final part of you to go – that ate into each of us, actors or watchers, like a scouring acid. Nobody spoke about the exercise afterwards. It would have been intolerable and harmful without the trust that had already been woven between everyone in the production, after eight weeks. But it informed and strengthened the work on those scenes, and gave US an emotional and spiritual backbone that could be expressed in action, and that held together its shrapnel-like scenes.

That was serious play. But US threw up an episode of another kind of play – mischievous, teasing, provocative. It was a quizzical game Brook invented to question people's need for authoritative interpretations and intellectual schemes. It happened a week after we had opened US. The production had been greeted with a chorus of extreme reactions: outrage, praise, scorn, excitement. We announced an evening of discussion with the public, in a Catholic church hall off Leicester Square, which was soon packed. Brook sat with us, the writers and production team, behind a long table facing the audience. Hanging from the front of the table were hand-painted signs, saying

OPINIONS COST MONEY. IT'S FREE IF YOU SPEAK. YOU MUST
PAY IF WE ANSWER. IF WE SPEAK FIRST, WE MUST PAY.

We sat there, and sat there. The audience waited, then grew
impatient. In the restless silence, a sound could be heard, the
sound of coins chinking in buckets, which were being carried
along the aisles by stage managers. Someone angrily asked a
question, like 'For God's sake, what do you think you're doing?'
Brook replied, 'Have you paid?'

Someone else asked a question about the play. 'If you've paid,
we'll answer,' said Brook. It became a stand-off. No one wanted
to put money into the buckets. After a while, the penny, as it
were, dropped, and people began to discuss the play, its politics,
its theatrical style, its relevance to Britain now, between
themselves. Discussion replaced indignation. We, the panel,
became the audience. It was a small Dada exercise in taking
responsibility for what one thinks and feels, not handing it over
to 'experts', a reminder that the flow within an audience can lead
to concrete but indefinable perceptions, which later definition
destroys.

Both pieces of play around US, the hypothetical suicide in the
rehearsal room and the game with the audience's questions in the
church hall, related to deep human questions. Talking to me
thirty years later, Brook sees a changed and less human art-world,
a world of instant image, celebrity and surface:

One has to bring into the question this enormous explosion
of art forms going off in every single direction and nobody
daring to say that this is better, this is worse, sheep in
formaldehyde is less valuable than something else. You can
see that there is a terror of falling back into old judgments,
which is very healthy. But what is lacking is the passionate
why. Say that you find that you can take a stone and put it
in a box, find a little mechanism that makes the box jolt so
the stone bounces about and go out in public and announce,

'This is my idea.' Then someone else says, 'Yes that's quite a good idea,' and someone else buys it. A process has started, but has the artist really brought the work back to the deep human question: 'I am bewildered by the world around me. I not only need to live well in it, but for my own survival I need to feel that I am discovering, moment by moment, a meaning. Not an intellectual meaning but that organic sense of being alive.'

One day, years ago, my painter friend Tom Phillips looked more closely at the colour he made when at the end of a day's painting he smeared together the remains of all the pigments left on his palette before scraping them off. Whatever colours he had been using, they always merged into a kind of grey. A different shade of grey each day. Slate grey. Battleship grey. Brain grey. Prison grey. Mist grey. He decided to paint a thin stripe of each day's grey at the edge of the canvas, around whatever image he was making. It would be an index of time passing, a sign of all the days' work, an in-built reference to the process of making the picture, qualifying the reality of the image. Cumulatively, the greys would be a goodbye. *Terminal Greys* was his name for these columns and borders of stripes. Eventually, he made paintings entirely composed from the end-of-day greys from other canvases. No image, just the accumulated stripes. You began to see a richness about them.

The rigorous distillation of Peter Brook's late work is like these strong terminal greys. First came the Dionysiac wildness of his theatre of the 1960s: the manic explosiveness of the inmates of the *Marat/Sade* asylum; the giant phallus and marching band he brought on stage at the end of his Old Vic production of Seneca's *Oedipus*, unseating John Gielgud's musicality with Bacchic rudeness; the American-musical exuberance of the big numbers in *US*. For the past few years, he has been doing miniature pieces about the mind, chamber plays developed in South Africa by Athol Fugard, Barney Simon, John Kani and Winston Ntshona and a minutely calibrated *Happy Days* with his wife Natasha. First the big transformations, like Prospero's cloud-capped towers, his gorgeous temples, the great globe itself. Now the monochrome trophies from the great ascents, drawn down from the heights to the pitiless, colour-drained truths of the workspace, Shakespeare's air, thin air. And finally, continually, the search to cross the threshold into moment-by-moment meaning, for which theatre has a special gift.

I found another essence of theatre far from the intellectually fashionable multiculturalism of Peter Brook's Paris, in the South Africa of Pieter-Dirk Uys. From the cruel absurdity of apartheid to the ironies of freedom, Pieter-Dirk Uys, a one-person theatre whose most famous creation is a dazzling woman, acts out an essential gesture of theatre: transformation. A satirical writer-performer, an impersonator and shape-shifter, he explores every contradiction: white and black, male and female, comic and tragic. Son of a Jewish mother, who came to Cape Town in 1938 as a refugee from Nazi Germany, and of an Afrikaner father whose family were cornerstones of the white Nationalist party, he's at the threshold between religions and races. A bald, polite, fifty-ish smiling man, when apartheid had the power he transformed before your very eyes into succinct impersonations of P.W. Botha, Desmond Tutu, and Nelson Mandela. He also traversed gender, turning into larger-than-life, lethally tongued women, from his waspish Jewish liberal Noelle Fine to his satiric masterpiece Evita Bezuidenhout, a sublimely prejudiced, irresistibly charming Afrikaner matron, who navigates the political switchback with effortless chutzpah.

He can turn on a sixpence and take you from riotous laughter to hushed attention, as he becomes an old Berlin grandmother in Cape Town, remembering Europe's fascism and measuring Africa's apartheid against it, or a brutally garrulous Afrikaner man, apologising to his torture victim whom he meets at a rugby match. As well as their political and social accuracy, these dramatic vignettes are his personal archetypes: beneath them lie his mother's membership of the persecuted, and his father's of a master race. But his cross-dressing and dressing-up is infectious fun, an irresistible invitation to join him in dressing-down killers and crooks, opportunists and hypocrites.

Today he casts a critical gaze on his reborn country, cleaving to his central belief that 'hypocrisy is the lubricant of political intercourse'. Imagination, fancy and carnival are the tools of his theatre, but his comedy, coming from a real front line, has substance. Its target is politics. Its enemy is racism and abuse of power. Its assumption is a scathing faith in democracy.

Each year he comes to London's Tricycle Theatre. In that galleried intimate space over six years, I have watched him rock audiences of expatriate South Africans, North London liberals, gays and young people. His show in summer 1999, *Dekaffirnated*, four years after the return of democracy to South Africa, was a kind of summation. He came on as a *sankofa*, a witch-doctor, a beaming storyteller in fairytale cap and robes, and told us the tale of how South Africa fell from its gods and timelessness into European time and control, when the Dutch settlers landed in 1652, 'and the sun lost its smile'. Then he announced that he was going to give a concert, walked across to a grand piano and did the oldest clown routine in the business, endlessly deferring the start of playing by clearing his throat, adjusting the stool, flexing his fingers – and then he shot into an explanation of the persistence of the word kaffir to a little golliwog, yes, a golliwog in a show about racism. Funny, but steely stuff.

We had a chilling flash of his favourite old monster, P.W. Botha, instantly sketched with a protruding lower lip licked by a reptilian tongue, porkpie hat and glasses and a stabbing forefinger. That forefinger is the tell-tale sign of the arrogance of politicians, any politician; Pieter saw it once in Mandela and is keeping his eyes skinned for any lapse by Thabo Mbeki and his team. But the twin peaks of his show, the routines everyone is waiting for, are the cross-dressed women. First, acid-voiced Noelle Fine, standing in a queue to register for the election, drawls a hair-raising story about locking herself out from her high-security mansion when she ventured out to pick fresh flowers for a dinner table. She managed to attract the attention of her neighbours' 'boy' to let her in, but he set off all the alarms, and the police arrived and shot him dead.

When he comes back in the second half as Evita Bezuidenhout, 'The Most Famous White Woman in South Africa', you can feel the pleasurable 'aaah!' and anticipation of an audience that knows they are in safe hands. She looks as elegant and self-assured as ever, in teetering high heels, bouffant spun-glass hair, crimson lip-gloss, long nails and lashes. Evita, as Pieter's friend Janet Suzman says, brims with 'hauteur and bonhomie'. She is wearing one of her vast wardrobe of cocktail party outfits. She favours whatever colours are politically correct. Now she sports the ANC colours, boasts of her long-time friendship with Mandela, calls him up on her cellphone to remind him to take his pills.

More than any postmodern icon, she's become an authentic fake. Only Evita would tip over into the political sphere itself, hosting a TV series immediately after South Africa's first free election, in which she interviewed Nelson Mandela and each of his ministers, who joined in the game as if she were a real and formidable woman, not a white Afrikaner Jew in drag. Only Pieter would put on his P.W. Botha porkpie hat and specs, and turn up at the Truth and Reconciliation Commission in place of the real Botha, who was refusing to do so. Only Pieter's Evita, crossing the line between theatre and life, would have her essential wit and wisdom published in a series that also anthologises Mandela and Steve Biko, as if she were as real as them. 'Politics', Evita wrote, 'is the art of getting votes from the poor and money from the rich, by promising to protect each from the other.'

The chatter comes thick and fast. The tongue spares no one. This is a dangerous customer. Even the most outrageous remarks seem to come from a brain in overdrive. 'The only way I can see my black grandchildren in the dark is when they smile.' Behind me at the Tricycle, a young woman from Soweto blows gleeful kisses at this liberating, extravagant, taboo-bending comic queen, who commands joyful allegiance.

Evita told the black grandchildren joke in one of the sixty towns she visited in spring 1999, in her pre-election trek to get people to vote. Pieter was concerned that apathy and the difficult election procedures would deter many from voting; 'but if we don't have a good second election, we'll never have a third one, and we'll be back where we were before.' Evita had already, at the invitation of the Speaker, delivered an historic televised address to the South African parliament, which made her nationally famous. Imagine Betty Boothroyd inviting Eddie Izzard in drag to speak to the House of Commons. Pieter/Evita travelled in a mini-bus – he had originally got South African Railways to loan him a train, but the offer was withdrawn, reputedly because a (black) board member said, 'We're not lending a train to that Afrikaner woman.'

At each town Evita would chair a meeting in which the candidates set out their wares, some of the more foursquare ones looking a little uneasy at sharing a platform with this Jewish transvestite. Little kids reached out to touch Evita's dress, mayors gave her motorcades. She stood up in towns across the country and apologised for apartheid. Desmond Tutu had told her that in the new South Africa she must confess: 'So let me get it out of the way. Look, Winnie Mandela apologised for Stompie in under three minutes and never looked back, no? So let me hereby apologise for apartheid on behalf of all white South Africans, and refugees from Rhodesia and the UK. Let me apologise for apartheid on behalf of all Coloureds and Indians who pretended to be Italians. We are very, very sorry . . . that it didn't work.'

This was the ultimate theatrical overspill: the most famous white woman in South Africa, who doesn't even exist, going out into the political arena, and getting the votes in. Evita's Ballot Bus Tour was cross-dressing for democracy.

At the end of one meeting, when Evita called for questions from the audience to the candidates, a young black man from the local township stood up. In the television pictures, he looks gawky, full of emotion, as awed as he is excited that the floor is his and he can say what he likes and people will listen.

'You promised us freedom,' he says to all the candidates, 'but what you gave us was . . . democracy.'

Evita, and Pieter's nomadic one-man/one-woman theatre tour, gave him the courage to say that. Hard to think of a better example of theatre as a vessel of transformation, a path to exercise freedom for the time being, and perhaps to remember what it feels like.

Pieter's creation Evita has acquired her own conquering presence, a kind of shameless female Falstaff, in the thick of 'real life'. He guards Evita like a precious double.

She has her own handwriting. When the press write about her they never write a.k.a. Pieter-Dirk Uys. She is asked her opinion on everything, from death to what cats should get when they have flu. She gets asked, not me. It means that she works as her own three-dimensional reality. When P.W. Botha retired she would send flowers to him and his wife on their birthdays – and get cards back, addressed Evita Bezuidenhout, c/o Pieter-Dirk Uys.

I had a big reaction from Afrikaner women who saw Evita as representing what they could not become, because Afrikaner women were not allowed that freedom of speech, that power. Gay kids were enormously inspired by her, she became their icon. Black people seemed to have enjoyed her enormously because she seemed to represent the worst of the people they wanted to smash. The irony was when I did my television series and met these ex-convicts, these ex-terrorists, these ex-Communists who were now my democratically elected leaders, they knew me because they had seen my videos in exile or even in jail. They had pictures of Evita on their walls next to their wives and girlfriends.

But there were chilling things, death threats. Maybe I should have been frightened, but how could I be? I was tarting around in a dress, talking crap. I felt so unthreatening. I was frightened once. There was I, in the Pretoria State Opera House – it was like doing *Fiddler on the Roof* in Nuremberg – a 2,000-seat theatre, the great temple of Afrikaner culture. President Botha was there, people were being hanged down the road, and the Opera House was jam-packed. I had it on video, I thought if they were going to kill me here I might as well record it. It was an extraordinary success. I took off the make-up and went down into the basement for my car and suddenly I could sense, oh-ah, feelings of dread, like a Tarantino movie. Suddenly out of the dark, from behind pillars, came these three bloody huge Afrikaner policemen. Not in uniform but you could see them . . . big, big, big. There was I pushed up against the car, and they said 'Pieter-Dirk Uys, you little bastard. You muck around with Afrikaans language. You mess around with our culture. You make us Afrikaners look like Nazis . . . bloody hell, you've got nice legs!' And they all burst out laughing. Then I thought, Oh hell, they're going to fuck me, Oh, Christ . . . Then they wanted signatures, but there was this constant sort of 'Hhhhh hhhhhh hhhhhhh', like 'But, don't go too far!' It was unimportant for them really. And I knew that there were so many people being imprisoned and killed. I was not in the front line of anything. I felt like the mosquito round the elephant's bum, making a lot of noise and shouting when the elephant farted. But I have this image of theatre as a cotton ball with a rusty blade in it, and suddenly your hand is bleeding, and you don't know where the blood came from.

Going Public

Not only did the audience *see* the actors and the
chorus but the actors and the chorus *saw* the
audience. They were all equally illuminated by the
light of the sun. The lighting grid was the great
globe itself.

Tony Harrison, Introduction to *The Trackers of Oxyrhynchus*

Play, dressing-up, pretending, make-believe, the pantomime
in the living room, the puppets at the bottom of the garden
– all may be necessary elements of theatre, but they are not
in themselves sufficient to seize its essence. A child plays with a
teddy bear. People in a therapy group do a 'role play'. Businessmen simulate hypothetical eventualities. The difference between
these acts of play and theatre is that theatre involves playing in
public. Not alone, or in the family, not in the sheltered, shared
privacy of therapy, not in the instituted groups of work. In public,
with strangers who for a while become your fellow travellers. And
theatre's public playing, at its utmost, goes beyond games or toys
or strategy or personal cure into the comic or tragic extremes of
human life.

Theatre is about going public, travelling through a dramatic
story with people with whom you have no links, except the ones
that are woven through the performance and the event. In a
theatre, you can be roughed up or kindled by the animal warmth
of other people's reactions to see more of yourself, among others.

People talk about 'being taken out of themselves' by a play. They don't have to mean that they were depressed or down when they arrived; simply that theatre moved them closer to other human beings.

The difficulty with this definition today is that we hardly know what a public space dealing with delicate or difficult life-aspects might feel like. We know about the mass spaces of sport, magnified and distributed to million-fold tribes by the media. We know about the commercial spaces of cities, branded with high-street facias and logos, with fragments of history peeping out between the frontages and atriums for lunchtime sandwich consumption, courtesy of the corporations. We know about the car parks and super-malls of the sad suburbs. Most town halls have become administrative rather than civic centres; they have lost the confidence of expressing a collectivity. And theatre for most people is part of an entertainment sector of city, cut loose from the role of a public platform, a sounding board for citizens, that was a vital part of its original nature.

A play is more public than a concert, because speech ties it more to our common human experience. *Waiting for Godot* connects at a more humble, visceral and down-to-earth level than Bach's *Goldberg Variations*, though both are severely distilled works of art. In a cinema, we are all in the dark, and we can hardly see each other. Cinema has the power of magnification and amplification, but it is a more solitary experience. Theatre is more public than watching television, which, except for live sporting events on public television, is less and less shared as it happens. It is more public than the personal, solitary act of reading, and its time cannot be turned back, as pages can. It is more public than the simulations of connection and contact provided on the Internet; the keyboard, mouse and terminal cannot connect 'the user' to another human presence.

For the actor, theatre is clearly more public than film or television. Each night, he or she steps on stage and goes on a journey with an assembly of people who can coalesce into an audience, with an audience's capacity to go further than its individual members. Actors, like the rest of us, thrive on being listened to. Unlike most of us, they have a profession which, if they do their job well, ensures that they will be listened to. In a theatre audience, actors receive the gaze of a thousand spectators. Benevolent strangers, not kith and kin; many, not one-to-one. On stage, the actors, unless they are fanatical naturalists behind an illusory fourth wall, know that they are being gazed upon, and work with that gaze. They are not in a private drama, being overseen by watchers. They are playing in public.

Perhaps the foundation of theatre in our nature is our desire to go public. Theatre is not simply the most social of the performing arts, it is the threshold across which our most personal intimations and impulses can become safely public.

In *Troilus and Cressida*, Shakespeare puts into the persuasive mouth of Ulysses a most arresting image of public presence nourishing and validating the individual. He has come to the tent of the great warrior Achilles, who is sulking away from the battlefield because he feels he has been slighted. Ulysses pretends that he has found arguments against withdrawal into privacy in a book he has been reading. Then, warming to his argument, he delivers a cascade of sensory images that are as much about theatre as their ostensible subject, real life:

> No man is the lord of anything,
> Though in and of him there be much consisting,
> Till he communicate his parts to others,
> Nor doth he of himself know them for aught
> Till he behold them formèd in th'applause
> Where they're extended – who, like an arch, reverb'rate
> The voice again; or, like a door of steel
> Fronting the sun, receives and renders back
> His figure and his heat.

An arch making the voice resonate; a steel gate, like a breastplate, both mirroring and reflecting back the sun. These are hot and excited images, of ear and eye and skin. They radiate from the most powerful word in the speech – 'extended'. Completing the circle of give and take in public extends us.

Shakespeare's images of sun, heat and reverberation in a play about the Trojan War irresistibly evoke the physical and social conditions in which theatre was born in fifth-century BC Athens, the historic moment which imprinted theatre's defining public dimension. It is no coincidence that theatre came about at the same time and in the same city that democracy was invented. The decisive condition for the existence of theatre was the confirmation in classical Athens of democratic rule in the city, and the creation of a new public category of being: citizens. It does not need stressing that citizenship was open only to free-born males, and that women and slaves were excluded. Democracy, it might be said, was forged in controlled conditions, and it has been the unfinished task of the subsequent 2,500 years to extend and enlarge the field of democracy. No reminder of the limits and exclusions of that first democracy can weaken its dynamic, foundational relationship between the amphitheatre and the assembly, the performers and the *polis*.

It was not a self-congratulatory one. The Athenian theatre festival was dedicated to the god Dionysus, the last arrival in the pantheon on Mount Olympus, and in some ways the most troubling and disreputable of gods. When his worship was a cult, his followers, many of them women who were described as 'maddened', embraced wine, song and ecstasy. He was perceived as an outsider, coming to Greece from Asia, and bringing 'Oriental' manners and modes with him. Although Dionysus had acquired mainstream acceptance by the time the Athenians chose him as patron of their festival, he was still not respectable, his previous wildness and transgression of limits somewhere clung to him.

'Public' in Periclean Athens was not the same as 'consensual'. Yet the Dionysian festival was also a civic occasion, and began with a commemoration of those who had died in battle for the city. A public and civic event in the fullest sense, before an audience of some 20,000 male citizens. This makes even more astonishing the content of the three tragedies and the satyr play that then had their unique, never-repeated performance over the rest of the day. Where 'official' art might have been expected as a follow-up to the civic and military ceremonies, what Aeschylus, Sophocles, Euripides and the many tragedians whose work has been lost gave them was hard, testing and confrontational, about violence and justice, family and identity, fate and free choice. And the finale of raucous satyr plays, featuring a chorus of priapic, drunken, half-human half-animal creatures, was a rude and irreverent release.

Theatre in its first incarnation was a fierce opening-up before all citizens of the stories, beliefs and structures of a society. In a city which loved argument, it staged the dialectic of gods and humans, men and women, citizens and outsiders. It probed conflicting allegiances and duties, it ventured to the frontiers of what could be known by living people. And all this was performed in a horseshoe-shaped hillside space which staged the rest of the audience as well as the protagonists of the plays. Masked actors, confronting the audience face-on with their ever-open eyes and mouths, showed that they knew the audience was there watching them. And as a final public aspect, the plays were in competition, and were judged, not by experts, but by a citizens' jury.

I am not a classicist. The person who taught me that the form and the values of classical Greek theatre could be as immediate as the latest avant-garde invention was Tony Harrison. In 1988, when I was head of arts at Channel 4 television, he rang from the rehearsal room at the National Theatre Studio in a state. I had already managed to get his version of Aeschylus' *The Oresteia* on television, full-face masks, all-male cast, alliterative verse and all. That had been in the early days, when Channel 4 under Jeremy Isaacs – a real Oxford classicist – was willing and able to chance its arm where other television would not go. Tony needed £12,000 to make sure his new play, *The Trackers of Oxyrhyncus*, got from the rehearsal room in Waterloo to its world premiere in the stadium at Delphi. We could have the world television premiere, he said. With my colleagues I twisted and turned and used every ounce of persuasion, but the budgetary walls were adamantine and the programme schedule less adventurous than

it had been, so I had to say no. With the help of private patrons
he got *Trackers* on and later, when I saw it at the Olivier Theatre,
I had one of my most gleeful experiences of theatre.

I was sitting in the balcony, behind an animated party of
teenage schoolgirls with their English teacher. *Trackers* is a play
prompted by the only surviving satyr play (and that in fragments)
that Sophocles wrote. Tony had encased it in the modern story of
its archaeological discovery in 1907 by Grenfell and Hunt, 'the
Holmes and Watson of British papyrology'. Under the spell of the
past and the site, they begin to mutate, Grenfell into the god
Apollo, Hunt into Silenus, the bedraggled leader of the satyrs.
Apollo summons his satyrs to hunt down the cattle-thief who has
rustled his herd. Nothing happens. He and Silenus cry out again,
in Greek. Silence. And then the most wonderful *coup*. Twelve
packing-cases, which we have seen carried on and stacked to
store the archaeological findings, split open forwards, backwards
and sideways to reveal a hysterical chorus of shaggy, half-
crouching, clog-wearing satyrs, an antic Crazy Gang from
antiquity, each equipped with the most monumental prick.

The girls' school group went mad, and continued giggling and
gurgling for the next half-hour. The English teacher looked
surprised, but not angry. For this was not some porn exhibition. It
was a funny, grotesque chorus-line, half-human, half-animal, all
underdog. As they swung into their first chorus, clacking their
clogs on the packing-case slats, they were irresistible, the way
George Formby or Eric Morecambe were irresistible. They got
under your defences – which meant that, within minutes, having
won over the audience with magical transformations and music-
hall routines, Tony was able to drive home the political point he
was making about the hostility of gods towards satyrs, and topdogs
towards underdogs, even now. The schoolgirls were as gripped as
I was, ready to take the most painful point the play makes.

Silenus tells the story of the torture of his brother, the pipe-
playing satyr Marsyas, by a jealous Apollo, who fancies himself as
a lyre-player and won't permit a satyr to win the music contest
over a god. Marsyas' punishment is to be flayed alive. Apollo's
decorous and triumphal lyre-playing as Marsyas is being tortured

becomes an emblem of high art used as an alibi for atrocity.
Tony's bitter, punchy couplets marked the distance we had
travelled, from amiable high jinks of ancient times to this
ferocious and timeless fable for a century in which concentration-
camp guards enjoyed Beethoven played by their prisoners:

They set up a contest, rigged from the start,
To determine the future of 'high' and 'low' art.
They had it all fixed that Apollo should win
And he ordered my brother to be flayed of his skin . . .
While Marsyas suffered his terrible flaying
Apollo looked on with his 'doodah' playing . . .
And the skinners applauded Apollo's reprise
As my brother's flayed nipples flapped on his knees . . .
Wherever in the world there is torture and pain
The powerful are playing the Marsyas refrain.
Wherever the racked and the anguished cry
There's always a lyre-player standing by.
Some virtuoso of Apollo's ur-violin
Plays for the skinners as they skin.

That's Tony Harrison's public voice, buttressed by strict rhythm,
rhyme and alliteration, strong enough to reach out to a 2,000 seat
auditorium, or to the street. Traditional and yet utterly modern,
he plays counter-currents and cross-rhythms with the street
virtuosity of a Mingus. Within scansion, he sets the informality of
vernacular. Against the expectations of heightened diction, the
patois of Leeds and Bradford.

The plot of his theatre life falls into three acts. In the first, he
makes translations and plays for an institution of public theatre –
the National Theatre, successively run by Olivier (*The
Misanthrope, Phaedra Britannica*), Peter Hall (*The Mysteries, The
Oresteia*) and Richard Eyre (*Trackers, Square Rounds*). In Act
Two, chafing against mainstream theatres, he breaks out and
tracks down his theatre truth by making pieces for industrial sites
(*Poetry or Bust*), historical locations (*The Kaisers of Carnuntum*),
sacred destinations (*The Labourers of Herakles*). In a third act, or

perhaps another play altogether, he body-swerves into cinema, writing and directing a feature film, *Prometheus*, owing much to what Tony has learned through thirty years in theatre.

Behind all these phases of work lies his long-meditated inheritance, artistic, ethical and social, from Greek theatre in fifth-century BC Athens. In all the diversity of his theatre work, Tony is replying to questions he has been asking himself for nearly half a century, since he started learning Greek at Leeds grammar school, enjoying music hall and wondering how he could learn from Greek drama: 'It was a drama open-eyed about suffering but with a heart still open to celebration and physical affirmation. In the late twentieth century, what clues to survival could be found in an ancient drama which managed to face up to the worst things it could imagine and yet not banish the celebratory?' Later, introducing the text of *Trackers*, he stakes out the life-giving importance of the outdoor, daylight Greek theatre: 'Greek texts are created with the performability for that known space in the conditions of shared light, and created to be spoken in masks to an audience that is *seen* and never cut off in darkened seats. Above all, since the expression 'to see the light' in Greek means to live, the final sense is of shared *life*.'

Seeking through the 'eighties to follow through this vision of theatre in terms of today, Tony began to chafe at the limitations of institutional theatre. The decisive shift came in 1993 with the move outside the National, to a succession of non-theatre venues where he created theatre events as director, writer and not infrequently producer, working with a regular group of actors, designer, composer, even clog-dance choreographer. The poet in the theatre became the poet as theatre-maker.

The move from mainstream subsidised theatre to 'kamikaze plays', as he calls them, in resonant public spaces, followed on Tony's Olivier Theatre production of *Square Rounds*, which was not a happy experience for him. A Meyerholdian dramatic disquisition about the creative and destructive powers of science, written in pyrotechnic couplets, it told the story of the inventors of the machine-gun and poison gas. Its theme was the power of science to make or to murder, and, in an act of transformation paralleling the chemical changes it describes, it was written for an all-female cast. Casting largely from the existing National Theatre company, Tony found himself uncomfortable with its naturalistic, motivated, character-driven ethos.

Square Rounds opened to very mixed reviews. I thought it was chillingly perfect, an astringent cabaret of carnage. But in a happier situation, it might have had heart as well as virtuosity. And by then, Tony should have had his own troupe, his own little society of theatre, his own public entity. It would have been a worthy successor to the troupes led by poets through history: the companies of Brecht, Lorca, Molière, Shakespeare, the Greeks. But at the outset of the 'nineties, when the Thatcherite market and the triumph of musicals and of management as a philosophy had eaten into the theatre, the idea, as Hollywood would say, did not have legs. So Tony took his theatre into the wilds, and in June 1995 made *The Kaisers of Carnuntum* for a rain-drenched ancient Roman stadium outside Vienna, for two performances only.

At the last performance, two bears broke loose backstage. Stagehands chased after them, one getting clawed. Barrie Rutter, playing Marcus Aurelius' thuggish son Commodus, was left alone on stage with three lions and a tiger, fortunately still in their cages. The actor who should have come on as Orpheus to impale Commodus on a cello-spike was busy chasing the bears, since he was also their trainer. Tony was about to step into the breach and deliver the death-blow himself, when the animals were recovered and order, of a sort, was restored. When you make theatre outside the walls of theatre, this is the kind of thing you contend with.

In *The Kaisers of Carnuntum*, Tony brought to the stage – in the person of Commodus, son of the philosopher-king Marcus Aurelius – the ultimate delinquent of the classical world. Marcus Aurelius mourned the transience of all things human in his *Meditations*, while commanding Carnuntum, a Roman frontier-post against barbaric Germanic tribes. His son Commodus was a serial killer in the very stadium where we watched this play.

Tony was drawn to him, as he has been to a long line of outlaws and underdogs. From writing a poem about the desecrators of his parents' grave, to dramatising this insatiable psychopath, Tony has followed theatre's gut instinct to test and challenge society by setting forth its villains – Herod, Tamburlaine, Richard III, Arturo Ui – in full, murderous flood. Finding that Commodus had been airbrushed from history, he wrote this play to make us confront chasms of the psyche we would rather deny. When it was performed in 1995, half an hour from Vienna, the Hitler-praising racist demagogue Jorg Haider had just won a quarter of the votes of an amnesiac electorate. Today his party has become the country's second largest in Austria. A play about historical forgetting and simplification touched a nerve of public concern. And not only in Carnuntum.

Tony and his sometimes overwhelmed producer assembled a cast of safari-park animals, a Czech lion tamer, hunting-horn bands, detachments of the local fire brigade and army, and choirs from Austria and adjoining Slovakia and Hungary. The night of the dress rehearsal, the heavens opened and torrents of rain and wind descended on the defenceless stadium, with its precious light and sound equipment. The pugnacity of the elements seemed to bring out Tony's defiant qualities. 'It was raining solid,' actress Siân Thomas told me. 'I thought we would never do it. But then I saw Tony, climbing aloft in the rigging like Ahab, wearing some ghastly cagoule, and his face was absolutely barmy, quite possessed, and I knew we were going to do it.' Composer Richard Blackford added, 'I will never forget, in the middle of the tempest, Tony saying, "I'd rather be here than anywhere else in the whole world."'

Saturday, June 3, 1995, the final performance at Carnuntum. Animals are displayed in enlarged mosaic images of men wrestling with wild beasts, but even more vividly in the pad-pad of the live lions and tigers, caged beneath our feet as we sit in the cold night. It's a long way from the soft seats of the Olivier.

High on a tower, counter-tenor Marcus Aurelius sings about the flow of the nearby Danube and the flux of empires:

Every empire, Reich and Raj
no matter how well-armed or large,

is but a moment's brief mirage.
All the emperors old and new
Caesar, Stalin, Ceauşescu,
transients all passing through.

With a swoop of searchlights and a stutter of gunfire,
Commodus thunders in, hauling a local road-sign with tragic
and comic masks indicating the arena we're in. Barrie Rutter's
imperial Roman bovver-boy is horrendous to behold: shaven
head, red Doc Martens, boxer's robe and a pop-eyed grin like Mr
Punch. He grows irate and hammers the road-sign designer to
death with his sign, for daring to portray this death-stadium as
an art-site:

Oh why
this modern squeamish need to Disneyfy
this space that was made for men and beasts to die?
This space wasn't built for tragic plays
for your Sarah Bernhardts or your Lord Oliviers
nor for your Cosìs or sopranos trilling,
but built just for one purpose: killing, killing, killing!

This beaming psychopath, stripping down to red lingerie, whips
the audience into Nuremberg Rally chants ('Thumbs down for
kill, thumbs up for save'); this rough, unstoppable spellbinder
becomes the garrulous, threatening voice in your head, the bully
in the brain.

Savage Commodus taunts his civilised father Marcus Aurelius
until he's ready to kill him. As he raises the club of Herakles high
in the air, we hear a woman character speak for the first time. It's
Faustina, Marcus Aurelius' wife, condemned by subsequent
history as a whore: gossip says she must have slept with rough
Roman trade to spawn the un-Aurelian Commodus. 'To deify the
one and demonise the other/in the end damns me, the blameless
mother,' she cries. Rising among the audience in the whipping
wind, Siân Thomas cries out the caustic pain of Europe's war-
widows, ready to accept lies if they lead to peace.

Would it help the world pretending your pure semen
did not create this blood-demented demon?
If it would I'd swear the nympho whore Faustina
fucked a fighting man from the arena . . .
If I agree to let these slanders thrive
will the future learn to hope, and thus survive?

Tony's play about Commodus resurgent, its subject matter, its
outcast presentation, its part-professional part-community cast,
its two performances and no more, captured the gravity and
intensity of his vision of Greek drama and planted them into the
world of sweet-savage Vienna, of Bosnia an hour's flight away, of
far-off Belfast or gun-crazy America.

Three months later, Tony pushed home Faustina's anguished
questions in a new play, *The Labourers of Herakles*, this time for
one performance only, in brilliant, lucid light, high in the
mountains of Apollo's shrine at Delphi – but in the building-site
which was to become Delphi's new 'millennium theatre'.
Immediately after the performance Tony was due to set out for
Bosnia in helmet and flak-jacket, to write poems for the *Guardian*
about the war. He was acutely aware of the discordance of a 'high
art' festival in Delphi while Sarajevo was being smashed and
Bosnian women mass-raped nearby. His chorus hammered out
agonised questions in the hard sunlight, using the myth of
Herakles' death-dealing shirt of fire to raise a public cry about the
war across the border:

Who wove the caustic camouflage no cooling water
    quenches?
Muslims that are mouldering in mass-execution trenches.
Who wove the blistering blouson that Herakles can't loose?
The fingers of the raped girl who wove herself a noose.
Who wove this caustic camouflage consuming Herakles?
Sarajevo children his shells made amputees.

Punched out by a bunch of building labourers trapped in the
cement foundations of the forthcoming European Cultural

Centre theatre, these lines had the power and pulse of Count Basie. But their dance-beat lifts the pain from self to society, making it more memorable than broken weeping or oratorical denunciation. On its tide a soloist can ride, as Barrie Rutter's Herakles did at Delphi, soaring out of the Nessus chorus like a bluesman to voice an anguish that spans centuries:

> I wear a fitted furnace. My scalded body squirms.
> My ethnic cleanser's conscience crawls with caustic worms.
> If you pull this garment from me, you'll pull away my skin.
> This is Europe's conscience I'm cremated in.

These etched couplets and triplets are the public music of Tony Harrison's theatre. Round and round it goes, rhymes clicking into place like clog-dance heels and toes. It carves words into space, roots them in bodies, rigorously places them in a space and time in which we can all, for a moment, fuse.

I asked him where the energy and conviction of the great tirades of his plays come from.

One is Milton, the greatest poet in English after Shakespeare. Milton's example of combining incredibly direct address and inwardness, inwardness and public declaration, has meant a huge amount to me. That's why his bust is in my hall, wearing a Polish steel-worker's glasses. Then there were the great speeches in *Phèdre*. People in Racine's time would often turn up to the theatre for the great tirade and the messenger's speech at the end. The other great example is the stand-up comic, who grabbed the attention of the audience and held it. Racine produced the same audience-binding performance that you got from someone who could hold the stage for half an hour telling jokes. And I thought, How do you use that, what is the equivalent of that? The great theatrical event is one person addressing a multitude. Try and tell most actors that, they're not keen. They hug the comfort of the proscenium and the eye-contact relationship between themselves. I always say to them, Look, there are so many more eyes in the audience, you've got at least two thousand eyes out there, go for them. We should always find a difference in the theatrical experience, find a way where being there means something.

When I speak of the impossibility of making theatre without a full public dimension, I speak of theatre at its optimal, as pursued by Harrison and countless other theatre-makers who have seen through the simulations of theatre to its real light. I do not mean theatre that has conformed to industrial or mercantile models, or taken refuge in the compounds of high culture, as so much classical music performance and recording has done.

It is a matter of an open public space, within which shared imaginative experiences can happen. Perhaps one of the decisive 'unique selling points' of theatre in our society of facile transactions will be as a precious site of the self in the company of others, of an audience as companions, of society as something more than machinery. Political parties in a society cut loose from place and shared history, obeying the rhetoric of media presentation, have lost much of their public ground. Party conferences resemble presentations licked into shape by salespeople and their focus groups. Churches, temples and mosques cater only for believers. Citizens are morphed into consumers, defined by their credit rating. Broadcasting fragments into narrowcasting. Communities become virtual. Theatre, despite its statistically low audience share, still seeks to speak to humanity in its wholeness, not to constituencies defined by allegiances and single interests.

I can imagine a future in which our needs for communication, information, management, publication, trading, education, conversation and even sexual and human contact are met by the new media. It would probably feel global, because the Internet is a many-to-many system, and cyberspace knows no boundaries. It would seem personal; users of the Net, the remote and other 'intelligent machines' are already able to customise their individual preferences, by repeating, or never straying far from, previous choices. What it would not feel is public.

Classical Comeback

The secret of Shakespeare's unique development
lies in this ability . . . to meet the inchoate, as-if-
supernatural actuality, and be overwhelmed by it,
be dismantled and even shattered by it, without
closing his eyes, and then to glue himself back
together, with a new, greater understanding of the
abyss, all within the confines of a drama, and to do
this once every seven months, year after year.

Ted Hughes, *Shakespeare and the Goddess of Complete Being*

The deeper you go searching into the heart of theatre for its essential qualities, the more that heart beats to the pulse of contradiction. 'Without contraries, no progression,' said Blake, and theatre thrives on such polarities: form and spontaneity, reason and ecstasy, order and excess, verbal and visual, feeling and thinking, structure and energy, Apollo and Dionysus. The polarity of left and right brain may have been supplanted by the many-sided maps of the latest neuroscience, but long before scanners imaged the brain's firings and spasms, theatre shaped itself to pendulum swings.

At one extreme is the Classical, which is nowhere near as steady and staid as it has been described. At the other is something equally hard to pin down, but which has been called the Experimental, the Alternative and the Avant-Garde. If the Classical has often been in danger of assimilation by Heritage

Culture and privilege, the Avant-Garde has proved to be no less vulnerable to takeovers – by commercials, music videos, billboards, fashion, musicals, wherever the mainstream has gone shopping at what it calls 'the leading edge'. In this and the following chapter, I want to explore the struggles around these twin tendencies which theatre, because it is rooted in human stuff, manifests.

In the theatre of this century, in Europe at least, the Classical has travelled from being a monument in societies of seemingly shared values to become a site for renewing long-lived meanings. On the way, classicism was cast by cultural guerrillas as a target for iconoclasm and as a pretext for experiment by directors, the aspirant authors of the modern theatre. In the second half of the century, as the culture became more visual, theatres began to reclaim the resources of the language of the classics, to relearn to read their codes and to root the visual or spectacular worlds of the stage in this reading. The classical disciplines were no longer seen as constraints on some native truth, but as a 'form and pressure' which could squeeze out truths bigger than the directors and performers could envisage.

But hardly had these rediscoveries got under way by the late 1970s than some countries, notably England, cut back funds needed to maintain the continuity of theatre ensembles in which the steady work of making a classical company, adept in language as well as motivation, could be advanced. In England at the end of the twentieth century, after more than a decade of standstill public funding – a cut in real terms – and reliance on sponsorship and the revenue from musicals, neither of which lasts forever, the Royal Shakespeare Company was facing a deficit of £1.3 million for 1998/9. Today, outside London, very few theatres can afford to employ enough actors to cast a Shakespeare play. In the light of these facts, it would be hard to maintain that our society cares about its living theatrical heritage, continually renewed for the present, as much as it does for the physical museums and monuments it has funded to mark the Millennium. All the world is not a Ferris wheel, and the continuity of what was presented to live audiences in the Globe by artists and actors deserves as much respect and care as what is being made, with the help of every media and design resource, in the Dome.

Meanwhile, it has become hip to put the Bard on the screen. The plethora of recent, and wildly unequal, Shakespeare movies backed by mainstream Hollywood shows that (a) the Bard (as the showbiz weekly *Variety* loves to call him) knew a thing or two about story and character, (b) if you choose the right plays, they will furnish you with some mighty picturesque locations, (c) if you underpin a contemporary story with the bones of a Shakespeare play, you are likely to have a better product, (d) he did write an awful lot of language, but if you cut it back, you can make a pretty powerful film.

On the pediment of the Burgtheater in Vienna, the classical pinnacle of Austria's theatre, a giant statue of Apollo, master of the muses, thrusts into the sky. It surmounts a bust of the Emperor Franz-Josef, flattering the ruler and underlining Apollo's connection with the powers that be. Below, a rather refined bas-relief Dionysus pipes in a procession of delicate Bacchantes, worshipped by swooning females who might cut an elegant figure at Vienna's New Year's Eve costume ball. Beneath these decorous revellers are the laurel-wreathed busts of the Classic Playwrights: Lessing, Goethe, Schiller, Nestroy, Shakespeare, Maeterlinck, Racine, Molière, Goldoni, Calderón.

This is the story of one of them: Shakespeare, now, in England, and beyond.

In October 1998, the day after Ted Hughes, the Poet Laureate, died, the British classical theatre – or a hundred or so of its brightest and best actors, directors, teachers and students – met in the National Theatre Studio to debate the crisis in speaking Shakespeare. What was billed as a 'Forum on Verse Speaking and Classical Text' became a sounding-board for the condition of British theatre.

The debate had started in the newspapers, with an article from Adrian Noble, head of the Royal Shakespeare Company, about new generations of actors coming to Stratford-upon-Avon less equipped than they used to be to deal with Shakespeare's

language. David Suchet, playing Salieri in *Amadeus* at the Old
Vic, replied with passion, targeting the defects of directors and
the shortcomings of drama schools. Trevor Nunn, director of the
National Theatre, about to start a classical ensemble company in
his theatre, picked up their exchange by organising this forum, a
prologue to three weeks of Shakespeare workshops.

The first half-hour was about where the tradition comes from,
and how it had been experienced by directors and actors in the
room. Trevor, who came to Stratford-upon-Avon from the
Belgrade Theatre, Coventry, recalled his terror at the first
rehearsal of his first Shakespeare play, *The Taming of the Shrew*.

Many years ago I undertook my first Shakespeare production
at Stratford-upon-Avon and I managed to persuade that
master of comic inner panic, Roy Kinnear, to join the
company and to play Baptista in *The Taming of the Shrew*. I
imagine everyone here has at one time or another
experienced the fear and dread that Roy and I went through
as we contemplated our first Shakespeare. Roy in particular
was ashen and petrified about going into the uncharted
territory of the iambic pentameter. I tried to calm his fears
by saying, 'Roy, it's very simple, it's just ten syllables to a
line, five stresses, it couldn't be easier. Ti-tum ti-tum ti-tum
ti-tum ti-tum. That's all you have to remember.' That
became a mantra for Roy. Whenever I passed him in the
corridor or cafeteria, he was repeating 'Ti-tum ti-tum ti-tum
ti-tum ti-tum.' He took to phoning me late at night or early
in the morning. 'It's Roy. Ti-tum ti-tum ti-tum ti-tum ti-
tum.'

The first day of our text rehearsal arrived and Roy took a
deep breath and started on Baptista's first line, and what
came out was 'GenTLEmen, IMporTUNE me NO
furTHER.' It couldn't have been worse, and the hilarity was
great, but a few days later Roy was inveigled into attending
a verse class given by John Barton. John, rather unfairly I
thought, set Roy as his test piece Hamlet's 'To be or not to
be' soliloquy. When Roy went through it for the first time

the laughter was overwhelming. John was impervious to this and began working with Roy slowly and methodically, through meaning, through phrasing, through breathing, getting him to discover where he could pause to coin the next phrase, where the antitheses were that gave it structure, that gave force to a particular word.

As this work went on, we all forgot the patent inappropriateness of the casting and eventually the moment arrived for Roy to do the whole speech. It was one of those moments when it's as if all the clocks have stopped. There was utter concentration and something of a revelation occurred; about the speech, the part, the language – certainly a revelation about that actor. But most of all it was a revelation about the teaching process that we had witnessed, passing from one person to another and causing a transformation.

Trevor situated 'this somewhat sentimental story' in the Stratford-upon-Avon of the early 1960s, when the RSC had been founded by Peter Hall, who, with John Barton, had questioned and renewed Shakespearean delivery. Now Peter, nearing his seventies, stood up and launched into a fifteen-minute speech, by turns personal history, manifesto and denunciation.

There are two reasons for the crisis. One, the perfectly natural and organic need of every generation to chuck out what's been done in the past and remake it. As we, like Moses, come down with the tablets saying, 'This is how you speak verse,' it is, of course, absolutely essential that every generation says, 'That is what you may have done, but we do this.' But there's something else. We don't like words as a society, we don't trust words. We are a visual society that doesn't like to listen.

So when we talk about the problem of handing on the baton of Shakespeare's verse, we're talking about something much wider. I believe that Shakespeare depends on a contract between the audience and the actor to play a game of make-believe. If I was good enough and I had a Shakespeare text I could make you believe that this was Rome. But if you put a camera there and filmed me, people would say 'It's not Rome at all, it's a crummy old warehouse.' Of course, if we go against the current of the time and make our speaking pompous, inflated, rhetorical, we will betray Shakespeare and ourselves. But unless we actually look at what he means, then we'll no longer succeed in playing him at all.

When I went to Stratford in the 'fifties, there were basically three types of actor in the company. The Old School, extremely orotund and very slow, marking the ends of the lines and doing their Shakespearean stuff. The middle-aged actors, brought up on Coward, on throw-away and realism; they tried to shoot the lines away. And the young brigade, who looked at the old with contempt and scorn, and said, 'I'm from the North and I want to be real and I don't fucking care about all this end-stopping.' And that's why John and I tried to bring some consistency to the question. We said, Let's go back to basics, let us be speedy, let us be light, let us be witty. What is wit? The combination, the clash of opposites which illuminates. It's ironic, it's funny and it helps you play the game of make-believe.

Peter explained how he learned about speaking Shakespeare. He and John Barton had had the good fortune to go to Cambridge, where they were taught about breathing, phrasing and line structure by George Rylands, a figurehead of the Bloomsbury set and of the Marlowe Society, founded at the beginning of the century by young Cambridge students, including Rupert Brooke. They were much influenced by William Poel, a great theatre reformer, admired by Shaw, who was agnostic about the cult of Shakespeare. Poel had said that Shakespearean speech should be quick, witty and light, not orotund or churchy; not like Henry Irving. 'Suddenly the plays lost about thirty minutes on their running time,' said Peter; 'suddenly they became communicable.' He asked Edith Evans, whom Poel had directed at seventeen as Cressida, to tell him everything Poel had taught her, and discovered it was an inheritance of great and often irreverent English actors. 'Poel said he got it from Macready, who got it from Kean, who got it from Garrick, who got it from Betterton.'

I watched the faces of the young actors and drama students, going out into a very different theatre in this visual and informational age, drenched in television. Now Peter drew a distinction between his and John's approach.

I have been called an iambic fundamentalist, and I am proud of that. When I started trying to do this, I was very tentative – 'Could you, if you feel it's possible? . . .' And John, fresh out of academe, was saying, 'No, no, do that!' Now we have rather reversed our positions. John will say, 'Do be careful, don't in any way let me invade your ego,' and I'm saying, 'If you don't want to do it this way, don't work with me.' Because forty years of it has made me understand that it's easier, quicker, clearer and it works, and finally, as far as I'm concerned, it's not negotiable. Shakespeare tells you when to go fast, when to go slow, when to come in on cue, when to pause, which word to accent, which antithetical meaning wants looking at, which rhyme wants banging. He tells you the entire dynamic shape, but not – and this is so important – why. That is for the actor. So the process is exactly like learning a dance or a duel or a song. A pointless, sterile exercise unless you can make it your own, make it absolutely true. So I hope we will not be discussing being real and being false. What is real, may I ask, about the act of learning a text, speaking it, and pretending to be someone else anyway? It's a fake. As George Burns said, 'The great thing about acting is truth. If you can fake that, you've got it made.'

The problem now, Peter believes, is that there isn't enough Shakespeare being done to suffuse actors with the sound and shape and sense of the language. 'They knew because they had heard. Now actors don't hear so they don't know.'

I had a picture suddenly, a map of language, culture and theatre practice. In some golden age of speech – place it where you will, in Tudor London, in eighteenth-century Dublin, in the halls of high art, the carnival of a red-blooded commercial theatre, the rhetorical platforms of pulpit or law court or pub – there was sufficient yeast of language and fever of emulation for Shakespeare's text, or any worked language, to live vigorously, to strut in touch with the energy of everyday talk. As the tide of inspired speech receded – not necessarily the same as learned speech, as Shakespeare's texts show – it became necessary to make rules and create theatre institutions, like the National Theatre that nineteenth-century intellectuals called for, and the twentieth-century Royal Shakespeare Company. Their motive, the opposite of heritage thinking, was not conservation but continuity, ongoing process rather than preservation. Peter concluded with an Agincourt peroration, spoken with the emphasis that has made him such a buccaneering force in the reform of British theatre.

We have to understand that this is a fundamental danger to the existence of theatre, not the existence of Shakespeare. If you accept the discipline of Shakespeare, you accept the discipline of the word as a means of communicating with the audience and making them imagine. If you don't, then you are simply people down one end of a room, muttering to one another, being real – and a camera is what we need. That's the crux: imaginative speaking embraced by the actor and made to look real, and therefore being true; or muttering – and then, of course, let's cut Shakespeare or rewrite him. Our responsibility is very grievous and heavy. We are partly moving against the current of our times, and partly against the professional needs of the actor. Why should you spend months and months training young actors to speak Shakespeare when they are very likely not ever to do it, when they need to get straight on to television in order to pay their mortgage?

John Barton shuffles into the centre, perches himself on a

convenient corner, peers into the rafters, and uses two of his
wiliest openings: apparent total agreement, followed by
disarmingly donnish joke.

I'd like to say first that I completely agree with every word
Peter and Trevor have said, but I would question some of the
methods and definitions. If Peter is proud to be an iambic
fundamentalist, I suppose I'm a bit more of a trochaic
revisionist. By which I mean that I think the foul word that
buggers us all up when we tackle the problem is the phrase
'iambic pentameter'. It's not an accurate description of the
text of Shakespeare. It is true that it is blank verse which
consists of five-stress lines. But the basic definition is not
true, it is not Shakespearean. It muddles and distresses and
confuses actors. There is something jarring for actors to use
that coinage, iambic pentameter, about what the Eliza-
bethans called blank verse. Blank verse is a very helpful tool
for the actor, Shakespeare was an actor, and that's why they
all seized on it. It's easier to learn, to find your way and
get your breathing right than the other forms they used or
the very convoluted Elizabethan prose that was fashionable
before Shakespeare.

I think there are rules, but there's no rule that ever was
that you cannot occasionally challenge, question and
modify. What I'm interested in is, How can I help actors
come to terms with Shakespeare's text? By showing them
the devices in the writing which Shakespeare uses over and
over, and there aren't that many. There are certain things in
his writing which are absolutely basic to how he handles
human thought and experience. Once the actor gets into
that, then I can hammer away at the verse the way I want to.

John threw up the first two lines of Brutus' soliloquy from *Julius
Caesar*:

It must be by his death. And for my part
I know no personal cause to spurn at him.

He recalled – in the bygone days, he says, when directors attended each other's rehearsals – Peter giving the actor a reading for this, which the actor doggedly followed. 'The thought didn't come out to me as spontaneous, human and real.'

Hall interrupted.

I don't know where you got the idea that that was my note. It wasn't. You haven't mentioned the most important thing about the first line: it is all monosyllabic. If you look at any page of Shakespeare, you, the actor, will find that 30 per cent of the lines are monosyllabic. He obviously didn't say to himself, 'I will write monosyllabics here,' but he heard something which is spread and measured and marginally slower than an ordinary line. And that is because the character is thinking. Shakespeare's luck was to be born at a moment when there was a verse tradition which he could make colloquial and easy and irregular, and that's why his verse is so living. But if you don't know the original basis that he's breaking, you're like a jazz musician ignoring the beat.

Barton came back, syncopating the beat:

I believe that all the best poetic lines in Shakespeare are almost invariably monosyllables. Polysyllabic lines vary the rhythm. Saying that is to me more important than talking about the verse. Shakespeare uses the verse form because it helps the actor, but actually at least 60 per cent of it is what I would call naturalistic. There are no similes, no metaphors, there's very simple language. When he uses a simile or a metaphor one has to say to the actor that he's not doing it to be poetic, it's because the character, at that moment, needs and finds a simile to express what they're handling. If you want to find what Shakespeare's poetry is, you have to let those monosyllabic lines breathe and feel them, they have a resonance. 'In sooth, I know not why I am so sad' opens a can of beans. It doesn't define, it resonates. 'You do me wrong to take me out of the grave': Lear's awakening is almost all in monosyllables.

This edgy Barton/Hall fencing-match was the after-trace of a key moment in British theatre. But as actors and actresses, directors, students and teachers continued affirming and arguing, it was clear that Shakespeare is the stamping ground for all manner of hopes about theatre itself. Michael Pennington, a leading Royal Shakespeare Company actor who became joint actor-manager with Michael Bogdanov of the English Shakespeare Company, toured visually radical and textually alert productions to young audiences throughout Britain. He paid tribute to the grounding he had at the RSC, 'a fantastic opportunity to play one of the most difficult houses in England for a year or two and develop the muscles necessary to deal with Shakespeare.' In their touring company, Pennington and Bogdanov were able to give young actors a similar graduation through teaching and experience. 'The greatest pleasure to me, looking back on that company's life, was that after a couple of years you saw young actors going into a different fifteen-hundred-seat theatre each week, here and abroad, checking the sound for five minutes, going off to have tea and coming back in the evening able to play it, effortlessly, with big open vowels. In a sort of traditionalist way, that seemed to me a terrific benefit.'

There was something of a collective confessional and unburdening going on this morning, a group gathering that was not just therapeutic or nostalgic, but something like a company meeting of Shakespeare and Sons and Daughters, conducting a quarter-century assessment. Adrian Noble, tousled in a big linen suit, recounted his journey to becoming director of the Royal Shakespeare Company today, and the tension between modern theatre's two traditions.

I was trained as a director at the Drama Centre, where the training was basically Stanislavski, counterpointed by the European tradition of Brecht, Copeau, Laban. Then I went to Stratford, after a period in rep at Bristol Old Vic, which was very fortunate, because I was given stacks of shows to direct. Then I went to Stratford as an assistant and became very conscious of another tradition. I quickly realised there was a tension here, which, in a way, has governed my life ever since. It is the tension of the actor in the twentieth century. It started when Freud opened up our selves and looked inside, and when Stanislavski analysed the interior life of character. It's to do with getting the character to cleave to oneself in tension with, but not contradiction to, Shakespeare's text. We know that Shakespeare's actors were given their parts, not the whole play, rehearsed over an absurdly short space of time for just two or three performances, discarded them and did another one. So there is a tradition whereby the text is almost like a mask that I put on like a Greek actor. Most of us have put on a mask and know that it will mysteriously lead you into almost uncontrollable actions. In the rehearsal room I try and make a creative marriage between the natural process of an actor, between Stanislavski and the sort of clues, hints, tips, that I was fortunate to get when I first went up to Stratford.

Looking round at the young faces of tomorrow's actors, Adrian enlarged the Shakespeare question to the biggest professional question of all: what does our society encourage, what does it want from actors, what does it seek from theatre?

How can people now get the nurturing opportunities that I was lucky enough to get? They don't seem to be around, and it's to do with the change of the actor's role in our society, which reflects what actors have to do in order to earn a living in front of the camera. We're in this mad situation whereby we seem to be in danger of losing a love of language. It's not just a load of sentimental tosh, I think it's to do with politics, with our ability to empower each other, with command of ideas. Ideas give you access to value. Without value you can't have democracy. That's absolutely fundamental to our society. And the actor's role in that seems to be not only one of a storyteller but also of a leader who should be propagating a love of language as a sensuous thing. We think of language only as a way of communicating ideas and thought and sense. It isn't only that. There were recordings of Ted Hughes reading his poems on television and radio last night. They communicate sensuously, through our guts. I find the situation now slightly more encouraging than Peter. I think actors feel that the ripping-up that seemed to happen in the 'seventies and 'eighties, not just in theatre but in many walks of life and most fields of education, has meant that they have lost out. I think there is a hunger there.

Mark Rylance, the actor-manager now running the Globe Theatre, wide-eyed and fervent, ended the session with a call for language as action, for almost Pentecostal speech, taking John Barton's tough-minded legacy and pushing it into almost evangelical realms:

I'm fascinated that today, in a session about verse, we have talked about people going to *see* a play, and what it looks like. If I learned nothing else when I played Hamlet it was that the dumb-show has no effect on Claudius at all. But when he *hears* the lines, he stands up and says, 'Lights, lights, lights, away.' It's laid down time and time again in the Shakespeare text that when you *hear* something it has a different effect than when you see it. Perhaps we should start saying, 'I'm going to come and hear your play,' 'I'm really sorry I haven't heard your play yet'.

There's a great need for meaning amongst most people I meet. I don't mean in an intellectual way, I mean satisfaction, soulful satisfaction in this busy life. Where can we find the language? Think of a baby. It doesn't learn the language it needs by reading or looking, it learns by listening. That's what Shakespeare can offer, the development of our skill to listen, so we will have the language to bring our independent and unique experience into any forum. This is the core for me of why we need theatre.

Next day, I ran into Michael Pennington in Soho, on his way to the Piccadilly to play a Saturday matinee. 'That was really good yesterday, wasn't it?' I said. 'It was,' said Michael. 'I didn't realise we have a theatre community.'

It was at the Royal Shakespeare Company of the 'sixties that I began to learn something of that community.

In 1962 I had written to Peter Hall, a letter of youthful chutzpah. I have walked on in a French troupe, I said, seen Brecht at the Berliner Ensemble, gone on the road with Arnold Wesker in a bid to widen the audience for the arts, and I think yours is the only theatre company in England that I could imagine working for. It was a letter with all the cockiness of the stirring 'sixties, when so much seemed possible that seems foreclosed today. It got a reply by return and, in those pre-fax or e-mail days, by telegram. 'Come 5pm Friday', read Peter Hall's message. So I turned up at his house in Montpelier Square.

Peter, ten years my senior, was then in the ascendant as a 'sixties celebrity, living the photogenic life, uniting fervour with glamour. But from the start I felt the recognition of one scholarship boy for another. Our generation stood in a line of cultural and social reform. Raymond Williams in his *Culture and Society*, which I'd devoured as a student, had begun his long alternative history of that cluster of art, trade, industry, religion and class which indelibly marks the English psyche even now, overlaid as it is with market standardisation and global packaging. The great unbuttoning of the early 'sixties had begun, with rock 'n' roll, street fashion, new British cinema, satire, an end to class deference, three television channels. Jennie Lee, as Harold Wilson's Minister for the Arts, created the Open University and extracted hitherto unimaginable public funds for a network of institutions and activities that began to give Britain a democratic national culture.

Within all this flutter and parade was Shakespeare, the most mercurial artist in any national pantheon. 'Shakespeare', as a concept, can be co-opted in any cause: imperialism, Toryism, cultural supremacy, commerce. That 'Shakespeare' has become a social and cultural phenomenon, the sum of its many uses and contexts, can be admitted. Shakespeare's plays, which Peter Hall and John Barton were eager to strip of accretions and assumptions, are something else: poetry in motion, speech in action, verse in story, essential theatre.

I was hired, not because of my fledgling efforts in theatre, but because I was a writer. At the start of the 'sixties I had helped edit and written for *Encore – the Voice of Vital Theatre*, a little magazine, which had become the platform and forum for a new wave of British theatre. In its pages writers, directors, reporters and critics fulminated and reflected and brought news of the reawakening of theatre here and abroad, fifteen years after the war had ended. *Encore* never reached more than 2,500 people, but they were the 2,500 people who mattered. Broadly on the left, with contributors including John Arden, Lindsay Anderson and Albert Hunt, it was never afraid to give room to sceptical voices like John Whiting's piece, 'At Ease in a Bright Red Tie', questioning the axiomatic left-wing-ism of Royal Court playwrights. Or to open its pages to the metaphysical questioning of Peter Brook, asking in the light of Beckett and Genet, just what was the 'reality' the theatre was meant to represent; or to the wise-cracking voice of American director and writer Charles Marowitz, who wrote about happenings and the hyper-naturalism of the Living Theatre, while earning a living teaching both Stanislavskian Method and Absurdist acting. With my occasional despatches from Europe – about Max Frisch and Grotowski – we covered the horizons of new theatre at the start of that impatient decade.

So Peter Hall hired me as a writer. He wanted to create a new kind of theatre programme, putting the play and production into contexts which would urge the spectator to think as well as to enjoy. With the benign but punctilious John Goodwin, the RSC's head of press and publications, we produced a series of Shakespeare programmes, studded with parallels and provocations to thought. I started an RSC newspaper, *Flourish*, in the spirit of *Encore*, and launched Theatregoround, a mobile group of 'actor commandos', taking out pocket-sized performances to schools and workplaces, evangelising theatre, in the spirit of the *théâtre populaire* that I had learned in France. And of the British democracy I had seen in action on the Aldermaston marches.

Many changes on many fronts took place with the birth and growth of the RSC, and they impacted on each other as Peter Hall must have hoped that they would. The 'revolution' in Shakespearean verse-speaking, which he and John Barton put in place, is often summarised as the ascendancy of 'sense' over 'musicality'. It was not only more complex than that; it was inseparable from the making of a company, a vessel whose components stayed together long enough for discoveries to deepen into a shared way of doing classical texts that could be passed on to succeeding actors and directors. The company in turn was inseparable from the *zeitgeist*, a moment of British history in which many people felt expansive, iconoclastic, active, brave, inquiring. This was the British climate in which a self-renewing Shakespearean company started to open to the world. The buzz-words which global business has now appropriated – 'synergy' and 'symbiosis' – acquired a tangible meaning. Pinter's shaped sentences and silences in *The Homecoming* were delivered with the same dialectic of form and feeling, of feeling secreted through form, as the rhetorical architecture of a Shakespearean speech.

I learned that there are times when classical theatre must renounce art and distance and assume its role as a forum for citizens, as the RSC did twice at the Aldwych. Rolf Hochhuth's *The Representative*, 'theatre of fact' based on investigative research, denounced Pope Pius XII for doing too little to save Europe's Jews in the war; I ran post-performance discussions in which the auditorium became a pressure-chamber for the rage and short-lived relief of concentration camp survivors at seeing some part of their experience brought into shared light. English people who had lived a long way in space or time from what happened saw their 'positions' overwhelmed by this release of pain prompted by minimal theatre based on events.

An even deeper catharsis came from Brook's three-hour staging of *The Investigation*, a 'dramatic oratorio' by Peter Weiss, based on the Nuremberg Nazi War Crimes hearings. Its circular, reiterated accounts of industrialised atrocity were given the ghost of a classical structure based on the design of Dante's *Inferno*, and actor after RSC actor came onto the bare, packed stage as witness or accused. It was staged for one evening only, simultaneously with theatres across Europe, in a collective act of bearing witness in public spaces, and pioneered, in this country at least, the stage as courtroom, which has since become David to the Goliath of 'info-tainment' media. Nick Kent at the Tricycle Theatre, staging the Stephen Lawrence and arms-to-Iraq enquiries, and Nuremberg and Srebenice war-crime trials, continues this moral and civic stance today.

The RSC of thirty-five years ago was a theatre that set out to revive blank verse as a living implement and went on to dig into the darkness of World War Two and Vietnam. The classical can be the hub of a tradition or a dead ritual, an alibi or an appeal to authenticity. An open and inquiring classicism, such as the RSC achieved for much of a decade, can be a torch in the moral labyrinth. Paradoxically, it was from this classical theatre, shaped by the undogmatic rigour of Shakespeare, not yet held in the embrace of 'heritage' and tourism, nor stunted by standstill funding, that I learned how all theatre could become contemporary, convivial and confrontational.

Thirty years later, still drawn to the classical, I came back to Shakespeare, in an attempt to explore the contention, by then widely contested in British academic and intellectual circles, that his plays had more universal appeal than any other dramatist's. Between the birth of the Royal Shakespeare Company and 1994, when I chose Shakespeare productions in foreign languages for an international Shakespeare festival at the Barbican Centre, and made a BBC series, both called *Everybody's Shakespeare*, a lot had changed in British theatre and culture, not much of it for the better.

Peter Brook told me about a wonderful Georgian troupe, the

Film Actors' Theatre Studio from Tbilisi, led by the octogenarian wizard, Mikhail Tumanishvili; I invited their *Midsummer Night's Dream*. From a small company in Israel, the Itim Ensemble, I invited *Romeo and Juliet*, directed by Rina Yerushalmi, whose intense, distilled dance-like work I already admired. From Japan, I asked Tadashi Suzuki to bring his *Lear*, a cruel ninety-minute crystallisation of the play performed by his actors grounded in the disciplines of Noh theatre but alert to the incursions of Western culture. His Lear sits in a sanatorium, dandled on a nurse's knee, recalling his story at his life's depleted end.

I went to the Dramaten Theatre in Stockholm to see Ingmar Bergman's *A Winter's Tale*, one of the most magical Shakespeare productions I have ever seen. In what was close to his swansong as a director, it was as if Bergman had merged the world of Shakespeare's late romance with that of his own late film of family crimes and reconciliations, *Fanny and Alexander*. The auditorium of the Dramaten Theatre is an oval, a jewel of art nouveau coloured glass and tendril-like wood. Bergman's first inspiration had been to complete the curve of the auditorium by carrying the auditorium design through onto the stage, so that we felt we were in the same room as the players. Arriving in this spacious, lofty room, we discovered the entire cast in turn-of-the-century dress, ballroom dancing. Old dowagers tottered down steps from the front of the stage into the front rows, which had been replaced by little golden chairs. We were part of this country-house weekend, as lavish as the Christmas party in *Fanny and Alexander*, and as threatened by explosions. In this convivial gathering, Leontes' sudden rage of jealousy was truly seismic, a grenade in a drawing room. But what was so seductive was Bergman's mastery of tone, the way he held the twined plots of the play in a joyful celebration of playing itself, lightness containing pain. Even the wild bear on Bohemia's romantic seashore became part of the ongoing charade, another fancy-dress costume in the weekend's costume ball.

But we never saw it in London. After anxious and finally reassuring talks with Bergman's cohorts, after his technicians had flown over, walked round and measured up the Barbican stage, after his manager had assured me all was well with the broody maestro, we received a fax from Bergman on his hideaway island of Faro saying he couldn't consider performing his *Winter's Tale* in such an unsympathetic modern space as the Barbican Theatre. Bill Wilkinson and I scurried around London, looking for auditoria with the required aura, found the Old Vic and the Lyric Hammersmith which might be free. But time ran out.

As in all festivals, there was one production that really got up the critics' noses, and it was almost inevitably the radical re-interpretation of *The Merchant of Venice* by American director Peter Sellars. I had known Sellars when he was the brightest student director of his generation at Harvard, staging *King Lear* in an automobile graveyard, Handel's oratorio *Saul* as an analogue to the Nixon Watergate hearings, and his opera *Orlando*, with the hero no longer a valiant knight, but an equally helmeted astronaut. He had been made the absurdly young director of Washington's Kennedy Center, where he did a four-hour version of Gorki's *Summerfolk* peppered with Gershwin songs and scandalised Washington's military elite by staging Sophocles' *Ajax* in the garbage disposal cellar of the Pentagon.

Sellars is a combination of Orson Wellesian chutzpah, and moral and political ardour. Small wonder then that he turned to Shakespeare's *The Merchant of Venice* right after the ferocious riots and looting in Los Angeles where he lives, with its global business and gilded, style-conscious youth chilling out in Venice, California. He mirrored the racial diversity and divisions in Los Angeles and in America at large by casting black actors to play Shakespeare's Jews, Asian actors to play Portia and her court, and Latinos to play the Venetians. The ethnic tensions in Sellars' Mahagonny/Los Angeles became parallel with the prejudice in Shakespeare's Venice, without changing an anti-Semitic word or action.

This interpretation took root as theatre for two reasons: it was driven by a real indignation about injustice, so that the play was mounted with urgency, and not as part of a cultural machine; and it fed into a native American performance style. Not the behaviourism of Method acting, but the self-aware, presentational skills of the actor in the age of the camera and microphone.

Sellars wrapped his performers in a web of sound. Cellphones, microphones and video cameras, with which they filmed each other, built an image of mercantile communication and of narcissism which illuminated many aspects of the play, gave the actors a chance to play in super-realistic close-up and to be exhibited at the same time.

When I saw a bunch of black eighteen-year-olds from Brixton in the Barbican theatre, digging the hip-suited young businessmen of this Rialto and relating to black Shylock's plight, I knew there was an audience beyond the parameters of the critical onslaught the production mostly received. It's perhaps no coincidence that this was the one production in the festival which was done in English, or at least Anglo-American. Unfamiliarity with foreign languages allows British critics to give visiting productions the benefit of the doubt. But when a foreign director working in English has the effrontery to take on the play as if it were as new as today's closing prices on the Dow Jones index, then well-worn reflexes of refusal click into action.

Quoting Noam Chomsky on capitalism and Eduardo Galeano on third-world exploitation (just what merchandise was on those ships of Antonio that were lost at sea?), Sellars went for his truth about Shakespeare with the energy of a street preacher:

People often remark that Shakespeare is so strange, so all over the map. He writes a kind of language of extremes, but also the plays themselves have no predictable form. And this has set up the Racine-versus-Shakespeare debate: this marvellous craftsman of perfect forms and then Shakespeare, spewing out all over the place. But where the level of consistency exists in Shakespeare, what functions from scene to scene, absolutely irrespective of questions of diction, characterisation or plot, is a moral vision. That is what makes one scene follow another, what makes an act have a complete shape, what gets you from the first to the last word of a play. And as a moralist, he goes beyond the conventional terms of religion or political theory because he's working in a laboratory with real human beings. And this is the gift that theatre can offer: it's not just what would we think would be correct but actually, in this circumstance with these people, what do we feel in our hearts is correct behaviour and when do we sense violation? It's the whole question of meeting life, you know, the wheel hits the pavement with a direct energy; not, 'This is taken for granted, this is an artistic experience'.

Doing this festival taught me that what we mean by 'Shakespeare' stretches beyond the culture wars within the English-speaking world, beyond the references and judgments of erudite Western Europe. While preparing the festival, I had gone out into the wide world for a BBC series to ask whether it made any sense to call Shakespeare the most universal dramatist in the world.

Luis Buñuel's screenwriter Jean-Claude Carrière relished the elusiveness of Shakespeare, which he explored when translating three Shakespeare plays for his closest collaborator now, Peter Brook:

Shakespeare himself doesn't speak out. I mean he doesn't take a position, he doesn't take sides. He gives the same talent to all the characters and the same reasons and the same beautiful language. In other words, it appears, you can work all your life long on Shakespeare's plays, as many people did, and you will never learn anything about the man himself. You will never know if he prefers living in the country or the city, if he is a Tory or a Whig, whether he likes men or women. It's impossible because he has reached the summit of glory, which is to be anonymous.

Ion Caramitru, the leading Romanian actor whose Hamlet became a rallying-point of resistance to the Ceauşescu regime, permitted himself an effusive figure of praise: 'Shakespeare, like just a few geniuses in the world, is probably that drop of God coming down to earth to make you feel richer and more important as a human being.'

Such effusions wouldn't make much impression on the new wave of British academic critics, like Professor Alan Sinfield of the University of Sussex, a leading exponent of 'cultural materialism'. Sinfield argued his corner with the rangy populism of a modern man at home in media and markets, who keeps his distance from actual theatre:

> The first phenomenon to question is that anything should be running across the whole world at all. Why should there be any such figure or sets of figures – and there are other figures, more often in popular culture – figures of Hollywood and figures of music, Tamla Motown for instance. People are doing Shakespeare at least partly in the same way that people do blue jeans and Coca-Cola. If you try and think of it on a market model for the moment – I'm not trying to say that's the only or the right way to do it – then you have to say that Shakespeare is now rather focused on a particular part of the market, so although he doesn't have the same density and indeed clarity of global push that Coca-Cola does, nevertheless you can quite see how he is calling forth a certain constituency.

I talked to Sinfield at the Shakespeare conference at Stratford-upon-Avon – the trade fair for Shakespearean academics the world over. He irresistibly recalled Malcolm Bradbury's roguish iconoclast The History Man, bent on dismantling and deconstructing any old certainty you might toss him, starting with Shakespeare's universality.

> The problem with the term universal is that it suggests we're all seeing the same thing, that there's some kind of core which is the real Shakespeare and the source of the truth, of which we all make our particular versions. But I see Shakespeare as endlessly malleable, and you can do entirely different things with Shakespeare. What you've got is a conglomeration of uses. Shakespeare is the sum of his uses.

There may be a kind of indeterminacy, a kind of shifting, allowing-you-to-have-it-both-ways quality in those texts, which may not be particularly admirable. There aren't any authoritative stage directions, directors are allowed to cut, put in business, stage what looks like a misreading. And why not? It's hundreds of years ago, the play still remains. But the fact that Shakespeare allows that to happen to his plays, may be a kind of shiftiness. Maybe it's a willingness to please all parts of the theatre, to compromise and negotiate. In certain circumstances this is a human quality we very much value, in some circumstances plainly what you want is negotiation. In other circumstances you really want people to come out and say what they damn well think about things. Maybe he doesn't do that.

Like all iconoclasts, Alan Sinfield has an initially bracing effect. Of course Shakespeare-worship has reinforced British power and class structures and Shakespeare's readily recognisable stories and characters can be used for dubious global purposes. But suspicion of Shakespeare can easily become as rigid a stance as making a cult of the man and his plays. For many foreign theatre people, and especially for those making theatre under oppression, the difficulty of pinning Shakespeare down to any ideological position is a great liberation. For Sinfield it's a limitation.

Peter Brook's views on Shakespeare seem to inhabit a different world. Over the past twenty years Brook has kept Shakespeare as a touchstone of his ongoing quest to seek the essence of theatre by working with multi-ethnic casts. In his cunningly dilapidated Paris theatre he has staged three Shakespeare plays: *Timon of Athens*, *Measure for Measure* and *The Tempest*. He agrees that to call Shakespeare 'universal' these days is risky.

One must understand what one means by 'universal'. It's easily misunderstood to refer to something bland; the worst of Hollywood is the destruction of cultural roots, making something accessible spread across the planet. That is one horrifying distortion of what is 'universal'. The universal truth is that every single being as yet discovered on this planet, unlike people from Mars, has the same anatomical and physiological structure. When Shakespeare has Othello say, I think there are men who have heads coming out of their stomachs, in fact, such people haven't yet been found on this planet. But as far as we know, black, yellow, white people, Jewish, Moslem people have their brains in the same portion of the head. When you operate on the stomach, the organs don't take on any colour. This universal reference of the human body is also an emotional, ideological, philosophical and spiritual reference. In other words, when a dramatic truth genuinely touches on what can be understood and felt within the human body in its most complete sense, it is 'universal'.

For Brook as for many directors and writers, Shakespeare's anonymity, his ability to allow the world of each and every character to speak in its own terms, is a great example.

Perhaps, apart from Homer and the Bible, there are few great works whose author has so little wish to be remembered by posterity by pushing his nose into every line he writes. The human necessity to see the world through one's own eyes and nobody else's, is natural, but it's a limitation, it's not a glory, it's a sadness. And anything that can open a human being's generosity so that he can really accept that another person exists, is in itself a minor miracle.

Brook, whose recent work has been much concerned with the human mind and its misfortunes, compares narrow-minded artists, who lack this Shakespearean selflessness, with autistic people, incapable of conceiving independent existences. It's the very openness, the fluidity of Shakespeare's plays, argues Brook, their wide sympathies and fierce contradictions, that carry them to so many different places and people. At times, Brook almost makes Shakespeare a measure of the rich possibilities of theatre itself.

Shakespeare goes beyond even what a painter can do, because a painter is only showing one aspect of life, the aspect you can put on canvas. A musician only shows one aspect of the mystery of what's behind life by capturing sound patterns. But a playwright is dealing with the whole of existential experience at one and the same time. And he is doing it through people meeting, talking and behaving with one another. I greatly admired Chekhov largely because, being a doctor, he was true to a doctor's sympathy and observation. Shakespeare goes beyond this, and however much one tries to find lines which seem to relate to Shakespeare's political views, to his view of the world, of love, this doesn't go very far. The plays are way beyond this.

What Peter Brook is attempting in Paris goes beyond translating the plays into French and making them work with French actors. He didn't need to leave England, to put himself into a plural frame of reference, for that. For what he seeks, Paris is a crossroads, where performers and traditions from the whole world seem more vivid and available. The way Peter Brook positions his work, both geographically and, if you like, semantically, is absolutely crucial to understanding Shakespeare in this time of shifting linguistic and cultural frontiers. The pool of actors with whom he works is multinational: English, African, German, French, Japanese and some ten other nationalities. They perform in French, often with marked accents, when they are in Paris. They do many of their shows, such as *The Mahabharata*, in English when they go on tour, although he's never toured in English any of his Paris Shakespeares.

The point of Brook's fifteen-year experiment is not to create some theatrical United Nations. Instead he brings together performers from widely different cultures whose interplay restores to theatre some of the polyphonic richness it loses whenever culture with a capital C becomes routine. And he sees Shakespeare, whose own world was a web of discoveries, new coinages and fresh connections, as a model to which he has continually to refer.

One of the things which has always fascinated him in

Shakespeare's plays is their supernatural dimension: the fairies in
A *Midsummer Night's Dream*, the ghost of Hamlet's father,
Prospero's magic, the spirit Ariel.

In 1968, at the first international workshop we did in Paris,
Yoshi Oida joined our work. He arrived, a Japanese actor,
with no English or French. Using his Noh theatre training,
particularly his understanding of the reality of all its witches,
sorcerers, spirits and demons, Yoshi got up and did a form of
movement that no Western choreographer could think up.
He used his body and his voice differently from the way any
actor could do just by using his own unrooted fantasy. He
caught everyone's breath by this image that he created. One
was convinced, just that, touched and convinced: 'Ah!
There is Ariel. This is not a literary invention. We're not
looking at it with slightly superior indulgent eyes saying, oh,
what a charming choreographer, what a clever director,
what a amusing actor! We're looking straight through it.
Ah! I believe – Spirit.'

In his most recent production of *The Tempest*, his third, Brook
cast Sotigui Kouyate, an African actor and storyteller, as Prospero.

It has become a cliché to say, 'Well of course a black actor
can play the slave, Caliban.' I think this is highly suspect
and very condescending towards black actors and a
complete misreading of Caliban, because the play is not a
document about colonialism showing how a wicked, right-
wing colonialist oppresses a poor slave, it's something way
beyond that, about essential human values. This was a
natural casting, not of a black actor, because I don't see that
has any meaning, but of an African, which is very different.
Somebody with a deep culture, that led to an understanding
of Prospero, with another African actor whose culture led to
a natural understanding of Ariel. This made a very natural
counterpart to the young German actor whose violent
adolescence corresponded truly with the nature of a

Caliban, who has the possibility one day, at the end of a very
long road, of coming out of his own violent adolescence and
approaching the understanding that Prospero has reached.

Seeing a Shakespeare play abroad, it's hard for a British person
not to feel some sense of loss. Without the layers and textures of
his English words, something crucial is missing. But other things
are lost which are worth losing – ritual reverence, over-
familiarity, heritage, solemnity, Bardolatry. So perhaps it's not
useful to think in simple terms of gain and loss, but of difference.
Shakespeare abroad is not a second-best copy of a radiant English
original but a different and sometimes equally valid experience.
The big obstacle to realising Shakespeare's depth and breadth is
reductiveness. This can take many forms: politics, puritanism,
nationalism or even just neatness. But the flower of theatrical life
can take root in these plays anywhere in the world as long as the
interpreter sees Shakespeare's limitlessness, not as a con-trick, or
conspiracy, but as a quality which, as Peter Brook acknowledges,
literally lifts you up.

It's very important constantly to be reminded of the poverty
of one's own work. I think that otherwise one has inflated
and unrealistic ideas about oneself. And this is the value of
contemplating great works of the past. To go to a museum
and stand in front of extraordinary paintings from several
hundred years ago, or to re-explore a play of Shakespeare,
brings one back to the fact that neither you nor I, nor
anybody alive, painter, musician, author, director, can today
touch that quality. That's very healthy for us. But it means
that one must then draw the positive and not the negative
conclusion: 'We see once again we can't do this, we're put in
our place and now we try to do once more the best we can,
do it a bit better.' And then because people like it, and give
us false illusions about ourselves, we return to this
unshakeable Himalaya, which is there to remind one that
some mountains can be higher than others, and some can be
the highest in the world.

The Vanishing Vanguard

If the world of sameness refuses to absorb the
element of otherness that every group and human
being unconsciously carries within themselves, just
as Pentheus refuses that mysterious, feminine
Dionysiac element that attracts and fascinates him,
despite the horror he claims to feel for it, then all
that is stable, regular and the same tips over and
collapses . . . The victorious eruption of Dionysus is
a sign that otherness is being given its place with
full honours at the centre of the social system.

Jean-Pierre Vernant, *Myth and Tragedy in Ancient Greece*

For the past century, the counter-current to the classical
mainstream has been a wave of provocations, inventions
and convulsions by a movement which borrowed its name
from the military: the avant-garde. This vanguard has challenged
conventions, shattered forms, contested culture and language
themselves.

A vanguard appeared in theatre, as in every modern art, not
just because the times seemed to require it, but because it is a
timeless rhythm, a cyclical turn of the mind. It represents a
longing to crack authority and uniformity, to turn inside out the
shape, gender, genre in which we are clothed. It descends from
Dionysus. But now that we are wrapped in a culture more
cunningly branded, targeted and marketed than ever before, the

shock of the new is already being swiftly and ironically absorbed by MTV, design, fashion and the countless varieties of industrialised innovation.

By the time I reached my twenties, I had already been inoculated with the modern passion for the New. Baudelaire, Rimbaud, Apollinaire, Meyerhold, Jackson Pollock, Charlie Parker, John Cage, Beat poetry, Happenings and William Blake were tucked into my baggage when I left the Royal Shakespeare Company and became the director of the Institute of Contemporary Arts. We opened the doors in April 1968, and I dreamed of a new motto above the lintel of the entrance in our Sir John Nash terrace on The Mall. It would be a quote from William Blake: 'The whole business of man is the arts, and all things common'. There was never any chance we would get permission to engrave these words in the stone of tradition, from either the Royal Parks authorities who governed our entrance or the Crown Commission, who were our landlords.

Out of the flood of invention and zest in theatre and cross-genre performance of that time, two theatre pieces, one by a courageous director, the other by an anarchic writer, have stayed with me as quintessentially vanguard work of that time.

Pip Simmons' theatre reached back to the spirit of Mayakovsky's confrontational plays and poems. When I went to his *Black and White Minstrel Show*, a grotesque assault on racism, I found myself handcuffed at the interval to a blacked-up actor who doggedly followed me to the bar like my personal slave, a bowing and scraping human rebuke.

But Simmons' most wrenching theatre event was *An Die Musik*, drawn out of his guts by the screaming contradiction between the atrocities of concentration camp guards and their love of German classical music. It is now a common reference that the SS formed concentration camp bands of Jewish prisoners, to play Beethoven and Schubert for them after days gassing babies. Pip, a gruff, tall, gaucho of an East Ender, decided to stage such an Auschwitz orchestra. His seventy-five-minute piece could hardly have been simpler. Its first part was an operetta, *The Dream of Anne Frank*. It was set around a Friday evening Jewish Sabbath table, with candlesticks and blessings, *challah* and *kiddush* wine. As the family performed the naïve, touching melodies of the operetta, a bunch of Nazi soldiers moved in and stripped them of jewellery, candlesticks, cutlery.'

In the second part Pip staged the degradation of the inmates, with a brutality that seemed to be just this side of tolerable, for the performers and for the audience. The prisoners were ordered to strip naked, an action that could have been the prelude to the gas chamber, the thought of which was in all our minds. Instead, they picked up instruments – woodwind, brass and violin – and, at first with difficulty, then with increasing assurance and finally with total confidence, played the innocent Romantic tenderness of Schubert's *To Music*. Then the Nazi commandant donned a gas mask, clouds of white smoke surrounded them, and they played Beethoven's *Ode to Joy* – *Alle Menschen Werden Bruder*, all men shall be brothers. I can still hear the sweet-sour, rough-edged sound they made. It broke your heart and made you rage, it said as much as volumes of analysis about European culture and European barbarism, its culmination was a theatre image that hammered itself into your mind with its simplicity, beauty and pain. *An Die Musik* was an exemplary work of alternative art, requiring a different kind of performer, more like a rock musician than a drama school product, arising from different networks (this was the period when the Mickery Theatre in Amsterdam was a lifeline for British vanguard groups), and fruitfully alien to mainstream theatre.

With Heathcote Williams' *AC/DC* in 1970, the decade found its infernal minstrel show, a play that, with its concerns about 'psychic capitalism' and 'media rash' still reverberates now, as we cross the engineered Millennium threshold. With *AC/DC*, the mind-bending tirades and dislocated drug-and-techno-talk of William Burroughs broke into the code-room of the English play. The play is an encounter between Sadie, Gary and Melody, a trio of sensation-loving tripsters in an electric games arcade, and Perowne, a psychic casualty of the media blitz.

Perowne thinks celebrities, magnified by the media, are stealing his instinctual patterns. 'THEY'RE STEALING THEM,' he cries, 'THEY'RE FORGING THEM. THEY'RE SLOWING THEM UP. THEY'RE SPEEDING THEM UP. THEY'RE REPRODUCING THEM TWENTY TIMES A DAY. THEY'RE UNLOADING YOU. THEY'RE OVERLOADING YOU . . .'

All the characters are as polymathic and besotted by wordplay as Shakespeare's language-intoxicated pedants in *Love's Labour's Lost*, and with just as far to go to reach reality. They have a laconic irony about the media landscape: 'Remember the time Sadie was so tripped out on Marshall McLuhan she sprayed the TV with communion wine and licked her way through the screen?'

Sadie steps in, to exorcise Perowne of his screen demons:

I killed Mick Jagger. I set it up. With a tantric spell. He's got some karmic debts to pay for, that's why. Poncing off a few back-dated revolutionary vibes to pay his Hilton Hotel bill. Writes a song Street Fighting Man, but when it comes to the crunch you know he couldn't fight his way out of a bag of smack . . . ALL these psychic capitalists are hustling Feedback all the time, more than anyone else, they're hustling Attention Molecules, and Validation Molecules, and Look at Me Molecules, and after a bit those molecules and that feedback gets TOO much for them to process, because they ain't that big enough to accommodate them you dig and so those attention molecules build up inside them, and get Radioactive, start overheating the whole fuckin Network and so those fat cats gotta be DIS-CHARGED, you dig, they gotta be Detonated. Psychic jiu jitsu. ESP terrorism, or just knock them on the head like rabbits. (*Sitting down*) Phew, I really hit the seed shit then.

You can't understand all the words in the geyser of speech, but it doesn't matter; you know you're watching a modern Morality Play as simple as the contest between Saint George and the Dragon: a hip Player Queen driving out technological addiction and media dependency. *AC/DC* remains a prophetic myth of modernity, in the form of a sassy, strutting, black-humoured

Pierrot show. It shows that theatre can go into the cage with the Dragon, provided it wears its own garb proudly. That is why it was resonant then, and has lasted.

In the largely permissive tolerance of the West at this time, we made our affirmations, our critique, as confrontations; in Central and Eastern Europe, they exercised irony and blasphemy. I rediscovered the gravity of theatre from that half of a Europe divided by the Cold War, when I brought Jerzy Grotowski and his company to the ICA in 1969, their first British visit.

I had discovered Grotowski fifteen years earlier, in his 'theatre laboratory' in the small Silesian town of Opole. With my friend Mike Elster, who was making a film about Grotowski, we drove to Opole, past sporadic horse-drawn wagons, driven by old peasants with immemorial faces. In Opole, a wrought-iron sign indicated the Theatre Laboratory. Grotowski was waiting for us, smoking at a small table, thin, excitable, dressed in black, with black glasses, very white skin and small, plump hands.

I am wary of mythologising that first meeting. But the force of his presence, the intensity with which he spoke, his still body and headlong voice, rising to falsetto as he punched home points in his punctilious French, have not been falsified by memory. I realised I was in the presence of a zeal that might as properly have been found in a Catholic crusader or a Communist militant. It seemed instead to grow out of a search that was at once spiritual – a way forward in a world seen as a wasteland – and yet utterly physical, rooted in the actions of the body, seeing many more possibilities than conventional acting required. As he wrote at that time, 'They have put a straitjacket on the theatre. We want to "let lose the madman".'

Next day, I watched his actors doing a three-hour session of exercises, in a long, low, black-painted room. They worked on breathing and voice – 'I am looking for resonators which European performers do not use,' said Grotowski, black-clad again as he watched his actors without comment. They worked on balance and acrobatics, putting the body into unfamiliar poses and painful positions which may release dimensions buried by habit and ease. Grotowski had spent two years in China, and brought Chinese and Hatha Yoga techniques to the 'bio-mechanics' of Meyerhold and Stanislavski's ethic of truthfulness, though not the latter's naturalistic recall exercises. For Grotowski was rebuilding theatre expression from the outside in, as in the rigorous sign-language of traditional Japanese Noh and Indian Kathakali theatre. But his voyage into the East was an agonised confrontation. He made his actor separate the parts of his body, 'so that his face can express heroism, his hands doubt and his feet panic.' A contrapuntal, discontinuous, fragmented expression, an irony made flesh.

His staging of Marlowe's *Doctor Faustus* in that catacomb of a room showed his constructive theatrical annihilation at work. Faustus embraced his sins with the glowing certainty of a pilgrim. He signed away his soul as a saint would renounce worldly toys, and cast off his robe, revealing a taut torso. These stage images were wrapped in a tapestry of sound. Words were spoken, chanted, whispered; sounds rose from strange regions of the throat or belly; medieval Christian hymns accompanied pagan actions; prayers sounded like threats. There were moments of sculptural beauty: Faustus borne to Rome to confront the Pope, held like a swan three feet above our heads, floating on the bed of a close-harmony motet. It could have been an image out of Dürer. But there was nothing pictorial or decorative in this work; it crackled with spiritual impatience and fierce yearning.

In Faustus' final monologue Rizsard Cieslak reached a crescendo of torment and contortion, in which fanaticism and belief could no longer be distinguished. As he froze in a trance of triumph, menacing paternosters broke out, and the twin Mephisto, now disguised as a priest, seized him as unconcernedly as if he were an object. From Faustus' mouth came a piercing scream and the panic blabbering of a torture victim. In that small black room, the martyrdom of this defiant dissident of the holy was absolutely terrifying, intellectually as well as viscerally.

When Grotowski and his company arrived in London, their presence was like the arrival of a slab of gravity in a teeming circus ring. To see him again, awkward in the buzzing ICA café, thin, black-clad and wearing shades, making his skin even more pallid, his voice still rising in excitement, was an immediate reminder of the stubborn loneliness with which he pursued his quest. In his memoir of Grotowski in Silesia, his friend and disciple Eugenio Barba evokes a scene of isolated artistic pioneers, dreaming up a holy theatre in conditions of Dostoevskian squalor:

> Almost every evening Grotowski and I went to the station restaurant which stayed open all night. It was our living room. We had supper and then, sipping continuous cups of tea – each with two bags – we talked for hours, often until dawn . . . We sat at that dilapidated table, fighting against the night, amid the rank smell of beer and cigarette smoke, the drowsy atmosphere and the grime, interrupted by the din of the loudspeaker announcing the arrivals and departures of trains. Then our narrations-confessions would resume and, as ineluctably as a river flowing into the sea, would end up in that India 'which exists before the eyes of our soul'.

Grotowski and his grave, slow-moving performers came to London from the country of my mother's parents, and in ways I could not express they had assumed the burden of being Polish: its sadness, its wariness, its resignation. But out of this burden, they had dug ecstatic expression, pushing their blood and nerves to capture the 'form and pressure' of their times. Nothing in London theatre at the time – or in Paris, New York or Rome, where they continued their journey – matched their work, or even shared any constituents with it.

Grotowski refused to play in the ICA theatre space. It bore the traces of too many other performances that claimed the name of theatre, and which he dismissed, with the scorn of a militant, as 'artistic kleptomania'. We found him the crypt of a church in Limehouse. He insisted, with great emphasis, that the place be scrubbed clean from top to bottom. It was as if these vaults were to become not just a theatre but an operating theatre, in which delicate and risky interventions of the body and spirit were to be conducted in strict conditions. If he said there would be only sixty-three seats, it would have to be sixty-three and not a single seat more.

When I saw the performance of *Akropolis*, I understood why. The Catholic-nationalist pantheon imagined by the nineteenth-century playwright Wyspiański had been brutally transposed into the concentration-camp universe. Its inmates, dressed in torn sackcloth, hair hidden, faces seemingly pulped beyond recognition, swung huge industrial pipes around the tiny space, building the hoped-for new Pantheon – and missing the audience's faces by inches. ' The resurrection becomes a cortège,' said Grotowski. 'It bears a corpse, not a risen saviour. But we do not just deride: we show the human needs which are met by what we deride.' It was theatre of another order. That is why these productions represented such a challenge, and why, even after Grotowski had left theatre to practise 'para-theatrical' workshops, the after-trace of these performances goaded so many theatre makers into creative dissatisfaction.

On the other side of the world from Europe, other codes were being undermined. I first visited America in the early 1970s, looking at theatre groups across the country. On the Mexican Day of the Dead, I drove out from San Francisco to San Juan Bautista, once a Spanish colonial town, now the home of Luis Valdez's El Campesino theatre, a Hispanic troupe that had started in the fields (hence its title) where the migrant grape-pickers were being turned over by their bosses. With short agit-prop *actos*, performed by a handful of actors with a guitar, Campesino had articulated demands and prompted action. Their style came from the fiesta of street theatre, the grotesque insolence of popular caricatures.

I arrived at the little town. You could see down the main street and out the other end into the desert. In the blazing noonday heat, a procession was forming up in the main square. Most of the marchers wore death-suits – home-made papier mâché skulls worn above black tights and top painted as a skeleton. A glass of something containing tequila was thrust into my hand, a rough Mexican band at the head of the line struck up, and we set out to march round the town. The death-figures jigged and jumped and cried, with howls of joy. Glasses were refilled by waiters who seemed to have risen from the mortuary. The sun beat down in rhythm with the band. We were no longer walking, we were syncopating, shuffling feet and flicking fingers.

Back in the main square we crowded into a big hall with a shallow stage across its long wall. A banner hung over it: EL FIN DEL MUNDO, The End Of The World. This was the title of the Day Of The Dead vaudeville. The lively street band went into an upbeat tune, and the show began. It was very simple, and devastating. A string of black-out sketches by active, agile actors of the trials and tribulations of migrants from Mexico – tangling with US Immigration patrols, failing to get work, struggling to learn English, being outwitted in a hundred ways – each ended in a setback, an accident, damage, destruction or death. Black-out. But instantly, lights up, and the victim leaps to his feet and joins in with the band singing the jaunty theme-song: 'It's the end of the world, the end of the world everyday, but it's never quite the end.' It was the matter of poor theatre, newcomers' theatre, the theatre of the downtrodden everywhere, anytime; in Sicily with Dario Fo, taking the masks of commedia dell'arte into the present-day world of bureaucracy and banks; in Gaza with George Ibrahim, carving up the classics in the town square to express Palestinians' oppression and dreams; in the Russian Pale of Settlement a century ago, the fiddle and accordion pit band playing the same jaunty kind of music to punctuate Yiddish family melodramas and tales of Cossack cruelty.

By the time I came back to America in 1980, to work for a year in American theatre, much had changed. Margaret Thatcher, who did not believe in the existence of society, was in power in Britain, Reagan, an actor who knew the art of ingratiating himself to an audience, was the soft-soaping salesman for big business, in America. The age of neo-liberalism, of free markets and privatisation, was beginning to bite into all the arts, cutting back public funding, encouraging censorship, shrinking public spaces, fostering sponsored and private ones.

American vanguard theatre, focus of so much life and talent, stripped down for survival, becoming sharper and more refined, but also more impenetrable and oblique. The Wooster Group's brainy dissections of contemporary classics, in Elizabeth LeCompte's glacially intricate staging, looked like the best of the new art in downtown Manhattan galleries. They were fierce, adversarial acts of theatre, playing to fervent enthusiasts in tiny spaces. They spawned the wry autobiographical solos of one of their actors, Spalding Gray, who cast a disabused eye on his profession, his teenage memories, his relationships. The 'eighties, when money for experimental theatre was scarce, were a growth period for the one-person show. Wallace Shawn's disturbing tales of shifty morality, Eric Bogosian's hoarse riffs on madness in the suburbs, Laurie Anderson's one-woman techno epic. In *United States I-IV*, she made a three-hour trip through the soothing nightmares of corporate, hi-tech America, her tiny body and white electric violin hooked into a network of the very technology whose seductiveness she was condemning.

But on any scale larger than the studio space or the one-person show, distinctive work was beginning to settle into exquisite mannerism. Robert Wilson had opened up a new theatre landscape: an infinitely slow unfolding action, characters like mutants, Philip Glass's racing music, an architect's sensibility in design and light. But the Wagnerian vision which had underpinned his first work gave way to pageants about modernism for a postmodern world, or pop-art pastiches, and as his style was copied, it looked more and more like the ascendancy of the designer.

In the last decade, not only in Wilson's case, there has been more and more visually breathtaking theatre which looks as if it were designed for the international festival and modern art museum crowd. By the end of the 'eighties, the vitality of vanguard theatre became a regular exhibit on the international festival circuit. Language-linked work gave way to the galloping global culture of images. The roots of adversarial, form-breaking theatre, its connection to its own place and idiom, were being loosened. Even a director as committed to renewing the classics as Peter Sellars, with his passionate reworkings of Mozart and Handel, Aeschylus and Shakespeare, was framed and to some extent tamed by the international festivals and opera houses that produced his work. This cannot be unrelated to the phenomenon we were beginning to call globalisation.

In London, there was one play – there is always one – which captured the groundswell of these times, and anticipated the new economic dispensation to come. In 1987, after a wave of work that broke out of the frames of definition, overflowed demarcations with dreams and deconstructions; after the roll-back of this wave by 'normalization', overtly political in France after 1968, repressive in Central Europe, and philistine in Britain; in these low times for the vanguard and heady times for business and marketable culture, along came Caryl Churchill's *Serious Money*.

The moment Alfred Molina as Zac, a London-based American banker, stepped downstage, shot his cuffs, shook his silk suit and hit us with his multinational money rap with its sawn-off sentences and slithery rhymes, you knew that theatre had collared the new *zeitgeist*, and was going to squeeze mirth out of it:

> The financial world won't be the same again
> Because the traders are coming down the fast lane . . .
> If you're making the firm ten million you want a piece
>   of the action.
> You know you've got it made the day you're offered
>   stock options.
> There are guys that blow out, sure, stick too much
>   whitener up their nose.
> Guy over forty's got any sense he takes his golden
>   handshake and goes.
> Because the new guys are hungrier and hornier,
> They're Jews from the Bronx and spics from Southern
>   California.
> It's like Darwin says, the survival of the fit,
> Now, here in England, it's just beginning to hit . . .
> England's been fucking the world with interest but
>   now it's a different scene.
> I don't mind bending over and greasing my ass but I
>   sure ain't using my own vaseline.

Now as a place to live, England's swell.
Tokyo treats me like a slave, New York tries to kill
     me, Hong Kong
I have to turn a blind eye to the suffering and I feel
     wrong.
London, I go to the theatre.

When *Serious Money* opened in 1987, first at the Royal Court and
then in the West End, the hipper City traders flocked to see
themselves impersonated. They laughed a lot, perhaps a little too
loudly to indicate comfort, for it was not a show they could
consider theirs, as they might a night out at the Royal Opera
House in the corporate box. In the West End we could afford to
get in. But by then, they knew things were going their way. For
the theatre, it had all begun to tip over, to turn around, in ways
that were not yet clear, except that there was less public money
for public theatre.

By now I had moved into the screen world, into television. At
the start of Channel 4, Britain's 'alternative television channel',
I became one of its first wave of commissioning editors. It felt like
moving to another planet, altering trajectory. The television
constellation lacked the gravity of the earthbound theatre world.
TV is a gathering of solitudes into networks of domestic viewers.
TV is domestic, not shared public space. TV is distant multitudes,
separate spectators. Except in pubs for the big match, they do not
share the space of experiencing something together, and less and
less do they share the time.

Helping to launch Channel 4 Television was hardly going into
the belly of the beast, for Channel 4 was a final and spirited
upturning of British television in its relation to fiction, fact,
audiences and art, before the forces of homogenisation, the
operations Caryl Churchill had dramatised with such bitter glee,
sucked most of the juice out of the least bad television in the
world. But entering it still felt like a journey into another
element, a Jonah-trip into a benevolent container tossed by
different waves, with a remembrance of a Promised Land.

I knew that in some sense I was playing truant at the age of forty, quitting theatre, and starting anew in the realm of – just what? I could not get away from the idea that the enterprise of Channel 4 was a last spasm, however socially, culturally and formally experimental its aims, however deftly a maverick Tory Home Secretary, William Whitelaw, had slipped it under the legislative wire before the Great Simplification got under way. What I was entering was the realm of screens and distance, machinery and markets. This didn't make me any less excited or impelled about what I was doing; just less prone to great expectations, more beady about the difference between innovation and mere novelty, and painfully aware of the huge cultural, political and artistic hopes that were being pinned on Channel 4.

There were many differences between theatre and television that struck me immediately as I started as the channel's Commissioning Editor for the Arts. In theatre, a group of people gets together to make a piece, and over weeks becomes at least a team, at best a mini-society. The activity rises to a peak, a discharge, which is the first night. The people making the work know immediately how it has gone, from the temperature and response of the audience.

In most television, the pay-off is deferred until the transmission date. If it's television drama, the work has been rehearsed and filmed, repeatedly and in fragments. The knitting together into a whole happens in post-production in small dark rooms with the director, editor and composer constructing the life of the piece. Months, sometimes years later, it goes out to the public. For the makers, there is no culminating discharge, no natural confrontation with a group of people they can sense and see under the same roof. Neither television nor film ends in a reinvented present tense.

I knew that if I was to make any sense of television I would have to carry with me, like some nomad with a bundle on his back, the ways of seeing and making I had learned from theatre, and apply them in this new medium. A good number of my fellow commissioning editors in the Channel 4 of 1982 came, like me, from outside television: from journalism, from community arts and cultural activism. So at the beginning Channel 4 was open to other preconceptions and assumptions as we sought to make a new kind of television – 'alternative', 'produced in a different way', 'innovative in form and content', to use the soon well-worn mantras we repeated. The wish to throw the familiar television categories and genres into a melting pot recalled the counter-cultural meltdown of rules and conventions I had lived through in the theatre of the previous two decades. Would it be possible to have the television equivalent of the Fringe venues and audiences in London in New York's Off-Off-Broadway? Or would these be regarded as too minority, even in an 'alternative' channel?

Other signs pointed to the fact that we were still part of the broadcasting industry, of broadcasting conceived as an industry, even if Channel 4 was a minority member among the big boys pulling the mass audiences. Each week at our programme review meeting, the channel's head of sales delivered reports on our performance – another word that had shifted meaning from stage to screen. Her measurements spoke of 'share', 'reach' and 'A.I.', which meant 'appreciation index'. I was especially interested in A.I. since my programmes scored high on this register, while often showing zero or not at all on the audience share register. I learned that programmes with 500,000 viewers or less would not register. Half a million people, in the world I had come from, would have meant a roaring success, full houses, smiles all around. In the world of ratings, it meant that you didn't exist. But the appreciation index from those paltry few hundred thousand people who did watch was consistently high.

I was interested to know how these measurements had been achieved, and learned, like some bemused Candide, that researchers would knock on front doors and if the 'respondents' were willing, get them to answer a series of questions about the programmes, on a scale of one to ten. This did not seem, to me, and still does not seem, a very good way to get reactions to work that is intended to shift perceptions, introduce new subject matter, derange the accepted codes of communication, estrange the medium, or whatever else some of us were attempting. Whatever further sophistications the market research industry has since produced, these methods still seem to have more to do with the retail world's self-fulfilling prophecies, with business confidence and consensus-building, than with the making of a relationship in which new things can be said in new ways through television.

I was much more interested in the man who phoned in when we put out the three hours of *1980*, a dance-theatre piece by the German theatre-maker Pina Bausch at nine o'clock on a Wednesday night in the early weeks on air. He said that he'd come home two hours earlier, switched on for the football on BBC, found the match had been rained off, switched over to Channel 4, and found himself watching Pina Bausch. 'I've been watching since then, I haven't the faintest idea what it all means, but I can't stop watching, and could somebody please tell me why?'

Making television from Pina Bausch's work raised most of the questions about drama on the stage and on the screen. Pina Bausch was making the most invigorating new work in the theatre of the 1980s, bringing her Expressionist formation as a dancer with Kurt Joos into the age of happenings and encounter groups, and rooting her work in a core company that by the time she came to London in 1982 had been together for over a decade. She melted the boundaries between dance and theatre, confession and drama, shaped movement and shared symptoms. She made the stage a great arena for her thirty-strong company of performers, beautiful and striking women and men, characteristically dressed as if for a ball in a Jean Cocteau film, haunted long-haired young women in gorgeous satin gowns slightly too old for them and high heels their mothers might have worn, young men in their best tailored suits for a night out, all of them trailing a long tail of love memories, childhood neuroses and lasting wounds. She would fill her stage with fantastic images out of Magritte, and yet all her own. Carnations wall to wall. An almost naked girl standing in the middle of this on-stage flower meadow with a tiny accordion across her breasts. A giant rhinoceros surfacing from craters of water on stage. Real grass that smelt sweet as it was bruised by the dancers under the hot lights.

A male dancer's pallid face plastered with luscious red lipstick kisses. A thin, firm male body in a tutu. The whole company fighting each other for a microphone to enumerate at the top of their voices all the scars they had on their bodies.

She never called what she made ballets or dance-works. They were 'pieces'. The word could be read as 'a piece by Pina Bausch' or 'a piece of Pina Bausch'. *1980*, made after the death of her lover, felt as if it were torn from her grieving flesh. She put her 'pieces' together intuitively, through games that became psychological space-probes, through scraps of music – a shaky but heartfelt recording of a Beethoven cello sonata made by Casals near the end of his life, Judy Garland's 'Somewhere Over The Rainbow'; kitschy close harmony by the Comedian Harmonists from 1920s Berlin.

Sometimes her stage reminded me of a playground for lonely children, only this enchanted playspace was full of sounds and surprises, games that recalled the first time you were kissed or you kissed. Or a quirky, angular chorus line would flower for a moment, then break down into the irredeemable loneliness of individuals. She fractured the codes of dance and theatre, the minefield between men and women, fathers and daughters, the end of parental security. Then she would surmount the fragility with a gleeful, slinky, sinuous routine, all doubts and fears subsumed in the self-confident twining of arms and sashaying of hips. Cheerfulness was always threatening to break through the gravity of Pina's pieces, as a smile could light up her bony Dürer face with its grey eyes.

Her pieces peaked in paroxysms of delirious action and sound, performers whirling through and across each other, in great bursts of energy. In the theatre, it was possible somehow to hold in your mind the overall long shot and many close-ups of detail, watch a mouth or a hand but not forget the enveloping cataclysm of bodies. All of these qualities, so enjoyable and rich in the theatre, went entirely against the grain of drama or performance on television in 1982. And they still do. Pina Bausch's pieces, like all rooted live theatre, rely on co-ordinates which cannot be matched on the screen. At best, the director, the cameraman and the editor can try to bring about something corresponding to the original by other means, or let themselves be spurred by the example of the theatre piece to make original film or television in another way. As television, *1980* sometimes looked like sport, like football or basketball, with bodies hurtling across the screen, and no perfecting framing as in TV ballet at Christmas. It was rough television, for sure, but its roughness matched the hoarse grief that drove Pina to make the piece at all. You didn't need to be interested in dance or in theatre to get something from *1980*, just interested in people, for her work opened up her performers to the audience, with all their skills and symptoms and narcissism and previously untapped childhood, experiences anyone could get involved with. I realised when *1980* went out, and went out in prime time, that I hadn't commissioned it in order to put a piece of theatre out on television in a cultural slot but to let this strong, cross-genre work punch through the norms of the television schedule with its unbridled physical and emotional life.

Working in television, I realised just how much it is in the nature of theatre to overflow, to breach boundaries and push limits; and by contrast, how television, because it is a medium of great accessibility and little identity – or rather competing identities in an endless Monty Python 'and now for something completely different' – tends towards formats, regularities, serial patterns. On the rare occasions it lets art, especially the performed arts, loose at prime time (often on public holidays when ratings drop anyway), it normally follows a sanctified notion of culture – the Royal Ballet, the Royal Opera House, Glyndebourne.

Most theatre that I chose to bring to the screen when I was at Channel 4 could not be assimilated to these codes of comfort or even cultural prestige. Peter Brook's *The Mahabharata*, nine hours and two evenings long in the theatre, based on the tenth-century Indian poem which is the foundation of Hindu drama and ethics, and performed by a multinational cast, was always going to be one of the channel's rule-breakers. It probably still holds the record for the longest gap between the first development payment for a project and its final production.

After going through the options of doing it in India, Australia or Tunisia, where Polanski had just shot a spectacular film very cheaply, Peter opted to do it on 35mm film in a Paris studio, and spend money for Chloe Obolensky to design a new film set, which would accommodate the camera's need for reverse angles and big movements, and offer up a succession of textures and colours.

What this film had, of course, which few others did, was the accumulated performing experience of his company who had played the material for two years, spun threads of deep connection and mutual knowledge between them, and could sculpt their work for close-up and cinematic tempi. This brought some special qualities to the screen, which could not have been reached from the mainstream production processes, and would have been more elusive if the film had been shot on location. There was the delicacy and detail of the playing, and the non-naturalistic casting, with an international group of actors bringing their own traditions to a specific and universal story. But there was also something that struck me about the gods.

Peter has always liked to use the word 'invisible' in theatre, and to talk about 'playing the invisible'. For him, the word seems to mean whatever force or presence or reality is beyond the world of our perceptions but can be made tangible in a performance. In theatre, this means gods and spirits: Ariel in *The Tempest*, a play he has done three times, most recently with very different African actors playing Ariel and Prospero, 'because their culture takes them closer to spirits and magic,' he says; Hamlet's ghost, to which he has returned in a recent chamber piece *Qui Est Là?*

Now in *The Mahabharata*, he found simple and mysterious ways of making the power and presence of the Hindu gods manifest. Sometimes it was as little as a non-narrative panning movement of the camera and a sound, which created a 'knot' in the threads of the story. Sometimes it was a light-change. These always took place in the chamber of Chloe's multiform set, which you knew was a material structure in one studio space. Had we shot in real locations, such magic would have had to be a costly digital special effect. What the film sacrificed in variety and mobility, it gained in another kind of intensity and steadiness.

In the small and tightly funded area of performance on screen
which I was exploring at Channel 4, I tried to look for the most
theatrical work I could find. Heightened language, transposed
rather than recorded reality, metaphor rather than slice of life. It
hadn't always worked: we shot Yuri Lyubimov's *The Possessed*, a
nightmare vision of extremism and terrorism, with a con-
structivist set and music by Alfred Schnittke, at the Almeida
Theatre, without an audience. Despite its cinematic structure as
a theatre-piece, it came across as merely Expressionistic.

But then I decided to make a television version of Aeschylus'
trilogy *The Oresteia*, translated into alliterative Yorkshire verse
and performed in masks by an all-male cast in masks. Peter Hall's
production for the National Theatre of Tony Harrison's new
translation had been a revelation to me, cutting away the
accretions of gentility that had gathered round Greek tragedy in
English. In the journey from stage to screen, it was the masks that
interested me, and the knotty text that Tony had hammered out
for them. Designer Jocelyn Herbert, who became Tony's
indispensable collaborator, created beautiful, sobering masks,
with large open mouths and eyes, masks of a smoothness and
pallor that removed the actor underneath from any possibility of
naturalism and frenzy, however extreme his character's plight or
pressure. Masks work well at a distance; how would these work in
close-up? Masks accentuate the architecture of stage space and
the groupings within it; would that formality and rigour survive
on screen? Masks contain and compress emotion; would the
camera eye just make them look inhuman and strange?

There was enough money to shoot three performances in
succession in the Olivier, with four cameras among the audience,
each night in different positions. From some fifty hours of tape,
Peter Hall began the long task of editing down to three and a half
hours. The other crucial element was the sound. We needed an
unblemished soundtrack. The mask alters or muffles the sound in
performance, a roughness that you take in your stride in theatre,
but which would be intrusive on screen. So on a Sunday morning
the actors came in and gave one not-to-be-repeated performance
of *The Oresteia* on stage but without masks. From the almost

empty Olivier stalls, they looked about a third as tall as when they had been masked. They found it unnerving, they felt exposed, and they could not have done it in front of an audience. They had become wedded to their masks.

When *The Oresteia* was transmitted, the first and probably the last time in British television that masks had filled the screen for over four hours, their effect was both strange and powerful. The editing had caught the masks with musical precision, cutting brutally to each harsh plectrum of Harrison Birtwistle's music, or mixing and overlaying in an oceanic cry which was to the screen what the chorus was to stage. People told me that something very strange began to happen. These unchanging wooden faces seemed to change. The movement of a head, of several chorus heads in rough unison, gave resonance to individual feelings. People watching began to project emotions into the blankness of these faces and their cavernous, never-closed mouths and eyes. Their impassiveness became eloquent. This had happened in the theatre, but on the screen, with factual, close-up reality, the effect was more surprising. Our Commissioning Editor for Sport, Adrian Metcalfe, watching *The Oresteia* for a second time with an appreciation he had not had at first, said the rigidity of the masks became more interesting than the over-expressiveness of so many human faces on television.

As the 'nineties began, Channel 4 found itself in a crossfire of deregulation and competition. Cable and satellite challenged it with 'narrowcasting'. A proliferation of outlets, far exceeding the provision of original programme material, had begun. Television companies stopped thinking of themselves as broadcasters, acquired other wings and limbs and re-baptised themselves 'modern media companies'. The science of market research, 'targeting' and 'demographics', moved in; the instinctive, felt sense of an audience, which real theatre has and television used to have, wilted.

Channel 4's innovations were reduced by its successors to a recipe for turning programme-makers and technicians into out-workers. Interdependent groups of technicians and programme-makers, co-operative and continuous, with shared skills and constant self-questioning, vanished from broadcasting. They were getting harder to find in theatre. Once upon a time, theatre elders would say, we used to have ensembles. But the *zeitgeist* was against it: neo-liberalism everywhere, and Mrs Thatcher in Britain, were going for radical individualism. The market, we were persistently told, could supply all goods. Except the ones that needed to be nurtured away from markets.

The fixtures we had always taken on trust were shaking loose. A great juddering had accelerated, like the wheel of death in a fairground. What had been solid and central was flung by irresistible centrifugal force to the walls of the spinning tower, flattened and thinned.

When did it begin? With the defeat of the sky-storming 'sixties? The Big Bang of 1986, is that when it began? Was it when young people in suits started trading in futures? No doubt about it, around the theatre and the arts, landmarks, references and funds were tumbling as fast as the ideas that had sanctioned them.

Management and Marketing had become the ends of public arts activity, not just its means. Social engineering, demanding perfectly justified advances in access and representation, took the place of a theory of art and a whole society. Theory of another kind, reductively critical, occupied the academy and blitzed the very idea of quality. Cities came more and more to resemble each other, with the same branded shop-fronts, the global logos and labels, architecture knowingly plagiarising the past. It was getting harder to find anything that wasn't shop-fitting, wasn't 'concept-driven', wasn't a quotation or a remix. Shops became stages for kits of shelves and counters and cabinets and tables and chairs and bars and lighting and sound-systems which could be recombined to make settings for themed Leisure. Retail had altered since the time of my father and his hand-painted window-displays; now the mall was sovereign. Small independent shops, and the modest theatres they resembled, began to feel the squeeze.

It was the squeeze of mergers and synergies, the roar of conglomerates, the caress of capital, a cool apocalypse.

Deregulation was the back-beat of the 1980s. Deregulation let in currency speculators, gambling on the rims of melting frontiers. A flock of traders out of Ben Jonson's *Volpone* became the masked creatures of mature capitalism's carnival. Every now and then there was a spasm in the markets of fictitious money. Millions got poorer, and then the system seemed to right itself, at least for the rich. But for a moment we had been vouchsafed a glimpse of pitiless warfare, as squads of hedge funds, liquidity locusts, black flocks of video-game vultures blitzed some Asian currency out of the water, like a Pearl Harbor in reverse.

Culture was given a make-over. Opera, for rich connoisseurs, and musicals, for the coach parties, ate into the space of original theatre, which was reliant neither on heritage nor hype. A lot of theatre adopted the devices of its opponents, as cutbacks continued. New playwrights withdrew to tiny studio spaces and casts. Movie stars mounted the boards to attract audiences to short runs of classical revivals, and then returned to their main métier, trailing cloudlets of glory. Meanwhile, full-time stage actors were derided as 'luvvies' and astringent columnists and pundits dismissed theatre as an art form past its sell-by date.

We began to be screened. Screens threaded the great skein of finance capital. Screens whipped its transactions around the world in microseconds. Screens crunched digits so traders could instantly comb their data this way or that. Screens instructed us that everything was data, and that data had no permanence, though it could always be accessed, reliably the same as it was before. Data, of course, meant 'the given', 'that which is provided'. Those who wanted more than the given were made to feel out of step.

We gave hours to reading screens. They logged our purchases, tagged our movements, fed fantasy games to our young. Screens accentuated solitude, they bore out the acid comment by a 'post-Yugoslav' critic, my friend Dragan Klaic, that capitalism was a machine for engineering loneliness. But screens softened the isolation by hooking us up with each other through simulation of contact. The hero of Mark Ravenhill's mid-'nineties play *Faust (Faust Is Dead)*, a philosopher, announced, 'Reality is over; simulation begins.'

A civilisation largely consisting of wired suburbs is not unthinkable. In this eventuality, the prospects will be grim for theatre, for real theatre, unco-opted into the Great Mall of the Universe. But talking about the effect of these changes on theatre in isolation is a bit like a story told to me by a research psychologist. He pulled down a bound volume of *Spirit News* for 1939 and showed me the front page for its issue of August 28, 1939. The headline read: SPIRIT DECLARES: THERE WILL BE NO WAR. He turned to the front page a week later, September 5, 1939. It read: WAR DECLARED: BLACK DAY FOR SPIRIT WORLD. Bad for spiritualists, then, but no mention of the rest of humanity. The developments I have described are not good for theatre, for what theatre stands for, and for the people who make and love theatre. But what threatens theatre bodes no good for the whole human race.

There is another alternative to these scenarios: that people will become so underfed and fed up by facsimiles and simulacra that they will begin to reclaim the truths of theatre, and the conviviality it enacts. But for that to happen, the infrastructure of companies and initiation and availability, what the American critic and producer Robert Brustein called theatre's 'fragile membrane', must be preserved.

One of the greatest, and in hindsight most prophetic twentieth-century poems, Cavafy's 'Waiting For The Barbarians', is like the ultimate shaggy dog story with an unexpected pay-off. For years, says its narrator, the city has been expecting the arrival of the barbarians. Now, today, they are due. The elders have assembled in the senate, where they used to pass laws. The emperor is preparing a ceremonial welcome, with ministers in full regalia. The orators have been sent home, because barbarians don't like public speeches. The whole city, like the Thebes of King Oedipus, is afflicted by a plague, a plague of waiting and blaming. And while waiting, it is going to pot.

The unexpected pay-off is that the barbarians don't turn up. Border guards report that there are no barbarians any more. As the city's population disperses, sunk in thought, the narrator comes to a crestfallen conclusion:

Now what's going to happen to us without barbarians?
Those people were a kind of solution.

It is tempting to let one's thinking take the shape of an
apocalyptic showdown. Since John wrote Revelations, we have
figured apocalypse as a final, defining battle against alien,
destructive invaders. We seem to relish such stirring, ultimate
conflicts, as much in cultural as in religious speculation about the
future. The great dystopian novels of this century, Huxley's *Brave
New World* and Orwell's *1984* offer images of treacly, anodine
mass entertainment, 'brain candy' in gruesome current parlance,
or of domineering mass communication, which Orwell
extrapolated from Stalinist films and radio. These are convenient
phantoms to justify warnings and rally resistance. But they are
seventy and fifty years old. At the turn into a new Millennium,
there are no such Manichean confrontations. Now there are deals
across dividing lines, and the villains may wear heroes' colours.
Instead of the arrival of the barbarians, instead of apocalypse, we
get the ambiguous phenomenon of Disney's musical, *The Lion
King*.

In autumn 1999 *The Lion King*, the latest venture of the
planetary entertainment corporation, comes into London
theatre. A hugely successful animated film for children, *The Lion
King*'s animal cast of characters has been theatrically realised by
Julie Taymor, who has been making gifted puppet parables,
visually entrancing holy theatre, in New York's alternative
spaces for the past twenty years. It shows how the culture and the
discoveries of the avant-garde can be taken up, well-fed, yet not
altogether appropriated.

With the engaging offhandedness of the seriously powerful,
Michael Eisner, Disney's chairman, said in a *New York Times*
piece just before the premiere, '*The Lion King* enhanced our
brand. We've been okay around the world, but in the intellectual
community in New York, we surprised them with *The Lion King*.'
Two boyish Disney executives, Peter Schneider and Tom
Schumacher, who went shopping for Julie Taymor, both grew up
in New York downtown theatre. But in the *New York Times* piece

Schumacher works to maintain his hard-boiled image. 'This is the essential difference between making movies and making theatre,' he announces wryly. 'With movies, they bring you water. With theatre, you bring your own.' The wriest remark in the article, however, comes from a seasoned Broadway producer, Rocco Landesman: 'No one on Broadway will ultimately either imitate or even attempt to compete with Disney because in the end no one else can afford to.'

Despite all my instinctive reservations about the Disney-fication of theatre, and disagreeable, reactionary Walt Disney, despite bad memories of being herded round a chillingly cute Disneyland, I am bowled over by *The Lion King*. At least my eyes are. For my eyes, it's an elating box of ravishing magic tricks, and its images stay with me for days. The most beautiful thing about Taymor's vision is her affirmation of the doubleness, the metaphorical force of theatre, where something or someone can be themselves and at the same time someone or something else. The menagerie of puppet animals, the carnival of gazelles springing on performer's arms, the rope-outlined elephant with operators inside, the panther padding softly on an elongated pram, the flocks of birds and buzzards whirled on thin wands; the imperturbability and energy of the operators; the soaring voice of an African praise-singer and the intoxicating rhythms of African percussionists in boxes either side of the stage, glowing with Richard Hudson's slatted silken sun; this is an ecstatic, elevating opening.

Like many of the century's leading theatre-makers, Julie Taymor has learned her craft as director and designer in the theatres of Asia. At many points she makes *The Lion King* more of a ceremonial than a musical. It is when the words and most of the songs that are not African take over that the piece settles back into sanitised, ecumenical spirituality. 'Look into yourself; you are more than you have become. Take your place in the circle of life', intones the old lion king to his son. Sententious ballads of New Age philosophy move in; the real sense of wonder that has been generated dwindles; the other side of Taymor's artistic inheritance, the political and moral puppetry she learned from the Bread and Puppet Theatre, vanishes, like the silken silver cloth pulled down a plug-hole in her depiction of drought in Africa.

The battle with the forces of evil feels more like a plot requirement than the kind of confrontation undergone by Hamlet with Claudius, or the protagonists of Peter Brook's *The Mahabharata* – another theatre fable of the search for wisdom in a cosmos of big powers and strong animals. You become aware that, as in every Broadway show, everything has been relentlessly amplified, and you feel fatigued.

Maybe there's another reason why the tale of a good king supplanted by a wicked brother is presented in such a dramatically unengaging way. Perhaps it cuts too close to a still aching Disney bone. For as well as straining after the universality so beloved of global corporations, this plot-line remorselessly echoes a conflict much more down to earth and closer to home: the feud between Jeffrey Katzenberg and Michael Eisner across the peaks of the Disney empire itself.

The facts are simple. Katzenberg was brought into Disney by Eisner, as the head, or vice-president, of its film division (we must not forget that the empire has many profit-centres – theme parks, hotels, model towns and merchandising being among its major principalities). In ten years, Katzenberg succeeded in turning Disney movies around, from a small to a mammoth profit. The animated film of *The Lion King* was one of his greatest successes.

Disney prospered. Eisner and Katzenberg became close friends, and looked like a winning team. One day, Katzenberg said to Eisner that he would like to become President of the whole Disney caboodle. After a brief reflection, Eisner told Katzenberg he couldn't.

An archetypal falling-out followed, complete with a prominent court-case in which Katzenberg sued Disney for $250 million for breach of contract, $250 million being the two per cent of profits of the films Katzenberg had overseen, which his contract guaranteed him. A settlement was made, and Katzenberg, in a final twist of the knife, left to help form Steven Spielberg's rival operation SKG, which set about beating Disney on its own animated territory.

You don't need to be a mythographer to see the parallels between the struggles of two lions to be king and the Katzenberg-Eisner vendettas, to sense that behind the overworked ritual afflatus of *The Lion King* and its obsessive appeal to the ennobling *Hamlet* story, lies the most rending corporate struggle in Disney's history. No wonder the storytelling is inhibited, no wonder the king's wicked brother is a campy, stereotyped sub-Captain Hook, no wonder none of the Kipling-esque ambiguities and resonances of a child's coming of age in a world of warring adults is ever sounded. The defeat of the Lion King's father by his uncle is too redolent of this recent corporate struggle for power and cash, which is not the stuff of uplifting family entertainment.

But Taymor's Brechtian/Oriental doubleness, the determination to show theatrical workings through beautiful demystifications of illusion, keep coming back to refresh the eye and the spirit. The stampede that kills the hero's father is realised with all the trickery and self-evident illusion any child could ask for: from tiny mouse-like silhouettes in a narrow canyon through icons on a revolving canvas thrusting downstage to leaping, crazed and malicious creatures, all pointed directly at us, a fearful image of unstoppable power. Her calculations of scale, proportion and perspective produce the magic of multiple seeing.

But it is mainly seeing. *The Lion King* is the descendant of the seventeenth-century theatre of spectacle, the masques designed by Inigo Jones for the court of Charles I, with words by Ben Jonson and music by Purcell. These neoclassical paeans of praise to the monarch, resplendent in imagery, song and dance, took the place of the visual restraint of Shakespeare's theatre. Pageantry replaced poetry, as it does in this culture; compare the Millennium Dome handed over to the interior designers with their synthetic sense of generalised wonder, rather than being imagined by the poets. Think of its Zones being devised and staged by poets of the theatre, like Ted Hughes or Tony Harrison, John Fox or Forced Entertainment, Adrian Mitchell or spellbinding Ken Campbell. But they're not committee people, they may not be sponsor-friendly, they're shaggy.

Julie Taymor's prodigious inventiveness has not been swamped by the reputed $10 million spent by Disney on *The Lion King*. She is too determined and canny for that, while being close enough to the feelgood ethos that is one of Disney's incarnations. But something of the rough, ragged, outcast honesty of the theatre in which she began has been lost. Impecunious secular theatre of the underdog has been replaced by big-budget holy populist theatre. To measure the difference, you only have to look at one of Europe's theatre pioneers, even more influenced by Oriental theatre: Ariane Mnouchkine.

No End But Perfect Happiness

To claim that theatre is ineffective would be the
same as saying that erosion has no effect, and that's
not true; you can see that erosion is effective. You
might say that theatre erodes barbarism, just a bit.

Ariane Mnouchkine

Ariane Mnouchkine calls her theatre Le Théâtre du Soleil,
the Theatre of the Sun. When I spend a weekend with
her, in August 1999, her living room is scattered with
videos, books and magazines about the forthcoming solar eclipse.
She's five months into rehearsals for her new production, four
weeks from the premiere. 'But if the rehearsals are going well on
the day of the eclipse, we will all take a couple of hours off to
watch it.'

It would be an appropriate move in many ways. The
togetherness, to start with. Ariane has succeeded in maintaining
a troupe for thirty-five years. Not with an unchanging group of
people; there have been new waves and departures. But a nucleus
has remained constant, and so has the 'field of force' which
Ariane has created with them.

If they watch the eclipse together, it will be apt in another way:
what the Théâtre du Soleil has been doing from the outset is to
stare into the molten heart of theatre through the lens of some of
its oldest forms. And it has sustained this solar probe by
embodying in its own structures as a troupe and in its welcome to

audiences, a vision of possible life in common. It's not a Utopia, it's not somewhere over the rainbow, but you come away from her theatre in the Cartoucherie on the outskirts of Paris with a taste of hope.

The lobby of the Théâtre du Soleil is one of the most seductive places to await a performance. Its size makes it luxurious, like an eighteenth-century London pleasure garden. The walls are repainted to suit each new show. A huge map of Asia, lovingly painted like street-mural, told about India and Cambodia, for the Soleil's two plays on their histories. For her play about Tibet, they were peppered with painted Buddhas, in colours that looked faded by sun and time. The food counter was selling spring rolls and delicious soup noodles.

Each night, Ariane herself opens the front doors to let the audience in, and tears their tickets. At the interval, she wanders around emptying ashtrays, while those actors who aren't needed at the start of Part Two serve at the bar. An actor tells a member of the audience that if he drops his fag-end on the floor, the actors will have to pick it up. If the Théâtre du Soleil is not a kibbutz or a commune, everyone has an equal duty to help keep the place clean and ready for theatre, everyone earns the same money, everyone goes on the dole when the rehearsals over-run and funds run low.

I have known Ariane Mnouchkine since we were both barely twenty. She had taken a year off the Sorbonne to come to Oxford and improve her English at Saint Hilda's College. I was an undergraduate taking my first steps in student theatre, along with John McGrath, Ken Loach, Anthony Page and other playwrights and directors-to-be in the great English amateur tradition of university drama, so rare in other countries, so productive for our own theatre. Ariane seized her opportunities, odd-jobbing on Anthony Page's *Coriolanus*, walking on in Ken Loach's *I Am A Camera*, and assisting John McGrath on *Bloomsday*, an adaptation of Joyce's *Ulysses*, in which I was acting. On a bus back to her college after a rehearsal of *Coriolanus*, she had what she describes as a *coup de foudre*, a revelation like a thunderclap that, whatever her family had in mind for her, she was going to be in, make and live theatre.

She came from an artistic, even raffish family. Her father, Alexandre Mnouchkine, was a Russian film-maker, and, after emigrating to France, one of the pioneers of French cinema. Her mother June had the devastating beauty of a Vivien Leigh, and came from a theatrical family – her brother, Nicholas Hannen, was a regular Shakespearean at the Old Vic. When I see her now, she still reminds me of a young Russian woman, out of Gorki rather than Chekhov. The same bustling energy. The same soft, even girlish voice, though in political debate it acquires edge and extra speed; she has learned to be a tough wrangler, as a theatre-maker must. Now the hair is greyer, the body fuller than when I met her. But the vivacity is undimmed, and the friendliness. Claude Roy, a vivid commentator on French theatre, called her theatre 'un atelier de l'amitié', a 'workshop of friendship'.

She returned from Oxford to the Sorbonne, founded a student theatre group inspired by Oxford's do-it-yourself student drama societies. Ken Loach wrote her a long letter of advice on strategy. She made the first of her many subsequent trips to Asia, which she sees as the fountainhead of the art of the actor. Back in Paris, her group played in a Roman amphitheatre, a Communist youth hostel. In 1964, she formed the Théâtre du Soleil, and in 1967 they had their first hit, Arnold Wesker's *The Kitchen*, played, along with *A Midsummer Night's Dream*, in an intimate circus-ring, the Cirque d'Hiver. I like the fact that these first productions mirror each other. The magic of the midsummer forest leads to realistic truths about love. The realism of Wesker's kitchen becomes microcosmic because every implement in the metal kitchen is mimed. 'I wouldn't have done the play if his stage direction hadn't specifically insisted on that,' she says.

The events of 1968 challenged Ariane and her young group. Their response was to channel the questioning right back into the most theatrical forms they could muster. Impelled politically and artistically, Ariane sought to plunge into the people's forms of theatre. A provincial town council gave them an abandoned salt factory for the summer. Here, above all, they learned how to use masks and play commedia dell'arte. One evening the locals asked them for an impromptu show. They set up street stages, lit them with candles and improvised simple situations. It worked like a dream, and the result, after four months' more work, was *The Clowns*, a show in which each actor strove to find 'the clown buried within him'.

Everybody's defences were pierced, social satire and self-scrutiny were forged into a bold language of gesture and sound. Now, equipped with a repertoire of popular theatrical skills, a hard-won group identity, and a first taste of the joy and pain of collective authorship, they were ready to tackle a big political subject. The Piccolo Teatro of Milan was ready to co-produce it. A Paris architect researching industrial spaces for art venues tipped Ariane off about the Cartoucherie, a former munitions factory in the Bois de Vincennes, where the Théâtre du Soleil now occupies two brick-and-iron hangars around a spacious military parade ground. The French army held the site from 1791. During the Algerian War, it housed imprisoned Algerian independence fighters. I re-read what I wrote in 1971 about the place and this inaugural production. It still conveys the elation felt by anyone who saw *1789: The French Revolution Year One*:

> The first thing you see when you go in, fighting your way in a clamorous queue which is likely to contain Sorbonne students, Left Bank Maoists and a party of workers from the Renault factory, is the actors making up and getting into costume in full view. No secrets here, and no conventional stage and auditorium either: instead, five rostrums are planted round the walls, leaving a football-pitch-size space in the centre. Here you stand to watch the show. Yes, stand – like a football crowd, like Speakers' Corner, like going to the fair, your attention grabbed by competing side-shows.
>
> A fairground is what this hangar will become: for *1789* is the story of the French Revolution played by fairground actors, travelling mimes and mountebanks, using all the

devices of the popular theatre to give the people's view of the Revolution. The lurid stereotypes of bourgeois history-books are banished – no tight-lipped Robespierre, no dashing Danton, not a guillotine in sight. Instead, *1789* gives voice to the people of the streets, not the bloodthirsty rabble of tradition, but inventive celebrants of change performing graphic scenes which move swiftly from platform to platform and often plunge directly into the audience, ploughing through the crowd. This theatrical marketplace also recalls irresistibly the ecstatic debates and feverish all-night meetings of May 1968, and the analogy is no accident. Both revolutions, the production seems to say, had to be contained and repressed by authority because the *fête révolutionnaire*, if allowed to reach its ultimate conclusion, might have brought absolute change.

Here comes an ailing fairy-tale King, bent over a crutch, flanked by bird-masked figures representing Nobility and Clergy. They sit on the back of a Donkey, the People. The Donkey-actor hees and haws and overturns King, Nobility and Clergy. Applause: the fairground players remove their masks and bow.

A puppet-theatre is set up, and these resourceful players present the political double-crossing of the Third Estate, Punch-and-Judy style. Then, just as the people of France imagined it, we see how Louis is seduced from the path of righteousness by a lubricious entourage of mistresses and the evil witch-doctor Cagliostro, the Rasputin of French historical legend.

And then, in one of the show's most riveting episodes, the lights dim, all goes quiet, and we gradually hear whispers. *Approchez, approchez*, whispers an actor, and we cluster round. With rising excitement, as if he'd just come panting from the event itself, he gives a blow-by-blow account of how he and his comrades took the Bastille. All round the theatre actors are whispering this precious story to little groups of listeners in the dark. Their voices weave together, mount into a triumphant crescendo of victory, the lights blaze on, and the whole place explodes into carnival, here and now, and we become the people of Paris celebrating la fête de la Bastille. Here, now, we shy coconuts at models of the Bastille: over there, minuscule David defeats gigantic Goliath. There's a wrestling match between Tyranny and the People, acrobatics, wheels of fortune, escapologists, pretty girls handing out tricolour sweets and nosegays, it's infectious, you never want it to end.

But – again the leitmotif of *1789* – festivity is a threat to authority, and must be kept in hand. A 'liberal' aristocrat, La Fayette, steps into the carnival: 'Friends, now it's time to go home, to remain calm and quiet: I ask you not to gather together. I order you to cease these reckless demonstrations: I forbid all public celebrations, all clamorous rejoicing, all impulsive displays of happiness which disrupt the order of property. And remember this: THE REVOLUTION IS OVER!' When the Paris police, the helmeted baton-swinging squads of *flics*, broke up 'gatherings' of young people in St Germain each night, they were making the same point, more brutally. And the audience is quick to seize the parallel: the night I went they booed La Fayette and drowned his threats by chanting and stamping out the most durable slogan of May '68, *Ce n'est qu'un début, continuons le combat.*

Three stern politicians carrying a black banner inscribed 'ORDRE' sweep Marat from the stage and reveal the victors of *1789*, the bourgeoisie, a grotesque collection of Gogolian grotesques, over-fed, over-dressed sophisticates posturing and twittering like mechanical dolls. Like a distorted parody of blasé theatregoers, they settle down to enjoy 'their' revolution: a penny-plain harlequinade in which the People, liberated by the middle class, routs the nobility and clergy and then goes quietly back to its leash. It's brilliantly ironic, a Chinese-box closing image.

On the night of *le quatorze juillet*, they gave a free performance. Five thousand people crammed into the Cartoucherie ('we felt we could take them with us to storm the Bastille all over again,' said an actress). When they reached the Bastille episode, they stopped the performance and the evening became one huge *bal populaire*, the multifarious crowd singing and dancing through the night to street-bands and Beatles records blasting the leaves off the trees of the Bois de Vincennes. It was a real fête, an ecstatic collective rejoicing, happiness let loose. So it must have been at times in 1789; now in 1971 it had been brought to life again, overflowing from the stage into the street, theatre becoming life and life momentarily elevated to the heights of theatre.

Since then, I have trekked out to the Cartoucherie many times. In 1975, for *L'Age d'Or*, about the odyssey, exploitation and survival of migrant workers in France, Ariane turned the theatre space into a great field of green grass, the space of an idyll for a story of a diaspora. Hills and slopes rose and fell under a sky festooned with strings of fairground lights, as we scrambled after the exiled families in their commedia dell'arte masks and costumes. There was a rural pleasure, almost the smell of outdoors, in these sad stories, joyfully and collectively told.

And as the shows progressed, so the theatre worked its way towards its archetypal space. A fairly steep slope of seats, for some 800 people, looking down on a bright-lit corrida-like playing space. At our right, a vast platform crammed with percussion, wind and string instruments, and with the Rasputin-esque figure of Jean-Jacques Lemêtre, the composer-performer of music for all Ariane's shows for the past fifteen years, a kind of multi-dimensional Roland Kirk. The torrent of drumming he released for the beginning of Soleil's *Les Atrides* raised the hair on my head. The exuberance with which thirty Kathakali-costumed chorus dancers and singers flung themselves yelping with excitement into Lemêtre's leaping, inexhaustible music energised the tragedy.

And from above the stage, flowing over this concurrence of space and performer, song and speech, perhaps the most miraculous scenic image of the Théâtre du Soleil: an unquench-able halogen daylight, almost white, almost never dimmed. As if daytime were in permanent attendance above the industrial skylights of the roof. In the final years of the century, this unblinking light illuminated another collectively authored show, this time exploring what theatre can do when the needs of the weak come crashing through its doors.

In 1996 the Théâtre du Soleil was occupied by immigrants. They were mostly Africans, caught out by a new law that would expel them if their papers weren't in order. These *sans papiers*, 350 of them, had found sanctuary in a church. But the police had attacked and thrown them on the street. At 10.30 at night, as Ariane's production of Molière's *Tartuffe* was reaching its climax, she was telephoned by a doctor involved in the struggle of the *sans papiers*. Could the theatre take them in? he asked her. He must have known she couldn't refuse.

Ariane doesn't like the word militant; she finds it too professional, and has never joined a party. But as a citizen she continues to take action on behalf of people pushed to the margins of society and the edges of the world. She says she cannot make sense of theatre without active engagement with life. So the *sans papiers* occupied the theatre:

The Africans kept on saying to us, You're going to make a play out of us, aren't you, you will make a play about us, won't you? And I kept on answering, We can't, it's too near, it's too real, it happened to us, in our theatre, so we can't do it. And later, when it was all over – well, it's not all over, the struggle of the *sans papiers* is still going on, although the theatre is no longer giving them shelter – when I wanted to start work on Tibet, suddenly their story was standing in the way. As if I couldn't tell the story of Tibet without telling at least a little bit of their story too. But it was not possible to do it as it happened. That would have been too realistic, too close. And we would have been under close scrutiny, *haute surveillance*, by everybody, and we needed freedom of style, of theatre. That's how the two stories got connected, the thing that had happened to us, and Tibet. What happened was this: there were three weeks, while we were performing

Tartuffe, when there were 600 people coming every night to see the play, and 365 Africans living there. And they never intruded on, never troubled the performance. It was so strange. And nice, in a way.

Two years after the theatre gave asylum to some people in need, Ariane opened the doors on the show that came out of the meeting of those two stories, *Et Soudain des Nuits d'Eveil* – And Suddenly, Nights of Wakefulness. It's about Tibet, but seen through the experience, through the lens, of that occupation by the *sans papiers*, which has been heightened and theatricalised. A Tibetan delegation has come to Paris to seek recognition for their country, and to stop the French government selling fighter planes to China. When the discussions go wrong, they come, 250-strong, to squat in the theatre in protest. When the situation reaches crisis-point, they threaten to immolate themselves one by one. The whole thing provokes a crisis within the troupe.

The leading actress is outraged by such a trespass on the temple of her sacred art. A hyper-anxious administrator agonises about keeping track of the refugees' blankets. In the audience, a yuppie businessman, won over to the Tibetan cause, is sacked from his Euro-corporation, via cellphone. Two exhausted aid-workers, just back from another black hole in Somalia, crash out, next to a comic pair of militants from the Seventh Collective – which, if you didn't know, was born out of the fission of the Sixth – who can't get their act together to print a protest leaflet with the right date and meeting-place.

The style of Ariane's crowded fresco is magnified, with commedia dell'arte elegance and Buster Keaton clowning. It lifts off from the plateau of documentary report. It celebrates as it stares the worst in the face, for the war-planes leave for China at the end. Her stage is a great white piazza – white like Greek light, clear, glowing, radiant. All the way through you think it's daytime, and are astonished to come out and find it's night.

What drives Ariane and her company, what makes them keep reaching to make theatre metaphors of the times we live in, what takes them to the edge of financial survival, what makes them unwilling to settle for anything less than the fullness of theatre language – is something as strong and simple as the subtitle of their formative *1789*: 'The Revolution Has No End But Perfect Happiness'.

Every evening I open that door, and there they are. And sometimes it's dark, it's winter, it's raining, it's cold, they've taken the Metro after their work, they pay – and they pay more than I would like them to pay, but we need them to. It's expensive, it's a long way, it's tiring, and also they know that they're not going to be passive, they know that by coming to the Théâtre du Soleil they're going to work in a way, their heart, their senses, their feelings, everything is going to be shaken. Even if they're going to laugh, they know they're going to be questioned, and that it's going to last four hours, and some papers have written that it's not good, and others that it's good, so they're not sure. And still they come. If they do, it must be because they need it, they expect something, they want something, they hope for something. And probably this is the most precious and immortal part of theatre. Hope. The hope of a woman or a man coming to the theatre. The hope when they come in. And also for the actors: Is it going to be a good performance? Are they going to love each other? Are they going to be better at the end than they were at the beginning? Are we going to get out this theatre a bit stronger than when we came in? Are we going to regain a little bit of confidence in humanity, in our humanity, in our strength of mind? Are we going to be pleased? Are we going to be [a long pause, then a pounce] happy?

On the last weekend of July 1999, when the French roads are already solid with getaway holidaymakers, and the few restaurants still open in Paris are Vietnamese, I sit in Ariane's house over breakfast and we talk. It's a converted light-industial workshop near the Porte d'Orléans. It feels like the Cartoucherie: a big open space, with the original iron pillars and girders. In the kitchen, bowls from China, Japan, Indonesia, some of the Asian countries she has visited, cane sieves and strainers from India. Books about Bunraku, Noh, Kabuki, Kathakali, the new circus, theatre photography, mime, gardening.

MK: *I've always seen you as a generous person. Suppose I said the theatre is a place where you can be at your most generous. Suppose I said the theatre is an enormous playground.*

AM: A very severe playground, but you're probably right. People in the Théâtre du Soleil are conscious that they have this enormous playground, so they try to share it as much as possible. I'm not saying it's generous, it's just fair. A theatre company's house, its means and methods, should always be celebrated as an enormous playground that has been given to them. It's a privilege. It should never be like a ministry or an institution, or a post office or a laboratory. Though it is a kind of laboratory – a kitchen. It's a field of experience.

MK: *A laboratory doesn't convey the idea of pleasure.*

AM: It depends on the idea of science one has. Whenever I speak to scientists, I tell them my difficulties, how we spend weeks making mistakes before finding what we want, and I say that this isn't a very scientific way of doing things, and they usually answer, You're wrong, this is exactly how it happens with us. We have to explore all the mistakes until suddenly a divine coincidence or an accident happens. And so it's just the same with artistic research, there's a mystery. You keep on banging away at the door for weeks, and then suddenly you see it's there, the right door, only we were trying to put the wrong key in the wrong hole.

MK: *You give yourself a lot of time.*

AM: That's where the money goes. For me, that's the most important, I need it, actors need it. Sometimes I look at the work of other theatres, and I feel they are doing on stage things we would do in rehearsal, which we would look at and say, That's interesting, let's go further. And when I see other people stopping short of what I would do, it upsets me, it makes me doubt. I wonder what it is that makes me give everyone a hard time for so long.

MK: *You're looking for metaphors on stage.*

AM: Theatre for me is the world ritualised, the world turned into poetry. If the flesh of the actor or actress – I mean their flesh, their bones, their calves, their eyes – doesn't become poetic, in every sense of the term, pictorially, rhythmically, if it's not like a fine drawing or a dance, for me it isn't theatre. It's an imitation of life, it may be interesting, but it's not theatre. In a workshop, I said to someone, As long as you treat the stage like a cowshed, you'll be like a cow.

MK: *What is the stage then?*

AM: The stage is . . . first of all, it's the space in front of a temple, it depends what you're doing, but it's the deck of a ship, the wing of a bird, it's a hand, it's whatever you can imagine. But it isn't a cowshed. It's not solid earth, terra firma. It's sublime earth. A spiritual earth, which actors only touch because there's a terrestrial attraction which they can't overcome. And that's the problem I'm fighting with this present play, where the actors have to become marionettes, and marionettes don't obey gravity.

MK: *Do you learn a lot from actors?*

AM: Of course. But an actor who begins to think he knows everything stops teaching me things. The ones who teach me things are gifted actors, but they don't yet know that they know, and so go on searching. And it's through their errors and triumphs that I find out . . . I'm thinking about *Et Soudain*, and an Italian actor, Duccio [Bellugi Vannuccini]. When we started rehearsing the new play, he was in such a state of anxiety, crying at the end of each rehearsal because he was so worried about what he risked losing. I said to him, You're not going to lose anything, and even if you lose, it will be in order to gain something else. For three months he was in acute difficulty, he couldn't manage anything. But I didn't lose confidence in him, nor he in me. He continued to listen and to follow me. And it turned out we were going down the wrong alley, both of us. But together. In the end, it came. But it was from him, he was the one who made it more radical. He heard what I was saying, and he thought, well, there's no alternative but to do it like this. He didn't hoard his forces. I learned from his mistakes.

Juliana [Carneiro da Cunha] teaches me a lot. She teaches me that without truth, there's nothing. You can find yourself working with a lying actor, a skilful and lying actor. At first it's dizzying, you find yourself tipped into a kind of vertigo. Then Juliana enters, says a line, and you say, Ah that's it, and she's stripped off the terrible brilliant skin that covers everything, and you can see the wound underneath. You forget, as you work with actors, that you're not just working with first violins. A troupe can't be composed of first violins.

MK: *Because if it was, it wouldn't be like a real society?*

AM: That's it, like a society. A theatre is like a society. Although it's a bit like a society made of skimmed milk. There's no terrible macho types, no vulgar people, only people who have a dream, which is already a big thing. You have very great actors and you have people who aren't very good, and you have to find out how to work with them. When it starts to weigh on you, a director can simply drown, lower her sights. That's what happened for a while with the new play. I began thinking that the bar wasn't set high enough, and I couldn't find a way to raise it. When I raised it, everyone passed under it. I was trying to lift it up too much, too soon.

MK: *You need a lot of patience.*

AM: Believe it or not, I'm very patient. Which doesn't mean I don't get angry. Maybe I'm even too patient. I always hope. And I don't know how to give up, or I give up too late. I accept too late that an actor isn't going to pull something off, that I'm not God. They're not my creatures; they're their own creatures. If the birth doesn't happen, in spite of forceps and Caesarean, it means there was no baby inside, and I can't do anything.

MK: *You talked about revealing the wound beneath the actor's skill. I sometimes think that at the heart of all good theatre, there's a wound.*

AM: If it's just a narcissistic wound, then it doesn't begin to count. Let me say something that may surprise you. The key word in Buddhism is compassion. It's a huge word, a master word, the nerve-centre. If there's no compassion, there's no human progress. Look, everyone is wounded, more or less, physically or morally, we all know what pain means, according to our age, our circumstances. What's important for an actor, an actress, is their ability to let in the wound, whether they are aware of it or not. When a character says something, the actor who says it may never have experienced it, but what's important is that the vision, the imagination, permit a total compassion, a suffering with, in the place of, the character. If that's not there, there's no actor.

And it's the same for the audience. Why do you tremble when you see a scene with Clytemnestra, even though you haven't killed your husband, or had your daughter murdered? When we did *Iphigenia*, somebody fainted at almost every performance. We were going crazy. Every other evening, we had to see out either a young woman – generally accompanied by her father, by the way – or a mature woman. Two thousand five hundred years after the play was written. I found myself saying, Look, you've fainted because Euripides wrote this play over two thousand years ago. The young women didn't understand what I was saying, they thought it was because the theatre was hot, but the older women, they knew what I was talking about. I've got children, they would say. Incredible.

MK: *But don't you think the context for them to do that is changing? Online life, getting things through the digital system, it's changing people's perceptions. There's no context, no history or place, around our incessant information. The Internet is beginning to change our codes of behaviour. And that will affect theatre.*

AM: I don't want to come out against the Internet. It opens up knowledge – for those who have it. Personally, I'm delighted that I can get into the library in San Francisco, find a book about Bunraku I've been looking for, which has already been digitised so I can download it, use my credit card – I don't see why I should be against that.

But although we talk about globalisation, there isn't one world, there are two worlds, moving away from each other, like two continents breaking apart in the worst moments of the formation of the earth. A continent of people like you and me, who know which buttons to press to get up on the Internet, with some difficulty, and a continent that doesn't have electricity. And, which is much worse, cannot get its knowledge and its culture into the digital system. We know that when printing was invented, many things were lost. It was in one way a cultural cataclysm, but of course it enabled another flowering to happen. Take Africa, for example, they have little or no chance of being able to digitise their stories, their recipes, their dances, the names of their plants – or what you call their codes of behaviour. I'm a great believer in conservation. Things are vanishing at great speed. We've made a sieve with enormous holes in it. What we are trying to do at the Théâtre du Soleil is to maintain tools, keep them clean and polished, even if they're tools we don't know how to use very well. At least the tool is there.

It's a question of preserving differences. You can't appreciate a difference, take pleasure in it, unless it's linked in the end to some similarity, to something universal. Why are you touched by something very different? Because you touch something central and essential through this filter of difference. When someone more skilful, more compre-hensive, comes along, they will understand what these tools are for. Music, language, all the things a body is capable of doing.

Difference. Perhaps that should be the second name of Dionysus, the patron god of Athens' theatre festival, who was treated by the city of Thebes as an outsider, a *sans papiers* from the alien lands of Asia.

Difference. The keyword of theatrical language, not happily

assimilated to the codes of screen drama or print fiction, to the
structures of media and the volatility of the Net.

Difference, the test of every society. Can it respect and give
recognition to outsiders even before its laws admit them as
citizens? Can the individuals who compose society face the
undiscovered countries of their own minds, and let them in?

Always difference, theatre's livery, as it knocks at the gates,
seeking to add its spice before the inhabitants' standard fare
becomes bland, predictable, packaged, no longer nourishment.

Part Three:

theatre@risk

Pictures from the Wired World

That same elevation of the spirit, which I had felt
almost two years earlier on first getting into e-mail,
that special lightness of hope and possibility which
caused people to look up from their screens and
yelp 'This is great!', presented a first-class
marketing opportunity. Look, a little window into
the consumer's soul! We'll just slip through this
little window and market these young souls into
oblivion!

John Seabrook, *Deeper: Adventures on the Net*

Japanese artists of the eighteenth century created a new genre
and called it, beautifully, 'pictures from the floating world'. In
thousands of coloured woodcut prints they celebrated the
new neighbourhoods of leisure and entertainment in their
expanding, affluent cities. People elegantly robed took pleasure in
the innovations of fashionable and popular sites. City tea-houses.
Refined whore-houses. Kabuki theatres.

If you wanted to leave behind images of our comparable new
sites of pleasure, you might make a suite of digital images, and call
it 'pictures from the wired world'. It would have some things in
common with the floating world. Sex, for a start, in the Internet's
heavily frequented pornographic sites. But thereafter there
wouldn't be much overlap. Neither tea nor any other kind of
beverage or cuisine has much presence on the Net. And of

theatre, there would be almost no sign at all, except links to book tickets for smash-hit shows. What your 'pictures from the wired world' would have to show aplenty would be images of business. The only floating things in this world would be currency exchange rates.

And if you ventured into that world of commerce itself, you would find that the dematerialised nature of the medium was affecting its users. As I did, when, in search of money for a new project, I visited the media division of one of the City of London's biggest international accountancy firms. This firm was involved in the new world of digital television, with its glut of channels. 'What's on Channel 400 Tonight?' sang a slogan on the wall of the conference room.

I mentioned some programme ideas to a woman in a power suit, and she said, 'The systems are very interested in content-providers like you.'

Content-providers. Somehow I can't see Shakespeare priding himself on being a better content-provider than Marlowe for the theatres on Bankside as the sixteenth century drew to its close.

There is a struggle between today's equivalent of Shakespeare's 'wooden O' and the webs of fluent transmission and communication that envelop the earth. As Gulliver's body was criss-crossed by the threads of the Lilliputians, the planet is circled by a lattice-work of digital connections. Is it a learning opportunity, or a silken prison?

The Internet grew out of the needs of military intelligence and academic conferencing to become one of the truly mutual and co-operative creations of the twentieth century. John Naughton, writing A Brief History of the Future, his history of the origins of the Internet, as an engineer and a critic, tells a compelling story of communication-obsessed programmers, problem-solving technicians and information-sharing inventors. It is fully as exciting and in a deep sense selfless as the story of the scientists who split the atom, or any of the clusters of artists who, working individually but connected as groups, made the great aesthetic revolutions of this century – Picasso, Matisse, Braque; Charlie

Parker, Miles Davis, John Coltrane; Stanislavski, Meyerhold, Brecht.

Naughton recapitulates the Internet's benefits, from uncensored publication in 'the marketplace of ideas' to access to a plethora of information from the most far-flung site of 'a distributed network':

> A force of unimaginable power – a Leviathan, to use a Biblical (and Hobbesian) phrase – is loose in our world, and we are as yet barely aware of it ... Like all powerful technologies, it has an immense capacity for both good and evil. It gives freedom of speech its biggest boost since the US Constitution got its First Amendment; but by the same token, it gives racists, paedophiles and pornographers a distribution system beyond their wildest dreams. The freedom it gives me to live and work almost anywhere is the upside of the freedom it gives employers to lay off office staff and contract out their work to tele-workers on the other side of the world. The Net enables us to create 'virtual communities' of geographically dispersed people with common interests; but the industries it supplants once supported real communities of people living in close proximity to one another.

The spin-offs and trade-offs which John Naughton explores, especially those about shared time and space, are central to questions about theatre's continuation in any recognisable form, and why it should matter. Compare the wired world with the theatre in terms of the body. Theatre is about embodiment, the bodies of the audience and the bodies of the actors in the same space and a constantly reworked web of 'call and response' between them. The wired world is about bridging distance and losing embodiment – or rather manufacturing replacements for the body. 'Virtual sex', conducted in digital overalls, is the ultimate substitute.

Another picture of the wired world is the rapidly expanding cyber-marketplace. In autumn 1999 the *Guardian* listed Britain's top fifty 'cyber-entrepreneurs', collectively worth some £13 billion. The young millionaires run companies with such names as Easyshop, Gameplay, Deckchair, Click Mango, First-e, all followed by the mandatory dot com, and they sell 'data warehousing', computer software, online banking, natural health products, last-minute air travel, online games. Apart from financial and business services or Internet upgrades all the better to equip the user for the global game, the sites deal with leisure pursuits (travel, air tickets, collectibles, fashion) that are emblematic of 'lifestyle' – that slippery neologism that has been superimposed on what we used to mean by 'life'.

Lifestyle is something you can buy. Life is what you have and what you make of it. But the two main outcomes so far of the technology whose anarchic and heroic history John Naughton describes are virtual communities of lonely sexual fantasists and networks of shoppers.

But the wired world is not a mere vehicle. It is also a model of life, of thinking and seeing and mapping experience. The new media, their icons and interfaces, their downloads and hyperlinks, twine into the psyche. They offer images that to many viewers or (bland word) users are indistinguishable from the real thing. They can colour perceptions as easily as a black-and-white movie of the 1940s can be digitally 'colorised' for cable TV.

This technological imprint on imagination has been at work for years. It began with the imprint of film and television. When I was working at the National Theatre twenty years ago, the Education Department organised 'theatre days' for schools. Parties of teachers and pupils would arrive in the morning, take part in a workshop about the play with the actors and director, have a packed lunch, and go into the matinee. One afternoon, I was standing at the entrance to the Olivier Theatre as an excited, expectant school party pushed its way in for the performance. Above the hubbub, I heard one teenager turn to his teacher and ask, 'Miss, is it going to be in black and white or colour?'

This story dates from the televisual, pre-digital, pre-computer age, but it says something about technological grip on perception and senses. Now theatre must increasingly play within the parameters of the wired world.

More recently, after a matinee at the Young Vic of Tim Supple's dramatisation of *Grimm's Tales* that was crammed with gleeful ten-year-olds, I went to a London cyber-café. I had just been among an audience of intent and active kids, delighted at watching actors switch roles before their very eyes, scared when one became the Big Bad Wolf, sad about the princess locked up by her father, delighted to see the workings of a performance revealed in the Young Vic's cradling, bowl-shaped space.

The cyber-café, a hi-tech coffee-shop, was filled with very low-key young people, glued to their terminals, their *caffè latte* tepid, tapping out texts to distant receivers, or near ones, no way to tell the difference. I began to ask people what their relationship was to the computer screen. Most of them used pseudonyms for communication in one of the favourite types of site, online 'chat rooms'. All of them said their alibis helped them 'to explore other aspects of myself'.

One of them, a young woman, told me about an online cyber-wedding she had attended in this café. 'The bride was here in London, the groom was in Australia, the priest was in America. When the priest pronounced them man and wife and invited them to embrace, she went up and kissed the screen.'

There is one graphic way of showing the different worlds of theatre and cyber-space, and that is the image of the Net itself. Theatre has one acid, unforgettable image of a net. It is the net in which Clytemnestra traps her husband Agamemnon and kills him, for having killed their daughter. It is the primal real-time – but off-stage – action of Aeschylus' *Agamemnon*, and its consequences will haunt and madden everyone else to the very end of the trilogy. Here is Ted Hughes' version of Clytemnestra's killing net, completed shortly before he died. The corpses of Agamemnon and his trophy woman Cassandra are trucked on, and Clytemnestra says:

How else could I have killed this man –
My deadliest enemy?

Lies and embraces were simply my method.
The knots in the net that enmeshed him . . .
I made no mistake. See, my work
Perfected. I don't disown it.
Every possibility of error
I wrapped in a great net –
Not a fish could have slipped from the shoal.
His struggles merely tightened the tangle.

How different is the grim, ironic acknowledgement of necessity in this net from the obstacle-free service promised by the Internet. In the pre-modern ethos of theatre, the knots in the net are the bared emotions which are the stuff of life and death – the rage for revenge, the fear that a cycle of violence may never end and yet the utter necessity of killing. Knots in the Internet would be obstacles and snarl-ups, not the volatile passions of humanity.

Theatres and their audiences now meet on new ground, sifted space. Lenin once defined communism as 'soviets plus electrification'. If he were around now, he might define global capitalism as 'multinationals plus information technology'. Theatre, having been pressured over the centuries by the power of monarchs, priests and tyrants, is now at risk from a more pervasive counter-force. Marx wrote famously and poetically about everything that is solid melting into air, under the irresistible impress of capitalism's volcanic forces. Now they dissolve into digits and bits. Will the old theatre faculties be rooted enough to withstand the simulations, the weightless and fluid interfaces of the new media and the wall-to-wall markets they propel? I decide to explore the new dispensation for myself.

In September 1998 I'm sitting at a conference in the Beurs Berlage, a cavernous brick, steel and glass building constructed in 1903 as Amsterdam's stock exchange. The conference organisers have chosen to call their event *Doors of Perception: Play*, borrowing from William Blake's epigram about reality seeming infinite if the doors of perception were cleansed. Blake might have spluttered to find his sentence strung up as a banner in a stock exchange, for a conference graced by Disney and Nickleodeon. But as a craftsman-engraver, he could well have been intrigued by the potential of the computer game: *Jerusalem* on the joystick, perhaps.

Ludic design students and digital game inventors predominate in the thousand-plus international audience. The bookshop stocks cyber-punk fiction, philosophical investigations of virtuality and boxed games like *Sim City Network Edition* and *Tomb Raider II*. The bar has been turned into a computer game arcade which is obligatory at these occasions. People hunch in the half-dark, driving images of cars at speed, pixel-warriors in ferocious combat, eerily smooth landscapes in seemingly infinite extension.

In the main hall, projections play on giant inflatables hung from the high roof, a back-beat pulses. It's the aesthetic of the motor show and the rock concert. The stage looks set to receive Janet Jackson. After a Nederlands beat poet has intoned, 'Fun never ages, fun never grows up!', Eric Zimmerman, a computer game designer and a fair clone for Woody Allen, bounces on stage wearing a neck-wrap mike, and announces, 'I design participatory experiences'. He body-swerves into French philosopher Roger Caillois's taxonomy of play ('Conflict, Chance, Mimicry, Vertigo') and concludes, 'In computer games, it's not so much the content but the actual navigation that's meaningful. Children are obsessed with process not product.'

Of course play is purposeless, that is its essence; and valuing the journey rather than the destination is a venerable spiritual, psychological and poetic position. 'I learn by going where I have to go,' said the American poet Theodore Roethke. Post-modernism, with its cult of surfaces and inexhaustible readings, would subscribe to the Sega and Nintendo approach, and loves to go metaphorically slumming in the game arcades. But a question remains: how much of an experience is this perpetual navigation, how much imagination does it stir?

The next speaker leaves little doubt about the indentured nature of play in the real world of the children's entertainment corporations. He's David Vogler, Vice President, Creative Director of Nickleodeon Media Works – Nick for short. 'Nick is a state of mind,' says this eerily slow, sallow young/old man in black crew-neck. Grimly playful, he reels out the TV, online and consumer products (toys, to you and me) which Nickleodeon manufactures. The crown of his speech is dissertation on Gak, a gluey, globby substance. Like every successful product, Gak has a unique selling point: squeezed into a crevice or through a small aperture, it produces the most horrible belches and burps and farts. With cross-promotion on Nickleodeon's TV and online outlets, it has sold eight million customised splats in its first year. 'The splat-shaped cardboard and cellophane wrapping we came up with blurs the border between the package and the play,' pronounces this philosopher of the market.

He puts on a video of him demonstrating the Gak fart-producing pump. He lays out the spin-offs of this reincarnated plasticine: 'Smell My Gak', with pizza, bubblegum and popcorn flavours; and 'Solar-Sensitive Gak', which changes colour as the sun hits it. I shout 'Enough is enough!', causing some surprise in the largely spellbound audience. This man comes from Nickleodeon, for God's sake! shriek their collective careerist reflexes.

Then comes Jogi Panghaal. He works mostly in rural India, using new media to help village craftsmen to relate to distant users they can't see or know, because the market for their craft work has dried up in the villages. Jogi, tall and bearded, projects silent images of the graphic make-up of a Kathakali dancer, the play of hands and fingers, saris and muslins that punch their colours into the air. 'Play has been understood in the Indian subcontinent as an activity that makes the body move in a certain way which produces joy,' he says, showing entwined bodies sculpted into temple walls.

Jogi is the first person to talk about the body. For the other speakers, it seems a given that the mind is dissociated from the body as the 'user', that peculiarly bet-hedging computer term, sits at a keyboard and terminal and minimally moves a mouse. 'You don't design play,' continues Jogi, 'you design playfully. Play generates meaningful moments in the field, like knots in a weave.'

I slip out to soak up the street of ordinary Amsterdam shoppers, then come back to hear Mitchell Resnick of the MIT Media Lab, a bushy-haired smiler for whom Elliott Gould would be good casting, announce that he believes in 'The Lifelong Kindergarten'. He demonstrates the blocks, beads, balls and badges his team have 'cyberized' to teach tiny tots size, shape and process. MIT sell their inventions to Lego. Resnick's proudest appliance is an electronic name-tag coded with its wearer's replies to a questionnaire. 'By rubbing two tags together when you meet someone, you can quickly find out what you have in common,' says the elated Resnick. 'For example, the first question might have been: "What do you consider the greatest danger for the Internet?" It makes starting conversations easier.' For some, perhaps.

Mitch makes way for a diminutive art-historian, Anne-Marieke Willemsen, who puts much of this techno-enthusiasm for teaching toys into perspective. She shows that tradition in play has always outlasted fashion, that the most enduring toys in history have been those made just for the fun of it, not as learning tools. The low-tech rag-doll has survived long after jointed and mechanised dolls have been left by the wayside, 'like elaborate but unwanted Christmas presents'. The rag-doll, that stained, battered, bruised, soft, first totem most children clutch close, still lives, says Anne-Marieke, 'because it can say whatever you want to make it say.' Unlike its over-specified successors.

Play, the very soil of theatre, is being appropriated by a new breed of designers and gamesters. There is a vast disparity between the confident pronouncements of the oracular techno-gurus revelling in the rhetoric of play, and their restricted experience. Most people at the Amsterdam conference – and they are the pick of their field – have slid from art school to game design to some well-paid niche in a cyber-corporation. Apple, Intel, Microsoft and Oracle are their household gods. They work obsessively. Their leisure hours are spent in health zones, themed restaurants and, I would guess, multiplexes.

The Amsterdam talk-shop makes one slight and late concession to another conception of play. Two theatre-people, my friends Dragan Klaic, and Tony Graham, who runs London's Unicorn Theatre for Children, are drafted onto an end-of-day panel, where designers and digital types easily outnumber them. Dragan talks about how children's plays are helping young Bosnian refugees and their Dutch peers to come to terms with exile and assimilation. Tony, using a simple, ancient example, speaks about what happens when an actor and a young audience agree to see a stick as a horse. A 'pivot of transformation', he calls such elemental theatre devices. He draws the distinction between 'mere motor activity' and imaginative engagement. But the young designers are drifting out in flocks.

In the final session of the conference, a troupe of Dutch dancers struggles pluckily to compete with the digital derring-do of Lara Croft, the computer-game heroine of *Tomb Raider*, projected in real time on the cyclorama around them. Lara has been chosen by Britain's science minister as 'an ambassador for British scientific excellence'. She wears a rubber vest and hot-pants, 'has an Uzi and is really hard, but is sexy too', in the words of a games developer from her software creators, and has sold 15 million copies worldwide. As she plummets and soars, surmounts horrendous disasters without consequence and impassively sidesteps catastrophes, your eyes go to her synthetic feats on the screen, not to the real, gravity-bound bodies of the dancers in front of them.

But that persistent rag-doll cuddled by a child, that stick horse animated by an actor, give me some hope that play, the seed-bed of theatre, has roots too deep to be permanently imprinted by the digital game-makers.

A few weeks later, in New York, I see a placard for a much-awaited video game in the Radio Shack store near Times Square. Its designer was hailed as a hero of interactive gaming at the conference in Amsterdam, where he demonstrated this new build-your-own-city-and-face-real-hazards computer game. The placard radiates fashionable empowerment language:

*Get Ready for The Power Trip of a Lifetime.
*Sim City 3000: Create and Control Your Own Urban Empire.

*Tool and Design – Everything from Bauhaus to Ranch-house.
*Real Landmarks which You Add:
A Piece of Paris or a Measure of Manhattan.

The screen simulations of urban living are doing well, while the real cities are re-zoned to divide the haves from the have-nots. The haves get their planners, architects and designers to give their zones a cosmetic makeover, choosing motifs from a style-box not unlike Sim City's. Security and surveillance devices wired into the city's nervous system keep these crisply confected compounds clear of aliens and undesirables. If there are any theatres within them, they are likely to have a homogenous audience and a safe programme. But most remaining theatres are outside the compound, at the rougher, untidier, more mixed and boisterous end of the inner city.

Theatre thrives on real cities, on their unpredictable mixtures and encounters, the way they bring you up against whoever is unlike you.

Public transport, public libraries, public spaces for celebration or protest are the stages for the city's acknowledgment of difference and diversity. Theatre thrives on this rich human stew, because theatre is fascinated by the outsider, the stranger, the exception. And because theatre itself is the Other, different from the drift of media and communications, a place of gods and ghosts, devils and an innate democracy.

If it is able to follow its own path, that is. In the second chorus of *Antigone*, Sophocles, invoking humankind as the greatest wonder on earth, praises 'the passions that raise cities' (in Timberlake Wertenbaker's version). Those passions are being tamed, pressured, standardised. Take away public space by crowding it with commercial messages, take away the jostling quality of crowds, put a financial or cultural intimidation in the way of people entering a theatre, and it becomes thinned, a simulacrum of its real self. Pull people out to the margins of the city by making the malls even more magnetic, and audiences in the centres will grow even more homogenised. Give or take a few years, e-commerce may empty shopping malls, as more and more transactions are made from home, and isolation, soothed by electronic information and entertainment, becomes normality.

There will then be two possibilities: either the faculty of making and enjoying theatre will wither, and tele-entertainment will supply all narrative needs; or theatres will start up again, in the spaces between the malls and the theme parks.

Either mass-audience sports in vast stadiums will supply all needs for sharing a big story together live; or people will seek something other than the adversarial immediacy of sport, in live performance of smaller stories, using language as well as spectacle, drawing on the new media perhaps, but not to dilute unaided dramatic encounter.

Either people will roam the Internet for interactions and relationships as well as information, using the anonymity of digital talk to rehearse fantasies and freedoms; or they will recognise their loneliness within the global market, and start to make and frequent places where individuals can become an audience, that brief paradigm of living together.

Is there a doctor in the house? was the cry in the medieval morality plays, calling for a surgeon to bind up the wounds of Saint George in his fight against the Dragon. The equivalent today might be: Are there theatre-makers in the house to evolve theatre to face up to the mutations of online life?

Theatre of Mutations

Having birthed your digital twin, you'll be able to
take it home in a bundle of software and load it on
to your computer where your surrogate self can
deliver e-mail messages to friends and colleagues;
serve as a size-accurate model to try on virtual
fashions; and even stand in for the star of your
favourite video game.

Andrea Moed, *Populate: Raising the Avatar Nation*

We live in an age of simple seeing; simple but cumulative; fantastically accelerated, but fundamentally simple. The language of theatre is made of alphabets of multiple seeing. Theatre semantics makes it possible for something to be both itself and something else, to be real and to be a metaphor at one and the same time. This is what makes it the antithesis of both camera and digital culture.

When Magritte painted a curly pipe and appended to it the phrase, *Ceci n'est pas une pipe*, 'This is not a pipe', he was wittily alerting us to the arbitrariness of language and categories. But when Shakespeare's Troilus, shattered by the evidence that his beloved Cressida is betraying him with a warrior from the Trojan camp, cries out, 'This is, and is not, Cressid', he is pointing to a painful truth of experience. He believes that she is the love of his life (though the language Shakespeare gives him warns us that his emotions may be over-effusive). She looks as desirable as ever, but the evidence of his eyes tells him she is betraying him. She is, and yet is not, his Cressida.

Life is ingrained with duplicity. Sartre was not wrong about the disparity between our imagined essence and our real actions. We are only intermittently in step with what we believe ourselves to be. The currents, as Hamlet puts it, turn awry. We can, in a Sartrean way, call this discontinuity, 'bad faith' or 'betrayal'. Or we can, as theatre does, make manifest the gap between life's script and its performance. In theatre, the sign and the signified are in a playful, perpetually renewed relationship, never a fixed contract of meaning.

Metaphor, the essence of theatre language, enables us to see around the edges of given reality, for it does not hide the make-believe of its pictures. Literalism, the mode of lens, film and videotape, stretches its captured segments of behaviour from side to side of the screen. Synthetic imagery, the vocabulary of the digital world, does not even try to mirror the real. At the flick of a keyboard key, the text, the image, the voice can be dislocated into its binary building blocks and tucked away.

There is no single species of theatre metaphor. The simplest – a common object made to stand in for a living creature by the actor's animation and the audience's concurrence – can be seen in the bundle-as-baby, in medieval mystery plays. But from early on, naïve make-believe is turned to powerful play. In the Wakefield Mystery Play, *Mak the Sheepstealer*, the hero conceals a stolen sheep as a baby in the family cradle, is then found out, and beaten. But this knockabout stuff leads to the nativity of Jesus, where a baby is represented by the same swaddling bundle.

The nursery illusion of the broomstick-as-horse in the hands of a bucking actor is turned to darker uses in Peter Shaffer's *Equus*, opening portals into the violence of the psyche. The movie of *Equus* makes it less resonant, more a literal account of trouble in the stables.

In the fourth act of *King Lear*, we are asked to look at a bare stage on which two old men have fetched up, during England's convulsive civil war. Gloucester has been blinded by Lear's son-in-law and daughter, and has decided to end his life by jumping

off the cliffs at Dover. His heartbroken son Edgar, disguised as a
wretched beggar, leads him to 'the cliffs of Dover' – in fact, to this
bare stage, to anywhere. The stage becomes a philosophical space
for an experiment about hope and despair. The entry ticket for us
to witness this test-bench of behaviour is to abandon our
everyday vision of things, and suspend our disbelief for a while.
There is even a grim reference to this different way of seeing in
Gloucester's half-line, 'I stumbled when I saw.' And in mad Lear's
bitter words of consolation when he sees blind Gloucester: 'A
man may see how this world goes with no eyes.'

We watch the actor playing Edgar, dissembling as a beggar, tell
his real father another lie. Gloucester asks him whether they
really are at the top of the cliffs, and Edgar comes out with a dizzying account of the view from the Dover heights. Trusting the
world beyond his blindness, Gloucester summons up his courage
and jumps.

Gloucester falls forward says the stage direction. What we
actually see is a body slumping from a kneeling to a lying position
on the stage floor. Edgar weeps, but has to stifle his tears and
pretend to be someone at the foot of the cliffs who finds the old
man miraculously still alive. We, the audience, have been given
a bitter display of the limits and fragility of our understanding of
the world and our trust in people and things. The instrument is
the multiple seeing of theatre language. This is what William
Blake meant when he called upon the readers of his illuminated
books 'to see not with, but through, the eye'.

But Shakespeare has one final trick in store: the trick of beauty.
Edgar's speech to his father about the view from 'the cliff-top' is not
just a clever commedia dell'arte routine. It is a beautiful vignette of
steady life in fertile nature, a reminder that whatever the horrors
before our eyes, life elsewhere goes on, and that the inventive language of theatre, facing the worst we can do to each other, will not
go dumb or deaf. Just listen to Shakespeare's sound-picture:

The murmuring surge
That on th'unnumbered idle pebble chafes
Cannot be heard so high.

In a prefigured response to impending digital culture, arresting visual pieces, visionary, painterly, sculptural, hi-tech, have begun to appear in the theatre, like updated Strindbergian Dream Plays. Theatre cannot ignore the perceptual changes of the new technology. So some of the best theatre-makers now are taking language through changes, mutations for the altered environment of digital networks. The Canadian director Robert Lepage mutates theatre language within a skein of technology and synthetic images. Mark Ravenhill's confrontational plays give voice to the mutilations and defiant mutations of emotional and sexual lives now. Both artists seek to renew theatre's fundamentally metaphorical nature.

Robert Lepage is making romantic theatre for the wired world. He has a screen sensibility and the capacity to do all the things a good film editor can do – cut and mix and montage and cross-fade. *Needles and Opium* paralleled his own unhappy love affair with the Paris romance between Miles Davis and Juliette Greco. Out of his Left-Bank hotel room, he hoisted himself into a trapeze harness and seemed to plummet in front of a brilliantly synchronised video screen of the frontage of buildings. Then he rewound his falling, so it became flying, and played with it back and forth, like a piece of tape or film between the heads. In *Elsinore*, another one-man show, sliding panels and mirrors moved and glided around him with limitless virtuosity so that he could draw every part in *Hamlet* into his solitude, until finally he was duelling against himself, through a tiny video camera on the end of his fencing foil. It recalled the pleasure of illusions, the power of playing with puppets, running a doll's house, turning pain into an elaborate toy.

Robert Lepage tells stories which have been altered by the new technology, but he cleaves to theatre's difference from circuits and screens. 'Theatre's cosmology is vertical,' he has written; 'it is in touch with the gods. Cinema is horizontal, its letter-box screen is at home with the things of the earth.' When I talked to Lepage, he saluted the new media, and their tonic effect on a complacent theatre:

The recording media, cassette players, film, TV and live performance – the now communications – are converging. We have to be ready for the outcome, we have to invite it in. When we talk about virtual realities and interactive video we are talking about recorded and electronic media borrowing from the theatre. Earlier in this century it used to be theatre borrowing from the other gangs. There is a dialogue and we have to see it coming, let ourselves go, see how we can be penetrated by the other forms, how that might merge into a new form of communication or artistic expression. If theatre dies or changes or mutates, so be it. New forms of communication and communion are going to be bumping into each other.

The audience of today is not the same audience as fifteen or twenty years ago. It's an audience which has become extremely film-cultivated, televisual, it's used to decoding stories which are told in a very jump-cut way now, so they come to the theatre, try to decipher stories that are beginning-middle-and-end, and they are used to running faster than the artists. People in theatre are still working to the old code of the early twentieth century, the old conventions. I think that the audience is going very, very fast. We don't have to run after them, but we have to consider that filmic vocabulary is part of theatre. Theatre is beginning to wake up and become more expressionist and impressionist and surrealist and cubist. In my own work, the difference is that my starting point is a strictly formal one: just trying to get a form on stage and to have actors and collaborators visit that space, that form, and try to find what stories it contains.

I spent a day watching his *Seven Streams of the River Ota*. He spent three years making it. The Ota is the river that flows through Hiroshima. The piece is about the fallout, in every sense of the word, of the atom bombs dropped on Hiroshima. I had gone to Edinburgh a year earlier to see it as 'work in progress', in a sports centre. About halfway through, the technology collapsed, and he called off the performance. But I'd seen enough to know I had to catch it wherever it next surfaced. Because it wasn't just technological, it was human. It grew out of collective work, out of the lives of his group of many nationalities – North American, European, Asian, their many languages, many professional and emotional experiences. It was handmade as well as delivered by switches and circuits.

What I remember is a mixture of people in situations and stage structures. A Japanese woman scarred by the bomb, ashamed of her ugliness. A soprano practising a yearning aria. A young man with AIDS who goes to Amsterdam, marries and kills himself. That is to say, he invites his friends to the wedding in the house of the doctor who is going to put him to death. They crack open some bottles, toast the couple, and the bridegroom is then hooked up to the dripfeed machine which will gradually kill him. We watched this. For hours, it seemed. A man hooked up to a medical machine. Everyone in their best outfits. It was the longest, most immobile time I've ever spent in a theatre. It was real, present time. You wouldn't have trusted it in any other medium.

And this unbearable material was framed and held in intricate staging, a use of space that acknowledges our knowledge of split screens, icons, logos, simulations. He loves playing with cramped space, and there's a delirious scene with twenty people in a rooming-house packed into its one bathroom. Or he sets strips of other action down the sides of the stage, like a window full of TV screens tuned to different channels. Or he uses the mystery of reflections, copies, lighting on the threshold of darkness, so we decipher faint signs. Or he borrows the clarity of Japanese space, sliding paper screens with black rims, light wooden floors.

And then he brings in the mechanics of theatre itself, the outrageous precision of farce. He injects a Feydeau farce – slammed doors, razor-thin coincidences, micro-second timing, battle-axe wives, frilly chambermaids and frisky husbands – into the subplot of a Canadian diplomat two-timing his wife in Japan. Feydeau's play-within-the-play is performed by a visiting Quebec theatre troupe. The diplomat lusts after the pouting soubrette, and they wind up in a hotel room in Osaka. Lepage could have made the troupe perform Racine, equally formalised but abstract. The calibrated hysteria of farce made his real theme – how to live after Hiroshima – even more immediate and rending.

In the plays of Mark Ravenhill – to choose just one of the recalcitrant gang of the new British playwrights – the values of glossy uniformity are subverted, counter-cultures are pitilessly set on stage, and the price of new lifestyles is spelt out in an unwavering, ironic voice. For a vital part of theatre's vocation is to push back the limits of language and representation, transgress decorum, crack open consensus. In times like ours, when new media and global business are installing a uniformity clothed in diversity, this instinctive boundary-breaking becomes confrontational. When artistic originality is rapidly snapped up and cloned into decoration, when non-conformity, within certain limits, becomes a commodity, theatre seeks to disturb. Playing dirty, infringing 'the decencies' can become means of breaking through the screens of simulation. It is playwrights, rather than directors seeking their own kind of authorship, who lead this charge.

Mark Ravenhill's first play, *Shopping and Fucking*, made shock-horror headlines when it moved from the Royal Court to the West End. There's a telling little scene early on, in which an out-of-work actress is forced to perform a Chekhov speech topless to a shyster who can give her a job. She removes her blouse and, in tears, delivers Sonya's final speech of affirmation from *Uncle Vanya*. 'One day people will know what all this was for. All this suffering. There'll be no more mysteries. But until then we have to carry on living. We must work. That's all we can do.' Halfway through her performance the sleazebag starts sobbing. Is he really moved? Is there a momentary hope for theatre? We never find out. When she has finished and put on her clothes, all he asks her is, 'Do you think you can sell?' He gives her a bag of pills, and she starts dealing in the clubs.

Mark Ravenhill's plays do not flinch from the swamp into which defenceless people in our society are sinking. *Shopping and*

Fucking takes place in a world of rent boys, drug dealing, shoplifting, junk food and telephone sex lines. At its climax, a young boy is sodomised to death. *Faust (Faust is Dead)* climaxes, after the affect-less sexual adventures of a postmodern philosopher in California, in the unmeant death through self-mutilation of a young boy, this time ordered up on the Internet. *Handbag* begins with an on-stage *in vitro* conception, as a gay and a lesbian couple decide to have a child. It ends with the choking baby being killed, as his junkie 'father' tries to jolt him into breathing again with a cigarette-end. Cross-cut with this contemporary horror story is a chilling take on the baby left in a handbag in Wilde's *The Importance of Being Earnest*. In Ravenhill's rewrite, the guardian of this foundling and of many other abandoned Victorian children turns out to be an agonised paedophile.

He told me about a Christian lady with blazing eyes who was leafleting the audience in Haywards Heath, urging them not to see *Shopping and Fucking* on tour. She was so indignant that she didn't realise she was talking to the author even after he had told her so. Yet an open response to Mark Ravenhill's plays would find that they have more to do with horror and compassion than opportunism and titillation; and it would find a quality of hurt and desperation in them, as in the violent and violently attacked plays of his now-dead friend and contemporary Sarah Kane, that belies tabloid descriptions of their content.

The pain which is Ravenhill's bedrock emotion comes from an impulse I would not hesitate to call moral. The thrust of his plays beyond consensus and comfort, coupled with tight structure and metaphorical rather than naturalistic vision, is a dialectical development of theatre's voice. The hyped installations of many of his equally notorious contemporaries, the *Sensation* generation of painters, sculptors and image manipulators, seem shrill gestures by comparison. But the art world, which has no defences against the rampant market other than such last-ditch exhibitionism, makes the state of theatre look positively healthy.

The often appalling actions of Ravenhill's plays occur in a wasteland of cynicism and distended individualism, a *tabula rasa* of alienation. This image of the world is Ravenhill's response, as he has said, to the seventeen years of Thatcherism, but his plays go beyond political riposte. It is clear who is the baddie in *Shopping and Fucking*: an entrepreneur who picks up – shops for – a pair of young people shoplifting in a supermarket and forces them into his sex-chat and Ecstasy-dealing activities. But the play ranges wider, into panicked and vulnerable areas of need, as the lonely young landlord brings home Gary, a rent boy with whom he has, tentatively, precariously, fallen in love. Gary, a survivor of a life that would have killed anyone less tough, finally can't take this love, and masochistically goes back on the game of shopping and fucking, being purchased and fucked, until a brutal client shoves a kitchen knife up his arse, and he dies.

I saw the play twice on Shaftesbury Avenue with a pre-dominantly young audience, taking their bottles of Becks into the auditorium, and picking up instantly on Ravenhill's style. There's a formal rigour at work, as well as outrage. The coiled-spring economy of the scenes, spliced by club music and neon slogans, makes a grid within which the most pitiful assaults on the minds and above all the bodies of the characters can be contemplated, not merely watched. A horrified face, mouth masked in blood, rising from between a boy's spread thighs is hugely distressing in itself, but it also becomes a formal sign in a theatrical depiction of devastation as taut and reflective as a Francis Bacon image.

You care for the lost rent boy Gary, as you care for his subsequent incarnations, another rent boy in *Handbag*, and Donny in *Faust is Dead*, who cuts up his own body on the Internet. The sado-masochism they have in common is not just a fling at a cheap thrill, but a last-ditch search for something real, something irreducible and shared, in a harsh, bare, terminal deadspace. 'Everything's a fucking lie, you know?' says Pete, another character in *Faust is Dead*, who is just about to pull off his shirt to show that he too is covered in cuts. 'The food, the TV, the, the music . . . it's all pretend. And this is supposed to be the one thing, one thing that's for real.' Everyone in these plays is at the mercy of more powerful people's appetites. *Handbag* ends with a situation of heartbreaking dependency. A junkie boy and girl are dependent on their dealer. The dealer wants to fuck their baby. They hold out. The dealer withdraws their supply. They give in.

'Cynicism is the starting-point for the under-thirty-fives,' said Mark Ravenhill, when we talked. 'It's the style of the times. I read a brilliant interview by Will Self, a demolition-job on Margaret Beckett, in which he said, "I'd do anything to make this column good. Why, I've even interviewed an actor." Irony and cynicism and flipness are all so valued. People like Self are anti-actor. But you can only act if you mean it, you can't be cynical about it. Well, you can, of course. Someone said, "There's a little bit of Angus Deayton in us all." Some young people in the audience at *Shopping and Fucking* laughed at the horror. I want to bring them from the cynicism to something more.'

Ravenhill knows – and this is where he has such a sharp sense of theatre language as a combination of fire and ice – that the process of crafting a play is very ordered. 'The subject may well be disorder, chaos, ambiguity, sexuality. But a lot of the time the playwright is engaging with order, form and structure. Yes, it's Apollo as well as Dionysus. I'm taking the audience on a journey which is quite structured but which leads them somewhere which is indefinable and often chaotic.'

Faust is Dead is the one play he has written which is not set in the cruel metropolis, but in gravity-free California, where experiment is a lifestyle, the sexual menu is extensive and Silicon Valley is voraciously and profitably constructing ever-new cyber-tomorrows. Old Europe, in the shape of a French philosopher modelled on Michel Foucault and Jean Baudrillard, comes to New America to confirm his theory that man, the concept of Man, is dead – and to sample the West Coast s/m scene by having sex with one of the post-human natives.

Scene Ten of its twenty tight scenes begins:

Desert. Night.

Alain   This is beautiful.

Pete   You like it?

Alain   Oh yes.
This is a very beautiful place.

Pete   I guess it's okay.
I kind of prefer it on the TV.
I prefer it with a frame around it, you know?

Alain   Okay.

Pete   Like you know, it stretches out, there it goes, on and
on – you get the point from the TV – but when you
actually see it, you know . . . it's a little scary.
Excuse me, I'm gonna have to . . .

Pete *takes out the camcorder, looks through it.*

That's better.
I kind of feel okay now.
This always works for me. Some guys it's Prozac, but with
me . . .

Alain   I understand.

Alain *starts to feel* **Pete**'s *genitals.*

And shortly after this, Pete, addicted to video documentation,
starts a running commentary on their sexual encounter, in order
to make the whole thing more like TV: 'Lost under the stars,
surrounded by the splendour of nature and the mysterious
awesomeness of Death Valley, the kid is initiated into the strange
world of the homosexual.'
Faust is Dead plants its greatest depth-charge in theatre's
ageless image of seeing and blindness. The horror of damaged eyes
opens a hot line back to self-blinded Oedipus, to blinded
Gloucester, Stanley's smashed spectacles in Pinter's *The Birthday
Party*. Alain tells Pete (whose questions I have removed here) the
story of a man who meets a woman, takes her to his apartment
and makes love to her:

Alain   They are making love and she asks him a question.
Which is:

Which part of me do you find the most . . . the most
attractive?
And he replies: the eyes.
It is the eyes he finds the most attractive part of this
woman.
So, the next morning he leaves. He works. But all the time
he is thinking about this beautiful, about making love with
this beautiful woman, yes?
The following day, he is woken by the front doorbell. The
doorbell is ringing, so he jumps out of bed. It might be her.
Maybe she can't bear to be apart from him.
But it isn't her. It's the mailman. Who has a parcel for him.
So he signs for the parcel and he takes the parcel into the
kitchen and he realises that the parcel . . . smells.
His hands are trembling with excitement as he pulls away
the packaging – he wants the moment to last, but also he
wants to discover the contents.
And as the packaging falls away, a box is revealed. A
cardboard box.
The sort of box in which you might buy shoes. The sort of
cardboard box that has a lid on it.
The lid is on. He waits for a moment, delaying the moment
of pleasure and then he lifts up the lid.
And inside the box are two human eyes.
She had cut out her eyes.

Alain tells the story to ask a philosophical question: Who is the
seducer and who the seduced? The man or the woman? With
eerie detachment, Pete shows his TV-naturalistic mind by asking
how the woman could have possibly seen to put her eyes in the
box if she had already cut them out.

What makes Ravenhill's use of the eyes metaphor even more
reverberant is the way it returns in the final moments of the play.
Pete has shot Alain, in order to get back the only existing disc of
a valuable software programme. He is tending his victim in
hospital. Just before leaving 'for a meeting', he hands Alain a
present. It's a shoebox with Donny's eyes in it. Donny is the boy

who has died in the scene before by accidentally cutting his jugular vein in a masochistic session.

Now Donny appears by Alain's hospital bed. Without eyes. Donny, the emblem of Ravenhill's abiding image of the needy defencelessness of humanity, the vulnerable and abused child, of love for sale, of bodies and lives treated as commodities. Donny has come back to be with disabused Alain, to cradle him. But Donny is dead. This actor with holes for eyes must, realistically, be a ghost. A revenant from another realm, reminding us, as theatre does, from Hamlet's father's ghost to Apollo to Ariel, that there are more things in heaven and earth than are dreamed of in the world's philosophy.

In Ravenhill's latest play, *Some Explicit Polaroids*, there is another returning ghost. It's the blond-dyed, white-suited ghost of an AIDS-infected boy who was in such despair that he did not want to treat his sickness. His trash toyboy tries everything to get him to take his medication, even performing up-stage cunnilingus on a lap-dancing woman flatmate. But he dies – and almost immediately seems to revive, asking his boyfriend to toss him off beneath the white hospital deathsheet.

The ghost of this desperate dead boy, the black hole of his nihilism, haunts Ravenhill's harsh and funny dissection of a society which has denied socialist hopes and turned ideals inwards. 'I don't let the world get to me,' says one of his characters, unthinkingly using a New Age cliché in the brave hope that they can opt out of a world that finally gets to everyone.

Ravenhill's plays circulate in a milieu of mutants. His characters are ready to put their sexual identities up for grabs. Many of them are cheerful all-purpose commodities for the market, shopping and being fucked. They are disposable, and the villains of his plays – in *Polaroids*, an asset-stripper with the ear of government – are all too ready to dispose of them. Their rooms and clubs and streets are transformable, morphing from one site to another at the kick of a techno-music track, the burst of a video stream.

Few playwrights of his thirty-something generation have captured so vividly and succinctly the anything-goes anywhere of the way we are now, the way places and people and beliefs can be installed and deleted like software. The old resources of theatre, rethought for a culture of jump-cuts and hyperlinks, provide the whetstone for his scalpel.

Last Acts

Everything changes. You can make
A fresh start with your final breath.
But what has happened has happened. And the
   water
You once poured into the wine cannot be
Drained off again.

What has happened has happened. The water
You once poured into the wine cannot be
Drained off again, but
Everything changes. You can make
A fresh start with your final breath.

Bertolt Brecht, 'Everything Changes'

Autumn 1999   London

I am back on the trading floor of culture, with my wares, which scarcely fit its norms, especially *Tantalus*. The production is now being prepared in Denver, since neither Britain, home of its author and director, nor Greece, where its gods and myths originated, have been able to come up with the funds to stage it. Denver Center for the Performing Arts will have put up close to six million dollars in cash and facilities by the time the first cycle opens there in October 2000. It will play in Denver until Christmas. My goal now is to create a life after Denver for *Tantalus*, so that the results of a decade of writing and six months' rehearsing are seen by the widest possible audience. I am putting together a European theatre tour, starting in England in 2001. The Old Vic is keen, and I am beginning talks with Manchester and Sheffield. There is some prospect of touring funds from the Arts Council, though Peter Hall is sceptical, and I start the search for a business sponsor. There may also be a chance of funds from the European Union culture directorate, which has given its programme a facelift with a new name, Culture 2000. I download a forty-five-page application form from their website, and see that only the name has changed.

I am sending blurbs and schedules to theatre festivals in Athens, Paris, Dublin, Brussels and other places. I don't yet know how much the production will cost any presenter, since Denver is still in negotiation with the cast. They have secured permission from American Actors' Equity for four leading English actors ('aliens' in the union's shorthand) to join the predominantly American cast. The English actors will be away from home, rehearsing and playing in Denver, for the best part of the year 2000. In view of this, they ask for more money. This would have a knock-on effect on all the American actors' salaries, and could put the touring price of the show out of reach. It will be worked out, but John Barton is desperate, prepared stoically to forgo this, probably his last and best chance of seeing *Tantalus* produced, rather than under-cast it. Like Richard II, the more he feels his back against the wall, the more last-ditch heroic he becomes. Peter grits his teeth. Money is redistributed in the budget to try to make it work.

After the European theatre tour, I am trying to set up a television version of *Tantalus*, as a ten-part drama series. I would like it to be shot on location in Greece, with sea and rocks and Mediterranean light. I write again to Alan Yentob at BBC Television and to Michael Jackson at Channel 4. I pitched it to them at the outset, and they turned us down. The good news now is that they will have the chance to see it, though only nine months before any shooting would begin. The bad news is that television drama has become even more naturalistic and formulaic, under the pressure of competition and sprouting digital channels, narrowcasting rather than broadcasting. Essentially,

Tantalus belongs to the deeply unfashionable public library model
of television, where chance discoveries can still be made. But
public libraries, as metaphors for the media, just as in reality, are
on the defensive. On the offensive is the entertainment industry,
the rampant purveyors of video-games, TV series, annual movie
blockbusters and theme parks, with all their synergies, sellable
formats, merchandising, cross-overs and cross-ownerships. With
incurable hopefulness, I continue flogging a fifteen-hour epic saga
about the Trojan War to theatre festivals more in love with postmodern pageantry than language, and television channels ner-
vously awaiting digital blanket-bombing.

Bill Wilkinson, former finance director of the Royal
Shakespeare Company and now working with us, adds up the
touring costs for our meeting with the Arts Council drama and
touring directors. Because of the requirements of American
Equity for American actors, the total touring guarantee needed is
much higher than usual, nearly £100,000 per week. We talk
about pricing and marketing and demographics. Once more I am
aware of the exceptional scale and nature of what John has
written, which will require a special effort from every theatre we
visit, a major drum-banging job in the media and a particular
approach to the schools and universities – although they will
have discounted prices, which doesn't help ends meet.

Much wooing of actors is taking place, and is needed. We are
asking four senior, classically trained English actors to leave
family and loved ones to rehearse leading parts for the best part of
a year in Colorado. They may well have played Broadway or
Brooklyn, but this will be the first time they have been out in the
American equivalent of West Yorkshire Playhouse for a year.
Understandably, there is some hard bargaining. There is also
some high-handedness. Peter calls one leading actor with whom
he has worked, makes the pitch, invites the actor's quite good
actress wife to join the company as well. It's looking good, until
the actor leaves a message next day, saying don't even bother to
send the scripts, darling. Some older actors still retain a sense of
courage and adventure; others prefer to stick around waiting for
the film or telly between good jobs.

To get through the material in the time and money we have,
Peter still needs two young co-directors. Characteristically, he
has gone for the brightest and the best, the most challenging:
Mick Gordon, the wiry, sparky Northern Irishman who, as
artistic director at the Gate Theatre, is making it a hot-house of
classics and European plays; and James Kerr, a quiet-spoken
director who is also a classicist, who did a poignant production at
the Gate of Aeschylus' *Suppliant Women* and is about to do
Sophocles' *Ajax*. They are two of the hot figures of their
generation, and Peter is worried they will be snaffled by the Royal
Shakespeare Company before Denver signs them up.

Peter has spent his summer holiday in Greece, near our
designer Dionysis Fotopoulos. He has worked on the plays every
day, and by the time he is back, he and Dionysis have made the
basis for a design:

Everything is monochrome. The floor of the stage is grey
sand, which can become a glamorous yellow under light or a
shit colour for the war. There is a rock pool two-thirds of the
way back with water. The back of the stage is black glass.
Projections of real and surrealistic images are shown on
these black surfaces which extend the full way across the
back of the stage.

Now come the problems: there are a large number of
effects. Rain, mist, fog should not be difficult. Fire may be. A
funeral pyre has to burn centre stage over the rock pool.
Neither Dionysis nor I want the great rock to hang over the
proceedings in too literal a way. We would like to explore
the use of a hologram for this. It is three-dimensional,
apparently now quite cheap and of course can have very
many variations of texture, tone, colour and presence.

A very gently moving seascape for instance, right across
the back of the stage, would give us something quite
elemental. The same goes for complex clouds. What we are
after all the time is the elemental things – the sun, the
moon, the stars, mist, fog, the sea, waves, rain, wind. If all
this is real enough, it will give a basis for our surreal images.

It sounds like they're cooking.

I go to Greece, first to the island of Paros, for a meeting about the return of the Parthenon Marbles. The meeting – an open-air dinner for potential patrons, under the moon, with a youth folkdance group and a choir singing Theodorakis – is kicked off by the Greek Minister of Culture, Elizabeth Papazoi – the one I hadn't been able to get replies from.

She listens and nods while I make a fairly impassioned speech advocating the return of the marbles for cultural reasons:

> Phidias' breathtaking sculptures of horses and centaurs and the Panathenaic procession, filled with the energy that William Blake called 'eternal delight', are the crowning piece of the most complex and democratic, serious and playful, religious and civic culture invented in Europe. In the Athens of 2,500 years ago, topped by the architecture and art of the Parthenon, there was, for a brief but hugely resonant period, an unequalled and dynamic wholeness. Not the stasis of authoritarian regimes, but a constant interplay and productive contest between actor and athlete, soldier and philosopher, civic and theatrical, politician and citizen. Quite simply, the cultural argument for returning the Parthenon Marbles to Athens, is that, properly presented, they will mean more there than in London.

Mrs Papazoi invites me to her table, and I am able to talk with her over dinner. She is clearly still interested in *Tantalus*, not least because it meets her aim to make the Greek theatre less insular, 'less Greek' when it tackles Greek classical drama. She invites me to see her in her office before I leave. At that meeting, the most important thing she says is that she would preside over a fundraising event in Athens for the Greek shipowners and business community.

The organisers of the Athens Festival drive me round the city to see possible performing sites. In Piraeus Street, just up the hill from that port of elated departures, I see a converted nineteenth-century factory with a roof open to the skies that has a lot of character, but small capacity and reduced visibility because of its pillars. Good for amplified music and wordless spectacle (Philip Glass and Robert Wilson have just played there), but not much good for text-based drama. I then see the open-air amphitheatre on the top of Lycabettos hill, a wonderful position, commanding views of the entire city, and giving the feeling of an island suspended in the air. It has a horseshoe raked auditorium, seating some 3,000, but so steeply raked it feels close to the marble stage, around which is stone and gravel, with rocks and scrubby vegetation behind, and the sky beyond. I think it could become the *Tantalus* island. We drive back, trying to figure out what the maximum audience might be in Athens for a fifteen-hour saga in English. Three nights of 3,000 people, they think. They had wanted to show me a third space, a quarry the other side of the city, where Peter Brook performed *The Mahabharata*. But it is currently a tent city for some of the 50,000 Athenians made homeless by their earthquake in early September.

Back in London, I go down to Butler's Wharf to see Art and Business (the new slimline title of what was the Association for Business Sponsorship for the Arts) about raising sponsorship for *Tantalus*. Butler's Wharf used to provide the warehousing for goods unloaded in the then busy Pool of London, whose ships I used to watch as a child. I walk along the river, past Tower Bridge where I stood gazing, and marvel again at its constellated massiveness, today glittering in the autumn sunshine. It always conjures up my father's retail toil in Tower Bridge Road. Now I am off to a meeting about a very different kind of selling: culture to rich patrons.

Butler's Wharf has narrow streets between close-packed former warehouses, stocky brick buildings with wrought-iron winches to hoist merchandise. It is a private-sector regeneration area, transformed so fast into offices for designers and architects, expensive apartments, glossy boutiques, restaurants and museums of its previous life that the street numbers can't keep up, and I get lost. The streets are eerily quiet as I finally find my way. This isn't a city district, it isn't a neighbourhood, it's a piece of real-estate engineering. One of those segregated, one-dimensional zones that I imagine will be defended with rooftop machine-guns and roaring helicopters if the dispossessed ever rise up.

Art and Business is in a renovated warehouse: whitewashed brick, polished plank floors, bright accessories. I meet their Arts Development Manager and their Business Development Manager, a man and a woman around thirty, and we have a speedy discussion about all the angles *Tantalus* presents. They suggest that we need high-profile politicians from Britain and America as patrons – 'because business will take it more seriously.' We talk about the prospects of the fast-growing world of e-commerce, which would need a very different kind of pitch from older business, seeking a gala performance for their clients. There's no doubt that, for them, the fine arts in a noble building such as the Royal Academy provide a better opportunity than a demanding theatre piece. Would the clients and their companions stay awake through one five-hour evening of *Tantalus*? When they ask me what kind of audience it will have, I am stumped, as I always am. As I start flannelling, the man says, 'What we mean is, is it an audience that has disposable income?'

The market, the market everywhere. On my way to the next meeting, I read about Coca-Cola's new vending machine. It is fitted with a temperature sensor. When the weather gets hot, the machine notes this, and increases the price in the coin-slot window. When it cools down, the price reduces. A perfect, homeostatic merchandising, profit-improving device. A company spokesman is quoted as saying, 'If there's an increased demand, it's only natural that the price should rise.' Well, it depends what you mean by natural. He's using the same argument as Lord Falconer of Thoroton, the cabinet minister now in charge of the Millennium Dome. Answering the charge that a £57 entry price for a family is too high, he said, much more candidly, 'As a result of no public money in this scheme there had to be a price to go in. The price we are charging is extremely reasonable.' Tell that to the average South London family, Lord Falconer. Coca-Cola or Dome, the result is the same: people are being treated like cattle.

I keep walking to my next meeting. In Soho, a ticket-tout outside the Prince Edward Theatre offers me a seat for tonight's performance of *Mamma Mia!*, a 'musical' concocted out of Abba songs, one of a number of knee-jerk shows based on pop music which have been confected for the coach-party trade. I don't like being bearded on the street, so I tell the tout that he would have to pay me to see the show, and that the sound of Abba makes me throw up. If it weren't for a long queue of people waiting for returns and watching us, he'd probably thump me. The new wave of carnival revolutionaries are right, when they cry: Reclaim the Street! More and more space is being grabbed for vendors. Sexy postcards in phone booths, banner ads on websites, all touting.

When I talk to Peter Hall next day, he tells me he's heard that the Stoll Moss group, owners of the Palladium, Theatre Royal, Her Majesty's, Queen's, Lyric, Apollo, Garrick, Duchess and the Gielgud, is about to be bought by the Shubert organisation, which controls most of Broadway. (Andrew Lloyd-Webber bought Stoll Moss in the end.) Apollo Leisure, the group controlling most of the remaining London theatres and the number one houses in Bristol, Liverpool, Manchester and Edinburgh, has already been bought by another American group, SFX, described in the *Independent* as 'the world's largest live-entertainment company'. SFX promotes pop and rock concerts in the forty of America's forty-six amphitheatres that it owns. It manages sports stars, it tours shows like *Riverdance*, which does for kitsch in the 'nineties what the Red Army Ensemble did in the 'fifties. SFX has bought up the management agencies of Elton John, Blondie, Michael Jackson, Barbra Streisand and Shirley Bassey.

Well, it's all live entertainment, isn't it? You can see what market sense it all makes, how the cash registers will ring with peals of 'synergy' and 'vertical integration'. What it's likely to mean is that the new owners will fill the big West End theatres with musicals they have successfully launched in America – or concoct shows based on pop-songs that can be sold to their customer databases. The smaller theatres will house classic revivals with big-name filmstars taking a break from the ardours of the screen to make a heroic – but very brief – return to the stage. You might call this the Almeida or Donmar formula, and it's clear how it provides 'product' for theatre landlords. The commitment and continuity from actors and audience that create true theatre are not foremost; the automatism of ticket-buying as part of an out-of-town or tourist itinerary takes over.

People are being treated like cattle. People are being sold short. Indeed, people are being sold 'squit', as Beaty Bryant, the heroine of Arnold Wesker's pioneering play *Roots*, shouted nearly forty years ago. It's got smoother packaging, a more seductive swing to it, but it's the same old squit. Theatre in the straitjacket of screen supremacy and corporate mergers is simply an updated and globalized example of Wordsworth's warning, two hundred years ago in his Preface to the *Lyrical Ballads*, against 'the combined force' of information and technology.

A multitude of causes unknown to former times are now acting with a combined force to blunt the discriminating powers of the mind, and unfitting it for all voluntary exertion to reduce it to a state of almost savage torpor. The most effective of these causes are the great national events which are daily taking place, and the increasing accumulation of men in cities, where the uniformity of their occupations produces a craving for extraordinary incident which the rapid communication of news hourly gratifies. To this tendency of life and manners the literature and theatrical exhibitions of the country have conformed themselves.

All that has changed, since William Wordsworth wrote this in 1800, is the sophistication of technology and the concentration of ownership.

At the interval of *The Lion King*, I asked an American couple who were ecstatically enjoying themselves whether they saw much theatre back home in Ohio.

'Quite a bit,' they said.

'Do you see any plays?'

Furrowed brows.

'I mean theatre without singing?'

The answer was no, in tones which indicated, What do you mean, theatre without singing? Who goes to theatre if there's no singing?

Down to the Gate Theatre at Notting Hill, a black box of a room above a pub, like so many small spaces in London and other cities where the lanterns of theatre are kept alight. Mick Gordon, who Peter Hall has invited to co-direct *Tantalus* with James Kerr, has staged *Marathon*, a new play by Eduardo Erba about two runners in training. There is nothing on the charcoal-coloured stage except two travelators. The whole play takes an hour. There are only two characters. And yet it excites because it is so condensed, and driven by the pulse of running, and the self-evidence of body and breath. And it rises from realism into metaphor, into metaphysics.

In the pub afterwards, Mick, a 28-year-old Ulsterman with a shaved cranium and fervent, twining speech, takes my compliments on the show, talks about his refusal to let the designer put any representational scenery on stage, and then embarks on his passion for *Tantalus*. He's just won The Empty Space Peter Brook Award, named after Brook's most influential book, for best experimental theatre, and he's a hot name, with offers on all sides. 'But I'm doing *Tantalus* because I will learn a lot from Peter, and because I will be challenging Peter and John. I don't want to let the material strangle itself. There's so much there, but there's also too much there. Peter took a bold step in inviting us in as collaborators. I believe he will have the strength to respond to questioning and challenge.' The more he talks, the more I feel his excitement, his awkward, sputtering passion. With Mick Gordon and the quieter but equally forceful James Kerr, a laconic Liverpudlian, we will have a combustible atomic nucleus at the heart of *Tantalus*. It makes all the pitching and manouevring worthwhile.

Steadily, all that continues, with Bill Wilkinson and I sharing the tasks. Crafting the approach to the Arts Council, without whose serious financial participation any private-sector funding will be unlikely. Getting the Royal Shakespeare Company to consider *Tantalus* in the main house at Stratford-upon-Avon in January 2001, and to give us time to adapt the production for a new space. Asking Sheffield and Manchester to calculate price structures and income projections. Talking to the Barbican about schedule and fundraising for spring 2001, to round off the British tour. Assembling a group of friends and patrons of *Tantalus*. Hunting down e-commerce companies as potential sponsors – how can I reach the president of amazon.com? Getting introductions to clubs of possible business sponsors. Trying to get replies from the Greeks.

In the thick of this round of planning and wheedling, some surge in my head makes me set down a sort of Martin Luther King dream-picture of how *Tantalus* might be at the Barbican. It takes the form of a festival – The Trojan War And Our Times – with *Tantalus* as a kind of benign bomb at the centre, radiating clusters of Trojan War-related activity in many directions.

While *Tantalus* plays in the main house, I imagine the Barbican Pit theatre presenting John Barton's dramatisation of Thucydides' *History of the Peloponnesian War*, Mark Espinall's production of Christopher Logue's *Iliad* version, performed in total darkness, the great Greek actress Irene Papas in her show of Greek tragic heroines. Staged readings and workshops of such Trojan War-affected plays as Goethe's *Iphigeneia in Tauris*; Seamus Heaney's *Cure for Troy*; Jean Giraudoux's *The Trojan War Will Not Take Place*; Heiner Müller's postmodern versions of the myths; *Oresteia* translations by Robert Lowell and Ted Hughes. In the cinema, movies made from the tragedies linked to the Trojan War – Michael Cacoyannis' *Iphigenia, Electra, Trojan Women*, and television programmes: the Peter Hall/Tony Harrison *Oresteia*, Michael Wood's archaeological series, *In Search of Troy*, and *King Priam*, Michael Tippett's opera.

In the concert hall, concert versions of Gluck and Berlioz and Strauss, Trojan War operas. Even Offenbach's *La Belle Hélène*. Birtwistle – *agm*, and other Greek-related pieces. Theodorakis – his popular and his art music. Vangelis, Maria Farandouri. I think up exhibitions for the galleries, lectures and debates on Myth and

Politics; Myth in the Information Age; the Classical World in a Modernising Age. An all-day symposium on The British And The Greeks, with especial reference to the Parthenon Marbles as a test-case. In the Barbican foyers, a children's painting competition of scenes from the Trojan War. *Rembétika* music, food, *kermesse* – that ancient word for festivity – from the London Greek Cypriot communities. Traditional dancing from Greek and Turkish villages.

This packed dream seems to cheer people up. It's so easy to get bogged down in the slog and minutiae, and forget just how big, how mountainous a peak we are attempting. Even easier to forget in times like these, of market tidiness and thoroughly reduced expectations.

And the times certainly are not propitious for theatre in these final weeks of the century. December is often the cruellest month for British theatre companies, for that is when they are informed of the Arts Council's decisions about their public funding. Two kinds of funding are to be applied this winter. Recovery Funds for immediate emergencies, to pull the patient off the brink-of-death list. And Stabilisation Funds, which will improve an organisation's annual grant, providing it carries out restructuring and rationalisations recommended by an inspection team. As with all management consultancies, there will be some cloth-cutting with fairly blunt scissors. Some recommendations will eat into the core achievements and essence of the enterprise. No one engaged in these would-be missions of mercy believes they are doing anything more than helping an under-funded and under-regarded public culture stagger on.

There are stories of everyday pain. A regional theatre that has managed to stay afloat by, among other things, narrowing its choice of repertoire to small-cast plays, one-third fewer actors than ten years ago. An orchestra that has been told that the price of stabilisation is to reduce the number of players in its string sections by a third. 'Nobody seemed worried about the orchestra's sound quality.' Everyone's getting cheated. The actors who can't practise their craft. The audiences whose ears are under-nourished, who never see big, public plays. The depleted culture of theatre itself.

The same day I learn of these lamentable stabilisations –
petrifactions might be a better term – the Theatres Trust, the
government's theatre watchdog, publishes its annual report.
Normally known for its campaigns to preserve threatened theatre
buildings, it is now sounding the alarm for theatre itself. 'I have a
dread,' writes its director Peter Longman in his conclusion, 'that
outside a few major cities we will have seen the slow death of the
regional repertory system, branded as elitist and starved of cash
and audiences. Live professional theatre will consist of miked
arena opera, two-handers in pubs and community centres,
American musical imports touring a closely controlled network
of dates, and pantos with ageing soap stars. The West End will
survive, albeit on a restricted and unadventurous scale and
classified as a tourist attraction.'

Meanwhile, the British government's Culture Secretary,
Chris Smith, hails Cool Britannia's new 'cultural industries' –
film, fashion, design and pop – from which theatre, neither being
nor wanting to be an industry of multiples but a vessel for
memorable and transient one-offs, is debarred. Theatre is
repeatable, up to a point, but it cannot be run off infinitely, as
can a CD, a film-print, a digital template. So it is an alien, a
stranger, in a world less and less kind to strangers or exceptions.
We reach the century's end devoid of an idea to justify public
funding for theatres, or indeed many of our art-forms. Our
society can encompass commercial art, or art that can be
assimilated to industry. Heritage still keeps familiar art
functioning, as does snobbery. But since management and
marketing became the prevalent philosophy in the world of arts
funding, where there was once an idea – even a paternalist, do-
gooding, BBC Reithian, public library idea – now there is a void,
filled with the chatter of cultural relativists. Their resentful
theorising, unwittingly hand-in-glove with neo-liberal
deregulation, has helped shake a few foundations and dug more
than one grave.

And above us all, as starved public theatres are tantalised by
prospects of improvement as long as they meet new management
and marketing yardsticks, the Millennium Dome swells with the

confections of well-paid installation artists called designers, selling simplistic ideas and synthetic awe.

Summer 1999   Oxford

I go to Oxford, to see the last preview matinee of Complicite's collectively-made show about memory, *Mnemonic*. The Playhouse is filled with a chattering, mostly young audience. Simon McBurney hurries in through the house, climbs the stage, sets off at a gallop into a stand-up disquisition, improvised, racing against some clock. Immediately, I'm grabbed by his scruffy urgency, and by what he's saying, so close to one thread of this book: the difference between remaking memory, as the human brain does, and retrieving or accessing data, as in a memory bank. Or, he proffers, the corpse-drawers of a morgue.

'When we remember it comes out slightly different each time,' he whispers. 'Modern theories of memory revolve around the idea of fragmentation. Different elements are, apparently, stored in different areas of the brain. And it is not so much the cells that are important in the act of memory, but the connections between the cells, the synapses, the synaptic connections. And these connections are being made and remade. Constantly. . . . They are being fabricated even as I speak. It's a process called sprouting.'

Simon scrubs his head, pings fingers to demonstrate the sprouting of brain cells and the keyboard playing of the hippocampus. 'What I'm getting at is that re-membering is essentially not only an act of retrieval but a creative thing, it happens in the moment, it's an act, an act . . . of imagination.' Like an act of theatre in the moment.

He leads us into the play, the piece, by remembering that his father was an archaeologist, which must explain his interest in origins. On each of our seats there is an airline sleep-mask and a leaf. Now he makes us put on the mask and hold the leaf to do a collective visualisation in the dark, to imagine time further and further back, to imagine our ancestors, and to think of the veins on a leaf as our family tree. He does dizzying sums with uncles and great-aunts and second cousins and great-great grandparents. 'Everyone in this house is related to everyone else,' he concludes.

Then his mobile rings and he steps out of the routine and starts
telling someone he has just come to the theatre to watch Simon
McBurney do some stupid party game when we all had to mask
our eyes and feel a leaf. And then the strangest thing happens.
His voice, amplified, goes on talking into the cellphone. But he's
no longer talking, he's packing up his things and moving off.
Dislocation, before our very eyes.

That's the overture to the two twinned stories of the piece.
One is a true story, I saw it in the newspaper, about the
disinterring in 1991 of a 5,000-year-old corpse frozen in a glacier
on the Austrian-Italian border. Simon, naked on an autopsy
table, becomes the corpse, and is fought over by rival scientists
and the two countries who want to claim him as their discovery.
The other story is about Alice, Simon's girlfriend, journeying
across Europe in search of who her father was. Alice only finds the
truth after a railway odyssey from Paris to Berlin to Prague to
Poland to the Baltic.

Because of the physicality of this mime-trained group, these
stories are not just cross-cut, they are intertwined. Simon lies
corpse-naked on a bed, as Alice makes love over and around him
on the bed to a Jew she meets on the train, who has decoded the
box of her father's belongings – shoes, a lighter, a tallith, that
gives rise to a haunting Yiddish song as Alice and the stranger
make love, or perhaps only do so in Simon's mind.

There are replays, rewinds, overlays, voice-separation, as the
thoughts go on inside the head of the speaker/spectator of his own
thinking. The show has all the paraphernalia of audio post-
production, and, at the same time, the physicality of stage space:
the mountain climbers who discover the corpse clamber over
Simon's bed, a collapsible wooden chair becomes the torso and
limbs of the corpse. Climactically, like an immensely tender
Bunraku operator, Simon cradles and manipulates this chair, re-
enacting his best guess of the imagined disaster that befell the
Stone Age victim. 'He only wanted a short rest but his need for
sleep was stronger than his willpower. He laid his head on the
rock. Soon his clothes froze to the rough ground. He was no
longer aware that he was freezing to death.' We are watching a

group of actors handling a pliable chair back into the memory of the man behind the bare-boned shrivelled corpse from the Neolithic age.

'What was violence in the Neolithic?' ask the participants at a scientific conference on the corpse, probing into why its ribs are bashed in. When the scientists report evidence of a mass grave in the Tyrol, we cannot but think of a Neolithic conflict, just like Kosovo, from which the corpse-man was fleeing. The parallel is lightly sketched in. But it is another resonant theatre metaphor.

The piece is so romantic: Simon flings himself around the stage, unable to sleep in any position, he calls his girlfriend across Europe, getting an anthology of answering-machine messages, he becomes a Schubertian wayfarer in a landscape of distance supposedly brought close. And it is so sophisticated and objective, the cry of lovers on cellphones when they do get through: 'You're breaking up, you're breaking up.'

Mnemonic reminds me of Lepage's *Seven Streams of the River Ota*, only it is even more metaphorical, it is as spatially eloquent and poignant as Pina Bausch, more human than the glacially brilliant postmodern New York group, Mabou Mines. It has the deftness and sorrow of a screen piece about memory, *Hiroshima Mon Amour*, and is constructed and edited like cinema. But it affirms the presence of the performer in the present – by conjuring up the life of a corpse from the past.

It touches current concepts: chaos theory, which tells us that a sandstorm in Africa can produce an avalanche in the Tyrol and pinion this man. In such vectors of thinking, this theatre is finding new forms. Like any good postmodernist, Simon McBurney can see life as a sequence of collisions and encounters on the networks. But that knowledge does not dissolve the body, and as an actor he is rooted in his trained body. He does not rest his weight on the fragile chair, but holds himself on his thighs, making us believe the chair is solid. It's a trick, of course, but theatre is made of such 'lies like truth', as the witches in *Macbeth* call them.

The piece comes to its unstable rest in reiterations of the body. Alice's voice repeats the question she asked when she made love, for real, or in Simon's imagination. 'What does nakedness remind us of? Dear God, what does nakedness remind us of? Naked, our needs are so clear, our fears so natural . . . Seeing a naked body of another person we make an inventory of our own. Shoulder blade, ribs, clavicle. We list the sensations we feel in each part of them, all of them indescribable, all of them familiar, all of them constituting a home.'

One by one the whole cast roll over onto the autopsy table, each taking the other's place, to stand in for the frozen corpse of the past, made human again in the present by our interrogations, each time slightly different, just as theatre is.

Towards the end of *Mnemonic*, an object, a chair, is manipulated by actors to reconstitute a human being. Three months later, I go to Paris to see *Drums on the Dam*, Ariane Mnouchkine's twenty-eighth production in the thirty-fifth year of her theatre's existence, and I see human beings become objects – actors as puppets handled by black-clad operators, in the style of Japanese Kabuki and Oriental marionette theatre. In both productions the fragility and interdependence of humanity is figured forth, not didactically but immediately and emotionally.

Autumn 1999   Paris

The Sunday matinee at Mnouchkine's Cartoucherie theatre presents its familiar welcome. The battered bus from the Métro through the woods at Vincennes, the walk across the parade-ground courtyard, bustling Ariane tearing tickets at the door, and once again the huge festive foyer, strung with lanterns, busy with people. A street scene, with its crossroads excitement and chance encounters translated indoors. A local habitation for a name: conviviality.

After the recent floods of the Yangtse, when the Chinese government flooded peasants' land to divert the waters from the cities, Ariane asked her habitual collaborator, Hélène Cixous, to write a play about a city threatened by a flood. She wanted it in the form of traditional Oriental puppet theatre. A long-time adept of Asian theatre, she was looking, not for an *exercice de style*, but for a metaphor for the victors and victims of any 'natural disaster'. The result is theatre poetry of the most refined kind. But nothing about it is antiquarian. Despite its overt exoticism, *Drums on the Dam* is a play of urgent actuality and plangent truth.

On a stage of polished planks, against silken cloths painted with soft-focus landscape and weather, brightly robed figures seem to spring forward, propelled by stage attendants dressed in black. The ruling Lord – for the action takes place in some unspecified feudal Middle Ages – courtiers, standard-bearers, warlords, fishermen, peasants, a Mother Courage-like noodle seller, seem to waft as weightlessly as birds. Levitated by their hooded operators, they land with a light bounce, like grasshoppers, then tilt and lean, reposing gratefully on the limbs of their puppeteer. Intermittently, you are aware of the black flocks of these operators; more often your mind deletes them and feasts on the life of their 'dolls'.

The spectacle of these puppets has all the enchantment of Julie Taymor's work in *The Lion King*, also shaped by Oriental theatre. But *Drums on the Dam* is about something more substantial than a New Age rite of passage. And these are not carved and modelled puppets manipulated by actors, but 'puppets' impersonated by actors, manipulated by other actors. And by impersonating a puppet, the actor's expressiveness is caught tight in a web of rules and limits – the rigidity of hands, the stiffness of arms, the immobility of a face – which paradoxically distil the character's emotion, make it more resonant. And between 'puppet' and handler there is a relationship of mutual trust and help which is itself a statement about human relationships.

Though set in feudal China, the story of *Drums on the Dam* is as acute as the morning headlines of Turkey's earthquakes, Orissa's cyclone, the broken bridges of the Danube. At stake are the lives and land of people who, in the eyes of their betters, don't count. Uncaring rulers, hypocritical politicians, the vulnerable poor, unregulated deforestation, ruthless speculators – it's an all-too-familiar cast of characters. Etched in sharp silhouettes and tableaux, like animated woodblock prints, these more-than-natural puppets speak to the make-believer in us all, while their displacement into a past age and from television news to heightened theatre reveals more clearly the complexities of the struggle against unchanging injustice.

But Ariane Mnouchkine's intricate theatre language in this piece goes beyond making allegories of the world as it is now. It also bears witness to our timeless fragility as human beings. The imaginary 'helplessness' of the actors, only able to act with the help of their puppeteers, which would be intolerable if it were real, breaks through into a flood of wordless emotion in a key scene of *Drums on the Dam*.

We are in the mountains, on a dam upstream of the river threatening to engulf the city. There a group of sentinels has gathered, armed with drums, to sound the alarm to the peasants ahead of the flood. A young woman, Duan, the leader of the watch, appears climbing up as if from a steep slope up-stage, bearing a drum almost as big as she is. Her struggle to mount the slope, aided by her operators, her unchanging features, tug at your heart. Swiftly, the stage fills with her twenty fellow-drummers, now governed by white ropes in the hands of puppeteers aloft. At her command they beat out their different signals, throbbing, subtle, syncopated, massive, fierce, a barrage of marionette sound.

As intoxicating as a military tattoo or African drumming, it also harked back, for me, to a cornerstone scene of twentieth-century theatre, when the dumb Kattrin in *Mother Courage*, unable to shout her warning about the approaching enemy, beats out her alarm on a drum on the wagon roof until the soldiers shoot her down. In Brecht as in Mnouchkine, the wordless drumming speaks for human solidarity, reduced under pressure to wordless gesture. Ariane pushes the tension even further when Duan's lover, come to join the rebels, rushes into the drummers and kisses her fiercely, their two hand-held bodies tilted to breaking point. Dazed by his passion, she breaks out of the clamorous group for a moment as if to take hold of her love, and then returns to drum even more fiercely, in a momentary image of self-sacrifice for the group.

At the end of *Drums on the Dam*, Ariane goes beyond the beautiful theatricality of her Chinese puppet play, and lets reality in. After an ambiguous series of victories and defeats, the topmost dam is breached, and water, real gurgling water, begins to seep through the planking stage, soon filling its central rectangle chest-high.

Into this deluge strides Bai Ju, a puppeteer who has been locked out of the city, along with all the other extra-mural refugees. From the sides the stagehands toss in bundles of cloth. They float and bob on the waters like distended corpses after a flood. The wizened marionettist, in the water with his young, now unmasked operator, tenderly picks up the bundles one by one. We see that they are tiny dolls with faces no longer Oriental, but like ours, and dressed in the multicoloured patchwork clothes of peasant refugees everywhere. Bai Ju lines up the tiny dolls along the front of the stage. They are the size of babies, victims still shifting with the waves that have killed them. They gaze at us like a mute accusation. Or like suppliants from another place, men and women seeking a haven, like the asylum-seekers in Aeschylus' *Suppliant Women* at the very beginning of European drama. Or like the displaced of Europe now, as theatre once more touches the nerve ends of the worst war of all, civil war. 'Perhaps all wars are civil wars,' Ariane says. Once more, she has displayed theatre's specific and unique way of reminding us of the care we merit from each other, by putting such care into the perilous balance of this play.

At the end of Ariane's play, as the flood waters rise, the River itself appears and addresses us. 'You had the earth as your vessel, and through lack of attention, through laziness of soul, you made holes in it. You had eyes for nothing around you. And yet, when I was framed by the forests, didn't I make a good mirror for you?'

Hamlet talked about a play as a mirror, held up 'to show the very age its form and pressure'. Do we really want to splinter the mirror of theatre by neglect and disregard? Isn't it a good enough mirror for our new impatience? Doesn't it still deserve its place in the ecology of our hearts?